AAT
NVQ TECHNICIAN

REVISION COMPANION Units 8&9

Managing Performance
& Controlling Resources

First edition 2002
Fifth edition May 2006

ISBN 0 7517 2613 3 (previous ISBN 0 7517 2241 3)

British Library Cataloguing-in-Publication Data
A catalogue record for this book is available from the British Library

Published by

BPP Professional Education
Aldine House
Aldine Place
London
W12 8AW

Printed in Great Britain by Ashford Colour Press
Unit 600
Fareham Reach
Fareham Road
Gosport
Hampshire
PO13 0FW

All our rights reserved. No part of this publication may be reproduced, stored in a retrieval system or transmitted, in any form or by any means, electronic, mechanical, photocopying, recording or otherwise, without the prior written permission of BPP Professional Education.

We are grateful to the AAT for permission to reproduce specimen assessments and examples from previous exam based assessments.

©
BPP Professional Education
2006

CONTENTS

Introduction (v)

Chapter activities

		Questions	Answers
1	Introduction to management accounting	1	177
2	Collection of data	9	189
3	Time series analysis and indexation	13	197
4	Standard costing	19	207
5	Standard costing – further aspects	25	217
6	Performance indicators	41	241
7	Quality	63	265
8	Budgetary control systems	69	273
9	Forecasting income	73	281
10	Forecasting expenditure	77	289
11	Preparing budgets	83	295
12	Reconciling budgets and actual figures	97	315

Practice exams

Unit 8

	Questions	Answers
Practice Exam 1: LNG Ltd	111	333
Practice Exam 2: Bell plc	117	341
Practice Exam 3: Blossom Ltd	123	349
Practice Exam 4: Brown Ltd	129	357
Practice Exam 5: Econair Ltd	135	367

Unit 9

	Questions	Answers
Practice Exam 6: Merano Ltd	143	375
Practice Exam 7: Arusha Ltd	151	383
Practice Exam 8: Jorvik Ltd	157	391
Practice Exam 9: Newmarket Ltd	163	397
Practice Exam 10: Tipton Ltd	169	405

INTRODUCTION

This is the 2006 edition of BPP's AAT NVQ Technician Revision Companion for Unit 8, Contributing to the Management of Performance and the Enhancement of Value, and Unit 9, Contributing to the Planning and Control of Resources. It is part of an integrated package of AAT materials.

It has been written in conjunction with the BPP Course Companion and has been carefully designed to enable students to practise all aspects of the requirements of the Standards of Competence and performance criteria. It is fully up to date as at April 2006.

This Revision Companion contains these key features:

- graded activities corresponding to each chapter of the Course Companion
- five practice exam based assessments for each unit, including tasks from AAT assessments up to and including December 2005.

All activities and practice assessments have full answers prepared by BPP Professional Education.

The emphasis in all activities and questions is on the practical application of the skills acquired.

A further bank of activities relating to each chapter of the Course Companion and practice assessments, with answers prepared by BPP Professional Education, is available in the Tutor Companion, available only to colleges adopting BPP's Companion material for the Unit.

chapter 1: INTRODUCTION TO MANAGEMENT ACCOUNTING

1   Explain the differences between financial accounting and management accounting. Ensure that you cover the following points:

- the main purposes of each form of accounting
- the users of each type of information
- the format of financial accounts and management accounts

2   Complete the following sentences:

i) The three main purposes of management accounting are ...*Planning*..., ...*Control*... and ...*Decision*...

ii) If production levels decrease then total variable costs will ...*Decrease*...

iii) The stores department in a manufacturing organisation is an example of a ...*Service*... cost centre

iv) Costs which cannot be directly attributed to a unit of production are known as ...*Indirect*... costs

v) When service cost centre costs are divided between the production cost centres this is known as ...*apportionment*... of costs

vi) The range of activity levels over which a fixed cost is anticipated to remain fixed is known as the ...*relevant*... range

introduction to management accounting

3. For each of the following statements determine if they are true or false:

		True/false
i)	Management accounts must be audited by an external auditor	False
ii)	As production levels fall fixed costs per unit will rise	True
iii)	A semi-variable cost is one which is fixed for a certain range of activity and then increases and is fixed again for a further range of activity	False
iv)	As production levels rise the variable costs per unit will remain constant	False True
v)	The salary of the production manager is an indirect cost	True
vi)	Absorption of overheads is the process of allocating overheads to relevant cost centres	True False

4. At a production level of 16,000 units a production cost totals £54,400. At a production level of 22,000 units the same cost totals £68,200. Is this a variable cost?

Semi variable

5. The following details are available for four types of costs at two activity levels:

Cost type	Cost at 1,000 units	Cost at 1,500 units
I	£7,000	£10,500
II	£11,000	£12,500
III	£12,000	£12,000
IV	£3,800	£5,700

Classify each cost by behaviour:

Cost I   variable
Cost II   semi variable / stepped
Cost III fixed
Cost IV   variable

introduction to management accounting

6 Given below are eight graphs illustrating a variety of cost behaviours. From the list of eight cost behaviours or descriptions given below (i to viii) match each graph to a cost behaviour or description.

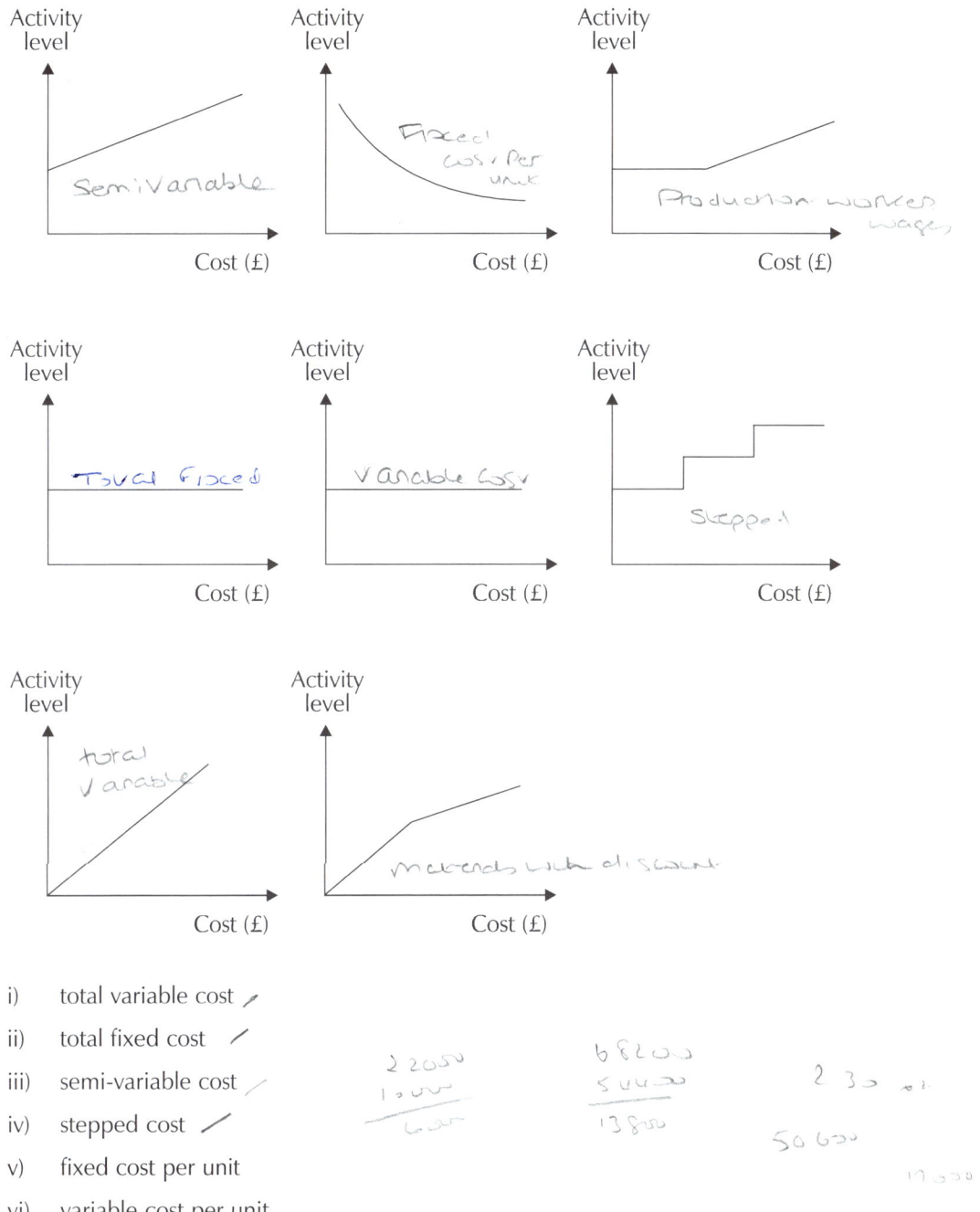

i) total variable cost
ii) total fixed cost
iii) semi-variable cost
iv) stepped cost
v) fixed cost per unit
vi) variable cost per unit
vii) materials cost with trade discount offered for purchases over a certain level
viii) production workers wages who are paid per unit produced with a guaranteed weekly minimum wage

introduction to management accounting

7. A manufacturing business anticipates that its variable costs and fixed costs will be £32,000 and £25,000 respectively at a production level of 10,000 units.

You are to produce a schedule showing the total production cost and the cost per unit at each of the following activity levels:

i) 8,000 units
ii) 12,000 units
iii) 15,000 units

Handwritten working:
× 3.20 = 25,600 + 25,000 = 50,600
× 3.20 = 38,400 + 25,000 = 63,400
× 3.20 = 48,000 + 25,000 = 73,000

8. Given below are a number of types of cost – classify each one according to its behaviour:

Cost behaviour

i) Maintenance department costs which are made up of £25,000 of salaries and an average of £500 cost per call out — Semi Variable ✓

ii) Machinery depreciation based upon machine hours used — Variable ✓

iii) Salary costs of nursery school teachers where one teacher is required for every six children in the nursery — Stepped ✓

iv) Rent for a building that houses the factory, stores and maintenance departments — Fixed ✓

9. A business produces one product which requires the following inputs:

Direct materials — 6 kg @ £4.80 per kg
Direct labour — 4 hours @ £7.00 per hour
Building costs — £18,000 per quarter
Leased machines — £600 for every 600 units of production
Stores costs — £3,000 per quarter plus £3.00 per unit

i) What is the total cost of production and the cost per unit at each of the following quarterly production levels:

a) 1,000 units — 82,000 £82
b) 1,500 units — 112,500 £75
c) 2,000 units — 143,000 £71.50

ii) Explain why the cost per unit is different at each level of production.

Not all costs are variable

4

10   A business produces one product in its factory which has two production departments, cutting and finishing. There is one service department, stores, which spends 80% of its time servicing the cutting department and the remainder servicing the finishing department.

The expected costs of producing 50,000 units in the following quarter are as follows:

Direct materials	£16.00 per unit
Direct labour	3 hours cutting @ £7.50 per hour
	2 hours finishing @ £6.80 per hour
Cutting overheads	£380,000
Finishing overheads	£280,000
Stores overheads	£120,000

It is estimated that in each of the cost centres 60% of the overheads are variable and the remainder are fixed.

Determine the cost per unit of production under the following costing methods:

i)   absorption costing – fixed and variable overheads are to be absorbed on a direct labour hour basis

ii) marginal costing

11   To help decision making during budget preparation, your supervisor has prepared the following estimates of sales revenue and cost behaviour for a one-year period, relating to one of your organisation's products.

Activity	60%	100%
Sales and production (thousands of units)	36	60
	£'000	£'000
Sales	432	720
Production costs		
Variable and fixed	366	510
Sales, distribution and administration costs		
Variable and fixed	126	150

The normal level of activity for the current year is 60,000 units, and fixed costs are incurred evenly throughout the year.

There were no stocks of the product at the start of the quarter, in which 16,500 units were made and 13,500 units were sold. Actual fixed costs were the same as budgeted.

Tasks

a)   Calculate the following using absorption costing.

   i)   The amount of fixed production costs absorbed by the product
   ii) The over/under absorption of fixed product costs
   iii) The profit for the quarter

b)   Calculate the net profit or loss for the quarter using marginal costing.

You may assume that sales revenue and variable costs per unit are as budgeted.

introduction to management accounting

12 a) A company absorbs overheads on a machine hour basis. Actual machine hours were 22,435, actual overheads were £496,500 and there was over absorption of overheads of £64,375.

Task

Calculate the overhead absorption rate to the nearest £.

b) When opening stocks were 8,500 litres and closing stocks were 6,750 litres, a firm had a profit of £27,400 using marginal costing.

Task

Assuming the fixed overhead absorption rate was £2 per litre, calculate the profit using absorption costing.

c) Actual overheads were £496,980 and actual machine hours were 16,566. Budgeted overheads were £475,200.

Task

Based on the data above and assuming that the budgeted overhead absorption rate was £32 per hour, calculate the budgeted number of machine hours (to the nearest hour).

13 You are employed as an accounts assistant in the management accounting department of Charleroi Aircon Ltd, the UK subsidiary of a major French group. Charleroi design and install industrial air-conditioning systems. The company is based in Birmingham.

Charleroi's usual pricing policy is to use direct costs (equipment and installation labour) plus a mark-up of 50% to establish the selling price for an air-conditioning installation.

Alice Devereaux, Charleroi's sales manager, is about to tender for a contract (quotation HMG/012) to install air-conditioning in some government offices in Exeter which are being refurbished.

Alice is also about to bid for a contract (quotation CFG/013) to install the air-conditioning in a furniture store which is being built in Gloucester. This job is very similar to an earlier one for the same customer.

Alice has asked Mark Langton, Charleroi's management accountant, to second you to the sales department to assist her in developing better pricing and cost models. Alice is particularly keen to experiment with activity based costing (ABC) as Mark is in the process of designing an ABC system for the company. She has asked you to investigate the profitability of quotations HMG/012 and CFG/013.

You have obtained the following information about the two jobs.

introduction to management accounting

Estimates related to contracts HMG/012 and CFG/013		
Contract number:	HMG/012	CFG/013
Equipment: cost	£175,000	£120,000
number of items purchased	650	410
Direct labour: hours	10,000	6,000
hourly rate	£13	£11
Design hours	1,280	620
Distance from Birmingham office (miles round - trip)	320	90
Engineer site visits required	30	10

You have managed to obtain the following overhead information from Mark's ABC working papers.

ABC details for overhead activities connected with air conditioning installation contracts

Activity	Budgeted cost pool £pa	Cost driver	Cost driver units pa
Design department	675,000	Design hours	25,000
Site engineers	370,000	Miles travelled	185,000
Purchasing department	105,000	Items purchased	15,000
Payroll department	75,000	Direct hours	300,000
Site management	750,000	Direct hours	300,000
Post-installation inspection	80,000	Items purchased	20,000

Tasks

a) Calculate the price for each of jobs HMG/012 and CFG/013.

b) Prepare a schedule setting out the activity-based overhead costs for each of jobs HMG/012 and CFG/013.

c) Write a memo to Alice setting out the profitability of each contract. Include a breakdown of costs into their main elements, plus details of the projected profits as a percentage of selling price and as a percentage of total cost.

7

introduction to management accounting

14 You are employed as a financial analyst at Drampton plc, a computer retailer. Drampton plc has recently taken over Little Ltd, a small company making personal computers and servers. Little appears to make all of its profits from servers. Drampton's finance director tells you that Little's fixed overheads are currently charged to production using standard labour hours and gives you their standard cost of making PCs and servers. These are shown below.

Little Ltd: Standard cost per computer

Model	Server	PC
Annual budgeted volume	5	5,000
Unit standard cost	£	£
Material and labour	50,000	500
Fixed overhead	4,000	40
Standard cost per unit	54,000	540

The finance director asks for your help and suggests you reclassify the fixed overheads between the two models using activity based costing. You are given the following information.

- **Budgeted total annual fixed overheads**

Set-up costs	10,000
Rent and power (production area)	120,000
Rent (stores area)	50,000
Salaries of store issue staff	40,000
Total	**220,000**

Every time Little makes a server, it has to stop making PCs and rearrange the factory layout. The cost of this is shown as set-up costs. If the factory did not make any servers these costs would be eliminated.

- **Cost drivers**

	Server	PC	Total
Number of set-ups	5	0	5
Number of weeks of production	10	40	50
Floor area of stores (square metres)	400	400	800
Number of issues of stock	2,000	8,000	10,000

Task

Prepare a note for Drampton's finance director. In the note, you should use the cost drivers to do the following.

a) Reallocate Little's budgeted total fixed annual overheads between server and PC production.
b) Show the revised unit fixed overheads for each of the two types of unit.

chapter 2: COLLECTION OF DATA

1   For each of the following sources of data state whether they are primary or secondary data:

    Primary/secondary

    i)   Retail Price Index — Primary ✗
    ii) Stock Exchange share price listings — Secondary ✓
    iii) Analysis of sales of a company by product — secondary ✗
    iv) Trade Association inter-firm comparisons — Secondary ✓
    v)   A company's aged debtor listing — Primary

2   Complete the following sentences:

    i)   The Retail Price Index is an indication of the level of ...INFLATION... in the UK
    ii) Quantitative data can be either ...financial... or ...non financial... data
    iii) The National Statistics are published in 11 separate ...13 separate themes...
    iv) A good alternative to pure random sampling are ...quasi random... sampling methods
    v)   When sampling, the name given to all items that are to be considered is the ...Random or Population...

collection of data

3   For each of the following statements determine whether they are true or false:

True/false

i) An analysis of purchase invoices to determine the average trade terms from suppliers is an example of secondary data ...FALSE... ✓

ii) The number of days holiday taken per year by qualified staff in a firm of solicitors is non-financial quantitative data ...TRUE... ✓

iii) A survey showing favourite holiday destinations is an example of qualitative data ...TRUE... ✓

iv) Quota sampling is an example of random sampling ...FALSE... ✓

4   What quantitative information can be found from the purchase invoices of a business and how might this information be used?

1. COST OF MATERIALS
2. UNITS OF PURCHASE
3. DISCOUNT VALUE

5   Suggest where each of the following sources of information might be obtained:

Source

i) Local planning applications — local council

ii) The previous year's financial statements for a competitor company — Companies House

iii) Previous month's discounts allowed — creditors history

iv) Industry average profit margin — trade assoc / national statistics

v) Information about a competitor's success — financial press

vi) Average sick days of employees per month — payroll

6   Explain what the National Statistics are and how they might be of use to a business.

10

collection of data

7   Explain the following sampling methods and give an example of the circumstances in which each might be used and how the sample would be chosen:

   i)   random sampling
   ii) systematic sampling
   iii) stratified sampling

   (handwritten notes: Population / 1st then 9 / Groups & batches)

8   For each of the following situations discuss any appropriate and practical methods of choosing a sample:

   i)   an auditor wishes to check whether purchase invoices in a business are properly authorised prior to payment

   ii) a train service provider wishes to assess the level of customer satisfaction with its service on a particular line

   iii) a manufacturing business wishes to assess the level of defective products that are likely to be produced in each batch of production

9   The adult population of your organisation's Northern sales territory is 500,000. The territory is divided into a number of regions as follows.

Region	Adult population '000
Northia	90
Wester	10
Southam	140
Eastis	40
Midshire	120
Centrasia	100

   In order to provide sales forecasting information, it has been decided to carry out a survey based on a 2% sample of the Northern sales territory's population.

   Tasks

   a) Describe how the sampling should be organised if the following methods are to be employed.

      i)   Simple random
      ii) Cluster
      iii) Stratified
      iv) Systematic

   b) Discuss which of these methods would be likely to give the most representative sample and why. Your answer should include discussion of the disadvantages of the other methods.

collection of data

10 One of the ways of conducting surveys is by the use of questionnaires.

Task

Discuss the advantages and disadvantages of conducting surveys by questionnaire using each of the following methods.

a) Personal interview
b) Telephone
c) Postal

chapter 3: TIME SERIES ANALYSIS AND INDEXATION

1   In the context of time series analysis explain what is meant by the following:

    i)   the trend
    ii)   cyclical variations
    iii) seasonal variations
    iv) random variations

2   Given below are the production cost figures for the last 9 months:

	£
March	104,500
April	110,300
May	112,800
June	109,400
July	117,600
August	116,000
September	119,200
October	122,300
November	120,500
December	119,300

Calculate a three month moving average for these figures.

time series analysis and indexation

3 A new restaurant has recently been opened which only trades for five days a week. The takings have been increasing rapidly over the first four weeks since opening, as given below.

		£
Week 1	Day 1	600
	Day 2	700
	Day 3	1,000
	Day 4	1,200
	Day 5	1,500
Week 2	Day 1	680
	Day 2	750
	Day 3	1,250
	Day 4	1,400
	Day 5	1,860
Week 3	Day 1	820
	Day 2	1,030
	Day 3	1,940
	Day 4	2,100
	Day 5	2,500
Week 4	Day 1	1,000
	Day 2	1,320
	Day 3	1,560
	Day 4	2,290
	Day 5	2,670

You are to:

i) calculate the trend of the results using a five day moving average

ii) calculate the daily seasonal variations on the assumption that the seasonal variations are additive

iii) comment upon how useful the trend and seasonal variation figures might be in this situation for forecasting future restaurant takings

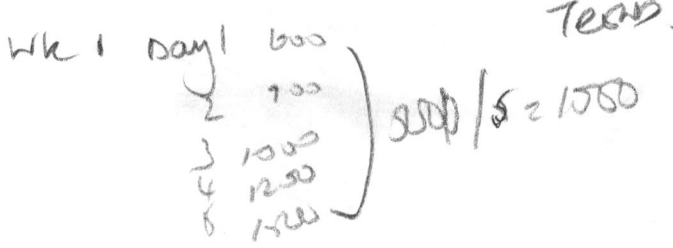

time series analysis and indexation

4 Given below are the quarterly sales figures for a small business:

		£
2003	Quarter 3	50,600
	Quarter 4	52,800
2004	Quarter 1	55,600
	Quarter 2	48,600
	Quarter 3	51,200
	Quarter 4	53,900
2005	Quarter 1	58,000
	Quarter 2	49,800
	Quarter 3	53,000
	Quarter 4	54,600
2006	Quarter 1	60,100
	Quarter 2	50,700
	Quarter 3	54,200
	Quarter 4	55,200

You are to:

i) calculate the trend of the sales figures using a centred four quarter moving average

ii) calculate the seasonal variations on the assumption that the seasonal variations are additive

iii) using the spreadsheet given below enter appropriate formulae in order for the spreadsheet package to calculate the trend using a centred four quarter moving average

	A	B	C	D	E
1					
2					
3					
4					
5					
6					
7					
8					
9					
10					
11					
12					
13					
14					
15					
16					
17					
18					
19					
20					
21					
22					
23					
24					
25					
26					
27					

time series analysis and indexation

5   A business uses time series analysis and has found that the predicted trend of sales for the next four quarters and historical seasonal variations are as follows:

	Predicted trend £	Seasonal variation £
Quarter 1	418,500	+21,500
Quarter 2	420,400	+30,400
Quarter 3	422,500	−16,700
Quarter 4	423,800	−35,200

What are the predicted actual sales figures for these four quarters?

6   Given below are the production cost figures for a business and the Retail Price Index for the last six months.

	£	RPI
January	129,600	171.1
February	129,700	172.0
March	130,400	172.2
April	131,600	173.0
May	130,500	174.1
June	131,600	174.3

i)   Express each month's production cost figures in terms of January's prices.

ii) Explain what the figures in part (i) indicate.

iii) Express each month's production cost figures in terms of June's prices.

iv) Explain what the figures in part (iii) indicate.

v)   Is this the same conclusion that was drawn when the production costs were expressed in terms of January's prices?

time series analysis and indexation

7 Given below are the quarterly sales figures for a business for the last two years.

		Sales £
2005	Quarter 1	126,500
	Quarter 2	130,500
	Quarter 3	131,400
	Quarter 4	132,500
2006	Quarter 1	133,100
	Quarter 2	135,600
	Quarter 3	136,500
	Quarter 4	137,100

i) Calculate an index for these sales with Quarter 1 2005 as the base period.

ii) Explain what the index indicates about the sales.

iii) You are now also given the industry average price index for each of the quarters:

		Average price index
2005	Quarter 1	135.4
	Quarter 2	138.2
	Quarter 3	141.7
	Quarter 4	142.3
2006	Quarter 1	144.4
	Quarter 2	146.2
	Quarter 3	147.5
	Quarter 4	149.1

Express each quarters sales in terms of Quarter 4 2006 average prices.

iv) Calculate an index using the price adjusted figures from (iii) with Quarter 1 2005 as the base year.

v) Explain what the index indicates about the sales. Is there any difference between the situation shown by this index and the situation shown by the index in (ii).

8 a) AB Ltd set the standard cost of material C at £3.50 per litre when an index of material prices stood at 115. The index now stands at 145.

Task

Calculate the updated standard cost.

b) Culver Ltd decides to buy a machine from a company in ABC country for 100,000 ABC dollars, when the rate of exchange is 10 ABC dollars to the £. Payment for the machine occurs when the exchange rate is 11.2 ABC dollars to the £.

Task

Calculate the difference between the planned cost and actual cost of the machine.

time series analysis and indexation

9 The following data show the sales of the product sold by your company in the period 2004 to 2006.

Year	Quarter 1 £'000	Quarter 2 £'000	Quarter 3 £'000	Quarter 4 £'000
2004	86	42	57	112
2005	81	39	55	107
2006	77	35	52	99

Tasks

a) Plot the data and comment on them.

b) By means of a moving average find the trend.

c) The seasonal adjustments are as follows.

Quarter 1	Quarter 2	Quarter 3	Quarter 4
+9	−32	−16	+39

Give the sales for 2006 seasonally adjusted.

d) Forecast sales for each quarter of 2007 using a 'rule-of-thumb' approach and comment on the likely accuracy of your forecasts.

10 You have collected the following data on your company's quarterly sales in recent years.

	Quarter 1 Units	Quarter 2 Units	Quarter 3 Units	Quarter 4 Units
2004	200	110	320	240
2005	214	118	334	260
2006	220	124	340	278

As part of the sales budget preparation you have been asked to analyse this data.

Tasks

a) Calculate a moving average of quarterly sales.
b) Calculate the average seasonal variations.

chapter 4: STANDARD COSTING

1 A business budgeted to produce 2,680 units of one of its products during the month of May. The product uses 5 kg of raw material with a standard cost of £4.00 per kg. During the month the actual production was 2,800 units using 14,400 kg of raw materials costing £60,480.

You are to calculate:

i) the total materials cost variance
ii) the materials price variance
iii) the materials usage variance

2 A business has the following standard cost card for one unit of its product:

Direct materials	4 kg @ £3 per kg	£12
Direct labour	3 hours @ £9 per hour	£27
Fixed overheads	3 hours @ £4 per hour	£12

The budgeted production level is 12,000 units.

The actual results for the period are:

Production 11,400 units
Materials 44,800 kgs £150,480

You are to calculate:

i) the total materials cost variance
ii) the materials price variance
iii) the materials usage variance

standard costing

3 Production of product Z1 for the month of November in a manufacturing business was 12,100 units using 54,900 hours of direct labour costing £410,200. The standard cost card shows that the standard labour input for a unit of Z1 is 4.5 hours at a rate of £7.30 per hour.

You are to calculate:

i) the total labour cost variance
ii) the labour rate variance
iii) the labour efficiency variance

4 A business has the following standard cost card for one unit of its product:

Direct materials	4 kg @ £3 per kg	£12
Direct labour	3 hours @ £9 per hour	£27
Fixed overheads	3 hours @ £4 per hour	£12

The budgeted production level is 12,000 units.

The actual results for the period are:

Production	11,400 units
Labour 34,700 hours	£316,400

You are to calculate:

i) the total labour cost variance
ii) the labour rate variance
iii) the labour efficiency variance

5 A business has budgeted to produce and sell 10,000 units of its single product. The standard cost per unit is as follows:

Direct materials	£18
Direct labour	£13
Fixed production overhead	£7

During the period the actual results were:

Production and sales	11,500 units
Fixed production overheads	£75,000

You are to calculate:

i) the fixed overhead expenditure variance
ii) the fixed overhead volume variance

20

6   A business has a single product into which fixed overheads are absorbed on the basis of labour hours. The standard cost card shows that fixed overheads are to be absorbed on the basis of 6 labour hours per unit at a rate of £7.60 per hour. The budgeted level of production is 50,000 units.

The actual results for the period were that fixed overheads were £2,200,000 and that the actual hours worked were 310,000 and the actual units produced were 52,000.

i)   You are to calculate:

   a)   the fixed overhead expenditure variance
   b)   the fixed overhead volume variance

ii) Split the fixed overhead volume variance into the efficiency variance and the capacity variance

7   A business incurred fixed overheads of £203,000 in the month of May. The fixed overheads are absorbed into units of production at the rate of £3.60 per direct labour hour. The actual production during the month was 13,200 units although the budget had been for 14,000 units. The standard labour cost for the production is 4 hours per unit at an hourly rate of £8.00. During the month 50,000 labour hours were worked at a total cost of £403,600.

You are to calculate:

i)   the budgeted fixed overhead for the month
ii)   the fixed overhead expenditure variance
iii) the fixed overhead volume variance
iv)   the fixed overhead efficiency variance
v)   the fixed overhead capacity variance

standard costing

8 The standard cost card for a business's product is shown below:

	£
Direct materials 4.8 kg at £2.80 per kg	13.44
Direct labour 2.5 hours at £8.50 per hour	21.25
Fixed overheads 2.5 hours at £1.60 per hour	4.00
	38.69

The budgeted production was for 1,100 units in the month of July. The actual costs during the month of July for the production of 1,240 units were as follows:

	£
Direct materials 5,800 kg	17,100
Direct labour 3,280 hours	27,060
Fixed overheads	4,650

You are to:

i) calculate the materials price and usage variances

ii) calculate the labour rate and efficiency variances

iii) calculate the fixed overhead expenditure, efficiency and capacity variances

iv) prepare a reconciliation statement reconciling the standard cost of the production to the actual cost

9 XYZ Ltd is planning to make 120,000 units per period of a new product. The following standards have been set.

		Per unit
Direct material A		1.2 kgs at £11 per kg
Direct material B		4.7 kgs at £6 per kg
Direct labour:	Operation 1	42 minutes
	Operation 2	37 minutes
	Operation 3	11 minutes

Overheads are absorbed at the rate of £30 per labour hour. All direct operatives are paid at the rate of £8 per hour.

Actual results for the period were as follows.

Production 126,000 units

Direct labour cost £1.7m for 215,000 clock hours

Material A cost £1.65m for 150,000 kgs

Material B cost £3.6m for 590,000 kgs

Tasks

a) Calculate the standard cost for one unit.
b) Calculate the labour rate and efficiency variances.
c) Calculate the material price and usage variances.

10 A manufacturing company has provided you with the following data which relates to component RYX, for the period which has just ended.

	Budget	Actual
Number of labour hours	8,400	7,980
Production units	1,200	1,100
Overhead cost (all fixed)	£22,260	£25,536

Overheads are absorbed at a rate per standard labour hour.

Tasks

a) Calculate the fixed production overhead cost variance and the following subsidiary variances.

   i) Expenditure
   ii) Efficiency
   iii) Capacity

b) Provide a summary statement of these four variances.

11 You are employed as part of the management accounting team in a large industrial company which operates a four-weekly system of management reporting. Your division makes a single product, the Omega, and, because of the nature of the production process, there is no work in progress at any time.

The group management accountant has completed the calculation of the material and labour standard costing variances for the current period to 1 April but has not had the time to complete any other variances. Details of the variances already calculated are reproduced in the working papers below, along with other standard costing data.

Standard costing and budget data – four weeks ended 1 April			
	Quantity	Unit price	Cost per unit
Material (kgs)	7	£25.00	£175
Labour (hours)	40	£7.50	£300
Fixed overheads (hours)	40	£12.50	£500
			£975
	Units	Standard unit cost	Standard cost of production
Budgeted production for the four weeks	4,100	£975	£3,997,500

23

standard costing

Working papers

Actual production and expenditure for the four weeks ended 1 April

Units produced	3,850
Cost of 30,000 kgs of materials consumed	£795,000
Cost of 159,000 labour hours worked	£1,225,000
Expenditure on fixed overheads	£2,195,000

Material and labour variances

Material price variance	£45,000 (A)
Material usage variance	£76,250 (A)
Labour rate variance	£32,500 (A)
Labour efficiency variance	£37,500 (A)

Tasks

You have been requested to do the following.

a) Calculate the following variances.

　　i) The fixed overhead expenditure variance
　　ii) The fixed overhead volume variance
　　iii) The fixed overhead capacity variance
　　iv) The fixed overhead efficiency variance

b) Prepare a report for presentation to the production director reconciling the standard cost of production for the period with the actual cost of production.

c) The production director, who has only recently been appointed, is unfamiliar with fixed overhead variances. Because of this, the group management accountant has asked you to prepare a brief memo to the production director.

Your memo should do the following.

　　i) Outline the similarities and differences between fixed overhead variances and other cost variances such as the material and labour variances.

　　ii) Explain what is meant by the fixed overhead expenditure, volume, capacity and efficiency variances, and show, by way of examples, how these can be of help to the production director in the planning and controlling of the division.

chapter 5:
STANDARD COSTING – FURTHER ASPECTS

1 What factors should be taken into account when setting the standard cost of labour for a product?

2 What are the main problems with using ideal standards in a business?

3 State possible reasons for each of the following variances which are all independent of each other:

　i)　a favourable materials price variance
　ii)　a favourable materials usage variance
　iii)　an adverse labour rate variance
　iv)　an adverse labour efficiency variance

4 State the factors that may be a cause of each of the following variances (either favourable or adverse):

　i)　fixed overhead volume variance
　ii)　fixed overhead efficiency variance
　iii)　fixed overhead capacity variance

5 i) A business has had to use a less-skilled grade of labour in its production process for the last week. What effect is this likely to have on the variances for the week?

　ii) A factory had a machine breakdown which resulted in three days of production delays last month. What effect is this likely to have on the variances for the month?

standard costing – further aspects

6 Given below is the operating statement for a manufacturing business for the last month:

Reconciliation of standard cost of actual production to actual cost – March 2006

	Variances Adverse £	Favourable £	£
Standard cost of actual production			672,500
Variances:			
Materials price	24,300		
Materials usage		6,780	
Labour rate	10,600		
Labour efficiency		10,300	
Fixed overhead expenditure		7,490	
Fixed overhead capacity		4,800	
Fixed overhead efficiency		6,100	
	34,900	35,470	
Add: adverse variances			34,900
Less: favourable variances			(35,470)
Actual cost of production			671,930

A number of factors about the month's production have been discovered:

- at the end of the previous month a new warehouse had been purchased which has meant a saving in warehouse rental

- six new machines were installed at the start of the month which are more power efficient than the old machines, but also more expensive, causing a larger depreciation charge

- there was an unexpected increase in the materials price during the month and when other suppliers were contacted it was found that they were all charging approximately the same price for the materials

- a higher than normal skilled grade of labour was used during the month due to staff shortages. The production process is a skilled process and the benefit has been that these employees, although more expensive, have produced the goods faster and with less wastage. This particular group of employees are also keen to work overtime and, as the business wishes to build up stock levels, advantage of this has been taken.

Suggest what effect the combination of the factors given above might have had on the reported variances and make suggestions as to any action that should be taken in light of these factors.

standard costing – further aspects

7 The standard direct materials cost for a business's product is:

6 kg @ £8.00 per kg   £48.00

During the month of October production was 7,400 units of the product and the actual materials cost was £397,400 for 45,100 kgs. The price of the materials has been unexpectedly increased to £8.50 per kg for the whole month.

i) Calculate the total materials price variance.

ii) Show how the total materials price variance can be analysed into the planning element that has been caused by the price increase and the control element caused by other factors.

iii) How would this affect how responsibility for the variance was assessed?

8 A business's product has a standard direct material cost of £26.00 (4 kgs @ £6.50 per kg). During the month of March the total production of the product was 2,500 units using 10,600 kgs of materials at a total cost of £73,140. During the month the price was unexpectedly increased due to a shortage of the material to £7.00 per kg.

i) Calculate the total materials price variance and analyse this into the planning variance due to price increase and the control variance due to other factors.

ii) How would the analysis of the sub-variances affect how the responsibility for the total variance would be assessed?

9 A business makes a product which uses a raw material which has a standard cost of £7.00 per kg. Each unit of the product requires 5 kgs of this material. The price of the materials for the last few years has been subjected to a time series analysis and the following percentage seasonal variations have been seen to occur.

Jan – Mar	–6%
Apr – June	+8%
July – Aug	+11%
Sept – Dec	–13%

During March 18,000 units of the product were made and the price paid for the 92,000 kgs of material was £631,200.

What is the total materials price variance and how can this be analysed to show the planning variance due to the season and the control variance due to other factors?

standard costing – further aspects

10 The standard cost of direct materials for a product is made up of 8 kgs of material at an average standard cost of £4.00 per kg. It has been noted over the years that the cost of the material fluctuates on a seasonal basis around the average standard cost as follows:

Jan – Mar	+12%
Apr – June	+18%
July – Sept	−16%
Oct – Dec	−14%

In the month of June the actual production was 5,000 units and 42,300 kgs of material were used at a cost of £194,580.

What is the total materials price variance, the planning variance caused by the seasonal price change and the control variance caused by other factors?

11 a) You are employed as the assistant management accountant in the group accountant's office of Hampstead plc. Hampstead recently acquired Finchley Ltd, a small company making a specialist product called the Alpha. Standard marginal costing is used by all the companies within the group and, from 1 August 2006, Finchley Ltd will also be required to use standard marginal costing in its management reports. Part of your job is to manage the implementation of standard marginal costing at Finchley Ltd.

John Wade, the managing director of Finchley, is not clear how the change will help him as a manager. He has always found Finchley's existing absorption costing system sufficient. By way of example, he shows you a summary of his management accounts for the three months to 31 May 2006. These are reproduced below.

Statement of budgeted and actual cost of Alpha production – 3 months ended 31 May 2006

	Actual		Budget		Variance
Alpha production (units)	10,000		12,000		
	Inputs	£	Inputs	£	£
Materials	32,000 m	377,600	36,000 m	432,000	54,400
Labour	70,000 hrs	422,800	72,000 hrs	450,000	27,200
Fixed overhead absorbed		330,000		396,000	66,000
Fixed overhead unabsorbed		75,000		0	(75,000)
		1,205,400		1,278,000	72,600

John Wade is not convinced that standard marginal costing will help him to manage Finchley. 'My current system tells me all I need to know,' he said. 'As you can see, we are £72,600 below budget which is really excellent given that we lost production as a result of a serious machine breakdown.'

standard costing – further aspects

To help John Wade understand the benefits of standard marginal costing, you agree to prepare a statement for the three months ended 31 May 2006 reconciling the standard cost of production to the actual cost of production.

Tasks

i) Use the budget data to determine the following.

   1) The standard marginal cost per Alpha
   2) The standard cost of actual Alpha production for the three months to 31 May 2006

ii) Calculate the following variances.

   1) Material price variance
   2) Material usage variance
   3) Labour rate variance
   4) Labour efficiency variance
   5) Fixed overhead expenditure variance

iii) Write a short memo to John Wade. You memo should:

   1) include a statement reconciling the actual cost of production to the standard cost of production;
   2) give TWO reasons why your variances might differ from those in his original management accounting statement despite using the same basic data;
   3) **briefly** discuss ONE further reason why your reconciliation statement provides improved management information.

b) On receiving your memo, John Wade informs you that the machine breakdown resulted in the workforce having to be paid for 12,000 hours even though no production took place, and that an index of material prices stood at 466.70 when the budget was prepared but at 420.03 when the material was purchased.

Task

Using this new information, prepare a revised statement reconciling the standard cost of production to the actual cost of production. Your statement should subdivide both the labour variances into those parts arising from the machine breakdown and those parts arising from normal production, and the material price variance into that part due to the change in the index and that part arising for other reasons.

12 (a) Pronto Ltd was recently established in the UK to assemble cars. All parts are sent directly to the UK in the form of a kit by Pronto's owner from its headquarters in a country called Erehwon.

The contract between Pronto and its owner is a fixed price contract per kit and the contract specifies zero faults in all of the parts. This fixed price was used to establish the standard cost per kit. Despite this, the managing director of Pronto, Richard Jones, is concerned to receive the following statement from the management accounting department where you are employed as an accounting technician.

standard costing – further aspects

	September 2006	October 2006	November 2006
Kits delivered	2,000	2,100	2,050
Actual cost invoiced	£12,059,535	£11,385,495	£10,848,600
Unit cost per kit to nearest £	£6,030	£5,422	£5,292

Richard Jones cannot understand why, with a fixed price contract and guaranteed quality, the unit cost should vary over the three months. He provides you with the following information.

- The contract's cost was fixed in Erehwon dollars of $54,243 per kit.
- There has been no change in the agreed cost of the parts and no other costs incurred.

On further investigation you discover that the exchange rate between the UK pound and the Erehwon dollar was as follows.

At time of contract	September 2006	October 2006	November 2006
$9.80	$9.00	$10.00	$10.25

Task

Prepare a memo to Richard Jones. Your memo should include the following.

i) A calculation of:

1) the UK cost per kit at the time the contract was agreed;

2) the UK cost of the kits delivered using the exchange rates given for each of the three months;

3) the price variance due to exchange rate differences for each of the three months;

4) any usage variance in each of the three months, assuming no other reason for the price variance;

ii) A brief discussion about whether price variances due to exchange rate differences should be excluded from any standard costing report prepared for the production manager of Pronto Ltd.

b) Pronto uses a highly mechanised and computerised moving assembly line known as a track to build the cars. Although individual employees are assigned to particular parts of the track, they work in teams. If the production of cars slows below the speed of the track, teams help each other to maintain the speed of the track and the production of cars. Because of this approach, labour is viewed as a fixed cost and machine hours (the hours that the track is in use) are used to charge overheads to production.

For the week ended 28 November 2006, the management accounting department has prepared a statement of budgeted and actual fixed overhead for Richard Jones. This is reproduced below.

Pronto Ltd: Budgeted and actual fixed overheads – week ended 28 November 2006

	Budget	Actual
Car production	560	500
Machine (or track) hours of production	140	126
Fixed overheads:	£	£
Rent and rates	16,000	16,000
Maintenance and depreciation	10,000	13,000
Power	75,000	71,000
Labour	739,000	742,000
Total	840,000	842,000

Richard Jones finds that the statement is not particularly helpful as it does not give him sufficient information to manage the company. He asks for your help.

Tasks

In preparation for a meeting with Richard Jones, do the following.

i) Calculate the following.

1) Budgeted overheads per machine (or track) hour
2) Budgeted number of cars produced per machine (or track) hour
3) Standard hours of actual production

ii) Calculate the following variances using the information identified in (i).

1) Fixed overhead expenditure variance
2) Fixed overhead volume variance
3) Fixed overhead efficiency variance
4) Fixed overhead capacity variance

iii) Prepare a statement for the week ended 28 November 2006 reconciling the fixed overheads incurred to the fixed overheads absorbed in production.

13 (a) You are employed as a management accountant in the head office of Travel Holdings plc. Travel Holdings owns a number of transport businesses. One of them is Travel Ferries Ltd. Travel Ferries operates ferries which carry passengers and vehicles across a large river. Each year, standard costs are used to develop the budget for Travel Ferries Ltd. The latest budgeted and actual operating results are reproduced below.

standard costing – further aspects

Travel Ferries Ltd
Budgeted and actual operating results for the year to 30 November 2006

Operating data	Budget		Actual	
Number of ferry crossings		6,480		5,760
Operating hours of ferries		7,776		7,488
Cost data		£		£
Fuel	1,244,160 litres	497,664	1,232,800 litres	567,088
Labour	93,312 hours	699,840	89,856 hours	696,384
Fixed overheads		466,560		472,440
Cost of operations		1,664,064		1,735,912

Other accounting information

- Fuel and labour are variable costs.
- Fixed overheads are absorbed on the basis of budgeted **operating hours**.

One of your duties is to prepare costing information and a standard costing reconciliation statement for the chief executive of Travel Holdings.

Tasks

i) Calculate the following information.

1) The standard price of fuel per litre
2) The standard litres of fuel for 5,760 ferry crossings
3) The standard labour rate per hour
4) The standard labour hours for 5,760 ferry crossings
5) The standard fixed overhead cost per budgeted operating hour
6) The standard operating hours for 5,760 crossings
7) The standard fixed overhead cost absorbed by the actual 5,760 ferry crossings

ii) Using the data provided in the operating results and your answers to part (i), calculate the following variances.

1) The material price variance for the fuel
2) The material usage variance for the fuel
3) The labour rate variance
4) The labour efficiency variance
5) The fixed overhead expenditure variance
6) The fixed overhead volume variance
7) The fixed overhead capacity variance
8) The fixed overhead efficiency variance

iii) Prepare a statement reconciling the actual cost of operations to the standard cost of operations for the year to 30 November 2006.

b) On receiving your reconciliation statement, the chief executive is concerned about the large number of adverse variances. She is particularly concerned about the excessive cost of fuel used during the year. A colleague gives you the following information.

- The actual market price of fuel per litre during the year was 20 percent higher than the standard price.

- Fuel used directly varies with the number of operating hours.

- The difference between the standard and actual operating hours for the 5,760 ferry crossings arose entirely because of weather conditions.

Tasks

Write a memo to the chief executive. Your memo should do the following.

i) Subdivide the material price variance into two parts.

1) That part arising from the standard price being different from the actual market price of fuel

2) The part due to other reasons

ii) Identify ONE variance which is not controllable and give ONE reason why the variance is not controllable.

iii) Identify TWO variances which are controllable and which should be investigated. For each variance, give ONE reason why it is controllable.

14 a) You are the assistant management accountant at the Bare Foot Hotel complex on the tropical island of St Nicolas. The hotel complex is a luxury development. All meals and entertainment are included in the price of the holidays and guests only have to pay for drinks.

The Bare Foot complex aims to create a relaxing atmosphere. Because of this, meals are available throughout the day and guests can eat as many times as they wish.

The draft performance report for the hotel for the seven days ended 27 November 2006 is reproduced below.

standard costing – further aspects

Bare Foot Hotel Complex
Draft performance report for seven days ended 27 November 2006

	Notes		Budget		Actual
Guests			540		648
		$	$	$	$
Variable costs					
Meal costs	1		34,020		49,896
Catering staff costs	2,3		3,780		5,280
Total variable costs			37,800		55,176
Fixed overhead costs					
Salaries of other staff		5,840		6,000	
Local taxes		4,500		4,200	
Light, heat and power		2,500		2,600	
Depreciation of buildings and equipment		5,000		4,000	
Entertainment		20,500		21,000	
Total fixed overheads			38,340		37,800
Total cost of providing for guests			76,140		92,976

Notes

1. Budgeted cost of meals: number of guests × 3 meals per day × 7 days × $3 per meal

2. Budged cost of catering staff: each member of the catering staff is to prepare and serve 12 meals per hour. Cost = (number of guests × 3 meals per day × 7 days ÷ 12 meals per hour) × $4 per hour.

3. Actual hours worked by catering staff = 1,200 hours

Other notes

The amount of food per meal has been kept under strict portion control. Since preparing the draft performance report, however, it has been discovered that guests have eaten, on average, four meals per day.

You report to Alice Groves, the general manager of the hotel, who feels that the format of the draft performance report could be improved to provide her with more meaningful management information. She suggests that the budgeted and actual data given in the existing draft performance report is rearranged in the form of a standard costing report.

Tasks

i) Use the budget data, the actual data and the notes to the performance report to calculate the following for the seven days ended 27 November 2006.

1) The actual number of meals served

2) The standard number of meals which should have been served for the actual number of guests

   3) The actual hourly rate paid to catering staff

   4) The standard hours allowed for catering staff to serve three meals per day for the actual number of guests

   5) The standard fixed overhead per guest

   6) The total standard cost for the actual number of guests

 ii) Use the data given in the task and your answers to part (a)(i) to calculate the following variances for the seven days ended 27 November 2006.

   1) The material price variance for meals served

   2) The material usage variance for meals served

   3) The labour rate variance for catering staff

   4) The labour efficiency variance for catering staff, based on a standard of three meals served per guest per day

   5) The fixed overhead expenditure variance

   6) The fixed overhead volume variance on the assumption that the fixed overhead absorption rate is based on the budgeted number of guests per seven days

 iii) Prepare a statement reconciling the standard cost for the actual number of guests to the actual cost for the actual number of guests for the seven days ended 27 November 2006.

b) On receiving your reconciliation statement, Alice Groves asks the following questions.

- How much of the labour efficiency variance is due to guests taking, on average, four meals per day rather than the three provided for in the budget and how much is due to other reasons?

- Would it be feasible to subdivide the fixed overhead volume variance into a capacity and efficiency variance?

Task

Write a memo to Alice Groves. Your memo should do the following.

 i) Divide the labour efficiency variance into that part due to guests taking more meals than planned and that part due to other efficiency reasons.

 ii) Explain the meaning of the fixed overhead capacity and efficiency variances.

 iii) Briefly discuss whether or not it is feasible to calculate the fixed overhead capacity and efficiency variances for the Bare Foot Hotel complex.

standard costing – further aspects

15 You are employed as a financial analyst at Drampton plc, a computer retailer. One of your duties is to prepare a standard costing reconciliation statement for the finance director.

The company sells two types of computer, personal computers (PCs) for individual use and servers for large organisations. PCs are sold by advertising in newspapers. Customers telephone Drampton to place an order and the telephone call is answered by trained operators. Drampton pays the cost of the telephone call. The total standard cost of one phone call is shown below.

Standard cost of one call

Expense	Quantity	Cost	Cost per call £
Telephone cost	1 unit	£0.07 per unit	0.07
Operators' wages	6 minutes	£7.00 per hour	0.70
Fixed overheads [1]	6 minutes	£6.50 per hour	0.65
Standard cost of one telephone call			**1.42**

[1] Fixed overheads are based on budgeted operator hours.

Drampton's finance director gives you the following information for the three months ended 31 May 2006.

- Budgeted number of calls — 900,000 calls
- Actual number of calls — 1,000,000 calls
- Actual expenses

	Quantity	Cost £
Telephone cost	1,200,000 units	79,200
Operators' wages	114,000 hours	877,800
Fixed overheads		540,400
Actual cost of actual operations		**1,497,400**

Tasks

a) Calculate the following information.

　i) Actual cost of a telephone unit
　ii) Actual hourly wage rate of operators
　iii) Standard number of operator hours for 1,000,000 calls
　iv) Budgeted cost of fixed overheads for the three months ended 31 May 2006
　v) Budgeted number of operator hours for the three months ended 31 May 2006
　vi) Standard cost of actual operations

b) Using the data given and your answers to part (a), calculate the following variances.

　i) Price variance for telephone calls
　ii) Usage variance for telephone calls
　iii) Labour rate variance for the telephone operators
　iv) Labour efficiency variance for the telephone operators

standard costing – further aspects

v) Fixed overhead expenditure variance
vi) Fixed overheard volume variance
vii) Fixed overhead capacity variance
viii) Fixed overhead efficiency variance

c) Prepare a statement for the three months ended 31 May 2006 reconciling the standard cost of actual operations to the actual cost of actual operations.

16 Croxton Ltd makes a specialized chemical, X14, in barrels at its factory. The factory has two departments: the processing department and the finishing department. Because of the technology involved, Croxton apportions both budgeted and actual total factory fixed overheads between the two departments on the basis of budgeted machine hours.

The standard absorption cost per barrel of X14 in the processing department, and the budgeted production for the five weeks ended 31 May 2006, are shown below.

Processing department: standard cost per barrel of X14			
Input	Quantity	Standard price/rate	Cost £
Material	10 litres	£60 per litre	600
Labour	8 labour hrs	£8 per labour hr	64
Fixed overheads	16 machine hrs	£20 per machine hr	320
Standard absorption cost per barrel			984
Budgeted production 5 weeks ending 31 May 2006			45 barrels

You are employed by Croxton Ltd as an accounting technician. One of your duties is to prepare standard costing reconciliation statements. Croxton's finance director gives you the following information for the five weeks ended 31 May 2006.

Total factory budgeted and actual data

- Factory budgeted machine hours   1,152 machine hours
- Factory budgeted fixed overheads   £23,040
- Factory actual fixed overheads   £26,000
- Budgeted **and** actual factory fixed overheads are apportioned between the processing and finishing departments **on the basis of budgeted machine hours**.

37

standard costing – further aspects

Processing department actual data

- Actual costs

	Total costs
Materials at £58.50 per litre	£23,985
Labour (328 hours)	£2,788

- Actual production output   40 barrels
- Actual machine hours worked   656 hours
- There was no work in progress at any stage.

Tasks

a) Calculate the following information for the processing department.

  i) Actual litres of material used
  ii) Standard litres of material required for 40 barrels of X14
  iii) Average actual labour rate per hour
  iv) Standard labour hours required for 40 barrels of X14
  v) Budgeted number of machine hours
  vi) Budgeted fixed overheads
  vii) Actual fixed overheads
  viii) Standard machine hours produced
  ix) Standard absorption cost of actual production
  x) Actual absorption cost of actual production

b) Using data given and your answers to part (a), calculate the following variances for the processing department.

  i) Material price variance
  ii) Material usage variance
  iii) Labour rate variance
  iv) Labour efficiency variance
  v) Fixed overhead expenditure variance
  vi) Fixed overhead volume variance
  vii) Fixed overhead efficiency variance
  viii) Fixed overhead capacity variance

c) Prepare a statement for the five weeks ended 31 May 2006 reconciling the standard absorption cost of actual production with the actual absorption cost of actual production.

d) Judith Green is the production manager of the processing department. You show her the statement reconciling the actual and standard costs of actual production. Judith then gives you the following additional information.

   - When the standard costs were agreed, a price index for the material used in making the X14 was 140, but during the five weeks ended 31 May it was 133.

   - Actual production output was 40 barrels but Croxton had to make 41 barrels of X14 as one barrel had to be scrapped on completion. This was because the barrel was damaged. The scrapped barrel had no value.

- If labour hours worked exceed 320 hours per five weeks, overtime is incurred. The overtime premium is £8.00 per hour of overtime.

- There is just one customer for the X14. The customer purchased 40 barrels during the five weeks ended 31 May 2006.

Judith believes there is no need to examine the variances any further, for a number of reasons.

- The material price variance clearly shows that the purchasing department is efficient.

- The labour rate, labour efficiency and material usage variances were entirely due to the one scrapped barrel.

- Fixed overheads are not controllable by the processing department.

Write a memo to Judith Green. In your memo you should do the following.

i) Use the material price index to identify a revised standard price for the materials used in X14.

ii) Subdivide the material price variance calculated in task (b)(i) into that part due to the change in the price index and that part due to other reasons.

iii) Briefly explain whether the material price variance calculated in task (b)(i) arose from efficiencies in the purchasing department.

iv) Explain whether the one scrapped barrel might fully account for the following.

    1) Material usage variance
    2) Labour efficiency variance
    3) Labour rate variance

v) Give ONE reason why the fixed overheads might not be controllable by the processing department.

chapter 6:
PERFORMANCE INDICATORS

1. Given below are the production figures for a factory for the last four months.

	November	December	January	February
Output in units	64,300	68,900	62,100	60,200
Budgeted output	65,000	65,000	60,000	62,000
Hours worked	98,200	107,300	90,200	92,000

   The standard time for each unit of production is 1.5 hours.

   Calculate the following performance indicators for each of the four months:

   i) actual hours per unit
   ii) efficiency ratio
   iii) capacity ratio
   iv) activity ratio

2. What is productivity? Does increased productivity always lead to increased profit? Give examples of increases in productivity that will lead to increased profit and examples that will not necessarily lead to increased profit.

3. Suggest possible measures of productivity for each of the following types of organisation:

   i) a taxi firm
   ii) a hospital
   iii) a motorbike courier service
   iv) a firm of accountants
   v) a retail store
   vi) a maker of handmade pottery

performance indicators

4 You are given the following information about a small manufacturing business for the year ending 31 March 2006:

Sales revenue	£1,447,600
Cost of materials used	£736,500
Cost of bought in services	£316,900
Number of employees	15

What is the total value added and the value added per employee?

5 Given below are production and sales figures for a manufacturing organisation for the last three months:

	January	February	March
Production costs	£552,300	£568,500	£629,500
Production wages	£104,800	£98,300	£110,800
Output in units	8,540	8,670	9,320
Hours worked	8,635	7,820	9,280
Budgeted output	8,500	8,200	9,500
Sales revenue	£916,000	£923,000	£965,000
Number of employees	55	55	58

Production costs are made up of the materials for production and the bought in services required in the month. It is estimated that each unit takes 1.1 hours to produce.

a) Calculate the following performance indicators for each of the last three months and for the three months in total:

    i) productivity per labour hour
    ii) efficiency ratio
    iii) capacity ratio
    iv) activity ratio
    v) cost per unit
    vi) value added per employee

b) Comment briefly on what the performance indicators show about the business.

performance indicators

6 Given below is the summarised production information for a manufacturing organisation for the last month:

Budgeted production in units	15,000
Actual production in units	14,200
Labour hours worked	46,000
Standard hours for each unit	3

a) Calculate the following performance indicators and briefly explain what each one means:

   i) efficiency ratio
   ii) capacity ratio
   iii) production volume ratio

b) Show how the three performance indicators calculated in part a) are related.

c) If the workforce had operated at 95% efficiency how many labour hours would have been saved last month?

7 A manufacturing organisation had a budgeted output planned for the quarter ending 31 March of 428,000 units but 467,800 units were in fact produced. The standard production time for each unit is 1.5 hours. The actual hours worked were 748,500 and the total production costs were £3,204,430.

Calculate the following performance indicators for the quarter:

i) cost per unit
ii) efficiency ratio
iii) capacity ratio
iv) activity ratio

8 Given below is the profit and loss account for a business for the year ending 31 March 2006 and a balance sheet at that date.

Profit and loss account

	£	£
Turnover		2,650,400
Cost of sales		
Opening stock	180,000	
Purchases	1,654,400	
	1,834,400	
Less: closing stock	191,200	
		1,643,200
Gross profit		1,007,200
Less: expenses		
Selling and distribution costs	328,400	
Administration expenses	342,200	
		670,600
Operating profit		336,600
Interest payable		36,000
		300,600
Tax		87,400
Profit after tax		213,200
Profit and loss reserve brought forward		374,300
Profit and loss reserve carried forward		587,500

Balance sheet

	£	£
Fixed assets		1,920,400
Current assets:		
Stock	191,200	
Debtors	399,400	
Bank	16,800	
	607,400	
Creditors	(190,300)	
Net current assets		417,100
		2,337,500
Less: long term loan		600,000
		1,737,500
Capital		1,000,000
Reserves		150,000
Profit and loss reserve		587,500
		1,737,500

a) Using the profit and loss account and balance sheet calculate the following performance indicators:

i) gross profit margin
ii) net profit margin
iii) return on capital employed
iv) asset turnover
v) fixed asset turnover
vi) current ratio
vii) quick ratio
viii) debtors' collection period
ix) stock turnover in days
x) creditors' payment period

b) If the creditors payment period was increased to 60 days what effect would this have on the cash balance?

9 Given below is a summary of a business's performance for the last six months:

	July £'000	Aug £'000	Sept £'000	Oct £'000	Nov £'000	Dec £'000
Sales	560	540	500	550	580	600
Cost of sales	370	356	330	374	400	415
Expenses	123	119	110	116	122	131
Interest payable	–	–	–	3	3	3
Shareholders funds	440	445	458	468	480	490
Loan	–	–	–	50	50	50

a) For each month of the year you are to calculate the following performance indicators:

i) gross profit margin
ii) net profit margin
iii) percentage of expenses to sales
iv) return on capital employed
v) asset turnover

b) Comment on what the figures calculated in part a) show about the performance of the business over the last six months.

performance indicators

10 Given below is a summary of the performance of a business for the last three years:

	2004 £'000	2005 £'000	2006 £'000
Sales	1,420	1,560	1,740
Cost of sales	850	950	1,080
Expenses	370	407	469
Interest	–	7	6
Capital and reserves	1,500	1,600	1,700
Long term loan	–	100	100
Fixed assets	1,100	1,300	1,500
Debtors	155	198	230
Stock	105	140	190
Creditors	140	162	193
Bank balance	280	224	73

For each of the three years you are to calculate the following performance measures and comment on what the measures indicate about the performance of the business over the period:

i) gross profit margin
ii) net profit margin
iii) return on capital employed
iv) asset turnover
v) fixed asset turnover
vi) current ratio
vii) quick ratio
viii) debtors' collection period
ix) stock turnover in days
x) creditors' payment period

performance indicators

11 A manufacturing business has three small divisions, North, South and Central. The figures for the last three months of 2006 for each division are given below:

	North £	South £	Central £
Financial details			
Sales	870,000	560,000	640,000
Opening stocks	34,000	41,000	34,000
Closing stocks	32,000	29,000	38,000
Purchases	590,000	380,000	420,000
Expenses	121,000	106,000	138,000
Capital	980,000	690,000	615,000
Creditors	103,400	42,600	66,700
Debtors	100,100	107,300	87,600
Non-financial details			
Factory floor area	500 sq m	400 sq m	420 sq m
Factory employees	18	12	15
Hours worked	8,500	5,800	7,000
Units produced	17,000	10,200	12,300

a) You are to calculate the following performance indicators for each division:

  i) gross profit margin
  ii) net profit margin
  iii) return on capital employed
  iv) asset turnover
  v) stock turnover in months (using average stock)
  vi) debtors' collection period in months
  vii) creditors' payment period in months
  viii) units produced per square metre of floor area
  ix) units produced per employee
  x) units produced per hour

b) Use the performance indicators calculated in (a) to compare the performances of the three divisions for the three month period.

12 i) A business operates on a gross profit margin of 48% and sales for the period were £380,000. What is the gross profit?

ii) A business operates on a gross profit margin of 34% and the gross profit made in the period was £425,000. What were the sales for the period?

iii) A business had sales of £85,000 in a month and with a gross profit margin of 40% and a net profit margin of 11.5%. What were the expenses for the month?

iv) A business has a return on capital employed of 11.6% and made a net profit for the period of £100,000. What is the capital employed?

47

performance indicators

v) A business has a net profit percentage of 8% and a return on capital employed of 10%. What is the asset turnover of the business?

vi) A business has opening stocks and closing stocks of £158,000 and £182,000 and made purchases during the year totalling £560,000. How many times did stock turnover during the year?

vii) A business has a debtor collection period of 48 days and the closing debtors figure is £96,000. What are the sales for the year?

13 A business has a gross profit margin of 42.3% for the year ending 31 December 2005 and had a gross profit margin of 44.6% for the year ending 31 December 2004. Suggest reasons for the change in gross profit margin.

14 Given below are the summarised profit and loss accounts and balance sheets of a business for the last two years.

Summarised profit and loss accounts

	Y/e 31 Dec 2006 £'000	Y/e 31 Dec 2005 £'000
Turnover	602	564
Cost of sales	329	325
Gross profit	273	239
Expenses	163	143
Operating profit	110	96
Interest payable	10	10
Profit before tax	100	86
Tax	40	26
Retained profit	60	60
Profit and loss reserve b/f	240	180
Profit and loss reserve c/f	300	240

Summarised balance sheet

	31 Dec 2006		31 Dec 2005	
	£	£	£	£
Fixed assets		709		632
Current assets:				
Stock	28		32	
Debtors	66		68	
Cash	2		3	
	96		103	
Creditors	55		45	
Net current assets		41		58
		750		690
Long term loan		150		150
		600		540
Capital		300		300
Profit and loss reserve		300		240
		600		540

a) For each of the two years calculate the following performance indicators, based on total capital employed when relevant.

    i)   gross profit margin
    ii)   net profit margin
    iii) return on capital employed
    iv) asset turnover
    v)   fixed asset turnover
    vi) current ratio
    vii) quick ratio
    viii) debtors' collection period
    ix) stock turnover in days
    x)   creditors' payment period

b) Comment upon the performance of the business for the last two years basing your comments on the performance indicators calculated in part a).

15   What are the main limitations of ratio analysis?

performance indicators

16 Melosoven Ltd is a subsidiary company of Rengbaud plc and manufactures motor components. It is run as a separate entity from the parent company, however. Rengbaud plc monitors the performance of subsidiaries using a quarterly financial ratio analysis. Melosoven Ltd's factory is in Swansea.

You are employed as a financial analyst in Rengbaud plc's corporate finance department at the group's Leicestershire headquarters. Louise Simpson, the managing director of Melosoven Ltd, is at group head office for a meeting. She has called into your office with the last quarter's summary results which have just been faxed to her. Louise needs to have these figures analysed as quickly as possible and has obtained the agreement of Rob Hutchings, your immediate superior, for you to assist her.

Melosoven Ltd
Financial results for quarter 4

Operating statement	£'000	£'000	Operating net assets at quarter end	£'000	£'000
Sales		4,759	Fixed assets (NBV)		7,253
Materials	1,583				
Labour	1,196		Current assets		
Production overheads	1,201		Materials stocks	305	
		3,980	Work in progress	224	
Gross profit		779	Finished goods stocks	1,326	
Admin overheads		427	Debtors	2,040	
Operating profit		352	Bank and cash	83	
				3,978	
			Current liabilities		
Stock changes			Trade creditors	2,362	
Materials		+ 43	Other creditors	758	
Work in progress		0		3,120	
Finished goods		+ 231	Working capital		858
			Net assets		8,111

Tasks

a) Given that there are 91 days in quarter 4, prepare a table containing the following performance indicators for Melosoven Ltd for quarter 4.

  i) The quarterly return on capital employed

  ii) The operating profit margin as a percentage

  iii) The quarterly asset turnover

  iv) The average age of period-end debtors in days

  v) The average age of period-end trade creditors in days

vi) The average age of period-end materials stocks in days

vii) The average age of period-end finished goods stocks in days

b) Louise needs a comparison between the quarter 4 results and those for the earlier quarters to take with her to a meeting at which Rengbaud plc's board will be reviewing the performance of Melosoven Ltd.

You are able to extract the following figures from Rengbaud plc's corporate information system.

Performance indicators for Melosoven Ltd for quarters 1 to 3			
	Q1	Q2	Q3
Return on capital employed	4.3%	1.2%	2.8%
Operating profit margin	9.0%	2.6%	5.3%
Quarterly asset turnover	0.54	0.55	0.52
Age of debtors in days	39	38	44
Age of trade creditors in days	192	167	158
Age of materials stocks in days	29	24	18
Age of finished goods stocks in days	51	41	28

i) Given that Melosoven Ltd's business is not seasonal, update the above table to include Melosoven Ltd's quarter 4 figures.

ii) Write a briefing note to Louise comparing Melosoven Ltd's quarter 4 figures with those for quarters 1 to 3.

17 Middle plc owns two subsidiaries, East Ltd and West Ltd, producing soft drinks. Both companies rent their premises and both use plant of similar size and technology. Middle plc requires the plant in the subsidiaries to be written off over ten years using straight-line depreciation and assuming zero residual values.

East Ltd was established five years ago but West Ltd has only been established for two years. Goods returned by customers generally arise from quality failures and are destroyed. Financial and other data relating to the two companies are reproduced below.

performance indicators

Profit and loss accounts year to 30 November 2006	West Ltd £'000	East Ltd £'000	Balance sheets extracts at 30 November 2006	West Ltd £'000	East Ltd £'000
Turnover	18,000	17,600	Plant	16,000	10,000
Less Returns	90	176	Depreciation to date	3,200	5,000
Net turnover	17,910	17,424	Net book value	12,800	5,000
Material	2,000	2,640	Current assets	4,860	3,000
Labour	4,000	4,840	Current liabilities	(2,320)	(1,500)
Production overheads*	3,000	3,080	Net assets	15,340	6,500
Gross profit	8,910	6,864			
Marketing	2,342	1,454			
Research & development	1,650	1,010			
Training	950	450			
Administration	900	1,155			
Operating profit	3,068	2,795			

*Includes plant depreciation of £1,600,000 for West Ltd and £1,000,000 for East Ltd

Other data (000's litres)	West Ltd	East Ltd
Gross sales	20,000	22,000
Returns	100	220
Net sales	19,900	21,780
Orders received in year	20,173	22,854

You are employed by Middle plc as a member of a team monitoring the performance of subsidiaries within the group. Middle plc aims to provide its shareholders with the best possible return for their investment and to meet customers' expectations. It does this by comparing the performance of subsidiaries and using the more efficient ones for benchmarking.

Tasks

Your team leader, Angela Wade, has asked you to prepare a report evaluating the performance of West Ltd and East Ltd. Your report should do the following.

a) Calculate and explain the meaning of the following financial ratios for each company.

   i) The return on capital employed
   ii) The asset turnover
   iii) The sales (or operating profit) margin

b) Calculate the percentage of faulty sales as a measure of the level of customer service for each company.

c) Identify one other possible measure of the level of customer service which could be derived from the accounting data.

d) Identify TWO limitations to your analysis in task a), using the data in the accounts.

18 a) You are employed by Micro Circuits Ltd as a financial analyst reporting to Angela Frear, the Director of Corporate Strategy. One of your responsibilities is to monitor the performance of subsidiaries within the group. Financial and other data relating to subsidiary A is reproduced below.

Subsidiary A

Profit and loss account year to 30 November 2006

	£'000	£'000
Sales		4,000
less returns		100
Turnover[1]		3,900
Material	230	
Labour	400	
Production overheads[2]	300	
Cost of production	930	
Opening finished stock	50	
Closing finished stock	(140)	
Cost of sales		840
Gross profit		3,060
Marketing	500	
Customer support	400	
Research and development	750	
Training	140	
Administration	295	2,085
Operating profit		975

Extract from balance sheet at 30 November 2006

	£'000	£'000	£'000
Fixed assets	Land and buildings	Plant and machinery	Total
Cost	2,000	2,500	4,500
Additions	–	1,800	1,800
	2,000	4,300	6,300
Accumulated dep'n	160	1,700	1,860
	1,840	2,600	4,440
Raw material stock	15		
Finished goods stock	140		
	155		
Debtors	325		
Cash and bank	40		
Creditors	(85)		
			435
Net assets			4,875

Other information

Notes

1. **Analysis of turnover**

	£'000		£'000
Regular customers	3,120	New products	1,560
New customers	780	Existing products	2,340
	3,900		3,900

2. Production overheads include £37,200 of reworked faulty production.

3. Orders received in the year totalled £4,550,000.

Task

Angela Frear asks you to calculate the following performance indicators in preparation for a board meeting.

i) The return on capital employed
ii) The asset turnover
iii) The sales (or operating profit) margin
iv) The average age of debtors in months
v) The average age of finished stock in months

b) One of the issues to be discussed at the board meeting is the usefulness of performance indicators. Angela Frear has recently attended a conference on creating and enhancing value.

Three criticisms were made of financial performance indicators.

- They could give misleading signals.

- They could be manipulated.

- They focus on the short term and do not take account of other key, non-financial performance indicators.

At the conference, Angela was introduced to the idea of the balanced scorecard. The balanced scorecard looks at performance measurement from four perspectives.

> **The financial perspective**
> This is concerned with satisfying shareholders. Examples include the return on capital employed and sales margin.
>
> **The customer perspective**
> This asks how customers view the business and is concerned with measures of customer satisfaction. Examples include speed of delivery and customer loyalty.
>
> **The internal perspective**
> This looks at the quality of the company's output in terms of technical excellence and customer needs. Examples would be striving towards total quality management and flexible production as well as unit cost.
>
> **The innovation and learning perspective**
> This is concerned with the continual improvement of existing products and the ability to develop new products as customers' needs change. An example would be the percentage of turnover attributable to new products.

Task

Angela Frear asks you to prepare briefing notes for the board meeting. Using the data from part (a) where necessary, your notes should do the following.

i) Suggest ONE reason why the return on capital employed calculated in (a) might be misleading.

ii) Identify ONE way of manipulating the sales (or operating profit) margin.

iii) Calculate the average delay in fulfilling orders.

iv) Identify ONE other possible measure of customer satisfaction other than the delay in fulfilling orders.

v) Calculate TWO indicators which may help to measure performance from an internal perspective.

vi) Calculate ONE performance indicator which would help to measure the innovation and learning perspective.

19 (a) Travel Bus Ltd is owned by Travel Holdings plc. It operates in the town of Camford. Camford is an old town with few parking facilitates for motorists. Several years ago, the Town Council built a car park on the edge of the town and awarded Travel Bus the contract to carry motorists and their passengers between the car park and the centre of the town.

Originally, the Council charged motorists £4.00 per day for the use of the car park but, to encourage motorists not to take their cars into the town centre, parking has been free since 1 December 2005.

performance indicators

The journey between the car park and the town centre is the only service operated by Travel Bus Ltd in Camford. A summary of the results for the first two years of operations, together with the net assets associated with the route and other operating data, is reproduced below.

Operating statement year ended 30 November	2005 £	2006 £	Extract from balance sheet at 30 November	2005 £	2006 £
Turnover	432,000	633,600	Buses	240,000	240,000
Fuel	129,600	185,328	Accumulated depreciation	168,000	180,000
Wages	112,000	142,000	Net book value	72,000	60,000
Other variable costs	86,720	84,512	Net current assets	14,400	35,040
Gross profit	103,680	221,760		86,400	95,040
Bus road tax and insurance	22,000	24,000			
Depreciation of buses	12,000	12,000			
Maintenance of buses	32,400	28,512			
Fixed garaging costs	29,840	32,140			
Administration	42,000	49,076			
Net profit/(loss)	(34,560)	76,032			

Other operating data	2005	2006
Fare per passenger journey	£0.80	£1.00
Miles per year	324,000	356,400
Miles per journey	18.0	18.0
Days per year	360	360
Wages per driver	£14,000	£14,200

Throughout the two years, the drivers were paid a basic wage per week, no bonuses were paid and no overtime was incurred.

In two weeks there will be a meeting between officials of the Town Council and the chief executive of Travel Holdings to discuss the performance of Travel Bus for the year to 30 November 2006. The previous year's performance indicators were as follows.

Gross profit margin	24%
Net profit margin	–8%
Return on capital employed	–40%
Asset turnover	5 times
Number of passengers in the year	540,000
Total cost per mile	£1.44
Number of journeys per day	50
Maintenance cost per mile	£0.10
Passengers per day	1,500
Passengers per journey	30
Number of drivers	8

performance indicators

Task

In preparation for the meeting, you have been asked to calculate the following performance indicators for the year to 30 November 2006.

- i) Gross profit margin
- ii) Net profit margin
- iii) Return on capital employed
- iv) Asset turnover
- v) Number of passengers in the year
- vi) Total cost per mile
- vii) Number of journeys per day
- viii) Maintenance cost per mile
- ix) Passengers per day
- x) Passengers per journey
- xi) Number of drivers

b) On receiving your performance indicators, the chief executive of Travel Holdings raises the following issues with you.

- The drivers are claiming that the improved profitability of Travel Bus reflects their increased productivity.
- The managers believe that the change in performance is due to improved motivation arising from the introduction of performance related pay for managers during the year to 30 November 20X1.
- The officials from the Town Council are concerned that Travel Bus is paying insufficient attention to satisfying passengers needs and safety.

The chief executive asks for your advice.

Task

Write a memo to the chief executive of Travel Holdings plc. Where relevant, you should make use of the data and answers to task (a) to do the following.

- i) Briefly discuss whether or not increased productivity always leads to increased profitability.
- ii) Develop ONE possible measure of driver productivity and suggest whether or not the drivers' claim is valid.
- iii) Suggest ONE reason, other than improved motivation, why the profitability of Travel Bus might have improved.
- iv) 1) Suggest ONE existing performance indicator which might measure the satisfaction of passenger needs.
  2) Suggest ONE other possible performance indicator of passenger needs which cannot be measured from the existing performance data collected by Travel Bus.
- v) 1) Suggest ONE existing performance indicator which might measure the safety aspect of Travel Bus's operations.
  2) Suggest ONE other possible performance indicator which cannot be measured from the existing performance data collected by Travel Bus.

performance indicators

20 You are employed as a financial analyst by Alderton Ltd, a chain of bookstores. Alderton's main competitor is Brandon Ltd. Extracts from the latest operating statements and balance sheets for both companies, together with other operating data, are shown below.

	\multicolumn{6}{c}{**Statement of net assets at 31 May 2006**}
	\multicolumn{3}{c}{**Alderton Ltd**}	\multicolumn{3}{c}{**Brandon Ltd**}
	Leasehold buildings	Fixtures and fittings	Total	Leasehold buildings	Fixtures and fittings	Total
	£m	£m	£m	£m	£m	£m
Fixed assets						
Cost	500	200	700	200	80	280
Accumulated depreciation	100	80	180	184	56	240
Net book value	400	120	520	16	24	40
Net current assets						
Stocks		150			140	
Debtors		30			40	
Cash		5			50	
Creditors		(65)			(30)	
			120			200
			640			240

58

performance indicators

Operating statements for the year ended 31 May 2006				
	Alderton Ltd		**Brandon Ltd**	
	£m	£m	£m	£m
Turnover		720		480
Opening stocks	60		200	
Purchases	450		150	
Less closing stock	(150)		(140)	
Cost of sales		360		210
Gross profit		360		270
Retail wages	60		40	
Depreciation buildings	10		4	
Depreciation fixtures and fittings	40		8	
Other expenses	70		80	
		180		132
Operating profit		180		138

Other operating data

	Alderton Ltd	Brandon Ltd
Square metres of floor space	240,000	200,000
Number of transactions	48,000,000	60,000,000
Number of employees	4,800	4,000

You report to Beverly Richards, the financial director of Alderton. Beverley has already calculated performance indicators for Alderton and these are shown below. She asks you to prepare similar indicators for Brandon Ltd. She tells you that Brandon did not have any bought-in services during the year ended 31 May 2006.

performance indicators

Alderton Ltd: performance indicators year ended 31 May 2006	
Sales margin	25%
Gross profit margin	50%
Asset turnover	1.125 times
Return on capital employed	28.125%
Average age of stocks	5 months
Average age of debtors	0.5 months
Added value per employee	£75,000
Average sales value per transaction	£15
Sales per employee	£150,000
Transactions per employee	10,000
Sales per square metre	£3,000

Tasks

a) Prepare the following performance indicators for Brandon Ltd.

   i) Sales (or net profit) margin
   ii) Gross profit margin
   iii) Asset turnover
   iv) Return on capital employed
   v) Average age of stocks in months
   vi) Average age of debtors in months
   vii) Added value per employee
   viii) Average sales value per transaction
   ix) Sales per employee
   x) Transactions per employee
   xi) Sales per square metre

b) Beverley Richards gives you two pieces of information about the directors of Alderton.

   - They are concerned about the differences in the performance indicators of the two companies.

   - They currently use the return on capital employed as the main measure of efficiency and the asset turnover as the main measure of productivity.

   She also tells you the following.

   - During the year the average cost of books purchased by retailers had been falling.
   - Alderton values stocks on a first-in-first out basis, but Brandon uses last-in first-out.
   - Both companies use straight line depreciation assuming zero residual balances.

   The directors have asked Beverley to prepare a report showing the reasons for the differences in the performance indicators and suggesting other possible ways of measuring productivity and efficiency. Beverley asks for your help.

Prepare draft notes for Beverley Richards. In the notes, you should do the following.

i) Explain what is meant by the following terms.

    1) Productivity
    2) Efficiency

ii) Give TWO possible reasons why there is a difference in the net book value of the fixed assets of the two companies.

iii) Show TWO ways the difference in the net book value of the fixed assets would affect the return on capital employed for Alderton.

iv) Explain the likely effect of the two different stock valuation policies on the operating profits and value of net assets of the two companies.

v) Give TWO limitations to using added value per employee as a measure of employee productivity.

vi) Suggest a valid alternative to asset turnover as a measure of employee productivity.

chapter 7: QUALITY

1 How would you define quality of products or services?

2 Define the four types of quality cost (prevention, appraisal, internal failure and external failure) and give three examples of each.

3 For each of the following state which type of cost of quality it is (prevention, appraisal, internal failure or external failure):

		Type of cost
i)	lost contribution on defective products sold as seconds	....
ii)	cost of replacing faulty products	....
iii)	claims from customers relating to defective products	....
iv)	products scrapped due to faulty raw materials	....
v)	training for quality control staff	....
vi)	maintenance of quality control equipment	....
vii)	performance testing of finished goods	....
viii)	costs of customer after sales service department	....
ix)	costs of inspection of raw materials	....
x)	costs of production delays due to re-working defective products discovered in quality inspection	....

quality

4 A clothing manufacturer has had a number of events occurring recently:

i) the internal designers have designed a new type of zipper that should last much longer than normal zippers and should reduce returns of products

ii) one line of jumpers produced over the last few months were produced on a faulty machine and have been returned by all the retailers who purchased them as the seams have come apart. Some of the retailers are considering suing the company for losses caused and it is almost certain that they will never purchase from the manufacturer again

iii) it has been discovered that the fabric used to make a large quantity of men's suits was flawed and these can now only be sold at a drastically reduced price as seconds

As a result of this discovery the manufacturer has introduced new inspection controls for raw materials.

Analyse each of these events and determine what effects they are likely to have on the various categories of quality costs – prevention, appraisal, internal failure and external failure.

5 Define explicit and implicit costs of quality. Give three examples of explicit costs of quality and three examples of implicit costs of quality.

6 A manufacturing business estimates that 3 out of every 1,000 of its products that is sold is defective in some way. When the goods are returned by customers they are replaced free of charge. It is estimated that 70% of customers who buy a faulty product will return it but that all customers who buy a faulty product will not buy from the business again. Each unit costs £10 to manufacture and is sold at a price of £15.

Due to quality inspections it is also estimated that 4,000 defective units a year are discovered before they are sold and these can then be sold as 'seconds' at a price of £11. The quality inspections cost £35,000 each year.

The unit sales of the product are 10 million each year.

Analyse and calculate the explicit costs of quality and determine whether there are any implicit costs of quality.

7 A manufacturing business estimates that it has to sell 7,500 defective units of its product at a 'seconds' price of £20 per unit. The normal selling price is £33 per unit and the inspection procedure that identifies these defective units costs £60,000.

What are the costs of quality and what type or types of quality cost are they?

8   A business estimates that one in 6,000 of its products are found to be faulty after sale. Of these it is estimated that 75% are returned by customers and can be repaired at a cost of £10 per product. It is felt that the customers who do not return the products will not buy the company's products again and the cost of advertising for replacement customers is £5,000 per annum. The customers that do return their products for repair are likely to purchase again from the business.

Total sales of the product are 8 million units each year.

List all of the costs of quality and the amount of that cost where possible. State into which category of cost of quality each cost falls.

9   A manufacturing organisation carries out quality inspections on its product and in the last year 5,200 defective units were discovered and had to be sold as seconds at a price of £108 compared with the normal selling price of £200. The costs of the quality inspections totalled £340,000 for the year.

Sales of the product are 1 million units each year and it is estimated that a further 1 in every 2,000 sales will be defective. Of these it is expected that 60% will be returned by customers and will be replaced free of charge. The cost of producing a unit of the product is £120. The customers who do not return their products are unlikely to buy the company's products again.

List all of the costs of quality incurred by the business and the amount of that cost if possible. State which type of cost of quality each cost is and whether it is an explicit cost or an implicit cost.

10   What is life-cycle costing?

11   Barnet Ltd is a small company owned by Hampstead plc. Barnet operates a job costing system making a specialist, expensive piece of hospital equipment.

Existing system

Currently, employees are assigned to individual jobs and materials are requisitioned from stores as needed. The standard and actual costs of labour and materials are recorded for each job. These job costs are totalled to produce the marginal cost of production. Fixed production costs – including the cost of storekeeping and inspection of deliveries and finished equipment – are then added to determine the standard and actual cost of production. Any costs of remedial work are included in the materials and labour for each job.

Proposed system

Carol Johnson, the chief executive of Barnet, has recently been to a seminar on modern manufacturing techniques. As a result, she is considering introducing Just-in-Time stock deliveries and Total Quality Management. Barnet would offer suppliers a long-term contract at a fixed price but suppliers would have to guarantee the quality of their materials.

In addition, she proposes that the workforce is organised as a single team with flexible work practices. This would mean employees helping each other as necessary, with no employee being allocated a particular job. If a job was delayed, the workforce would work overtime without payment in order for the job to be completed on time. In exchange, employees would be guaranteed a fixed weekly wage and time off when production was slack to make up for any overtime incurred.

Cost of quality

Carol has asked to meet you to discuss the implications of her proposals on the existing accounting system. She is particularly concerned to monitor the **cost of quality**. This is defined as the total of all costs incurred in preventing defects plus those costs involved in remedying defects once they have occurred. It is a single figure measuring all the explicit costs of quality – that is, those costs collected within the accounting system.

Task

In preparation for the meeting, produce **brief** notes. Your notes should:

a) identify FOUR general headings (or classifications) which make up the **cost of quality**;

b) give ONE example of a type of cost likely to be found within each category;

c) assuming Carol Johnson's proposals are accepted, state, with reasons, whether or not:

   i) a standard marginal costing system would still be of help to the managers;
   ii) it would still be meaningful to collect costs by each individual job;

e) identify one cost saving in Carol Johnson's proposals which would not be recorded in the existing costing system.

12 (a) You are employed as the assistant management accountant with Local Engineering Ltd, a company which designs and makes a single product, the X4, used in the telecommunications industry. The company has a goods received store which employs staff who carry out random checks to ensure materials are of the correct specification. In addition to the random checks, a standard allowance is made for failures due to faulty materials at the completion stage and the normal practice is to charge the cost of any remedial work required to the cost of production for the month. Once delivered to the customer, any faults discovered in the X4 during its warranty period become an expense of the customer support department.

At the end of each month, management reports are prepared for the Board of Directors. These identify the cost of running the stores and the number of issues, the cost of production and the number of units manufactured, and the cost of customer support.

Jane Greenwood, Local Engineering's management accountant, has just returned from a board meeting to discuss a letter the company recently received from Universal Telecom, Local Engineering's largest customer. In the letter, Universal Telecom explained that it was determined to maintain its position as a world-class provider of telecommunication services and that there was serious concern about the quality of the units delivered by your company. At the meeting, Local Engineering Ltd's board responded by agreeing to establish a company-wide policy of implementing a Total Quality Management (TQM) programme, commencing with a revised model of the X4. Design work on the new model is scheduled to commence in six month's time.

One aspect of this will involve the management accounting department collecting the cost of quality. This is defined as the total of all costs incurred in preventing defects plus those costs involved in remedying defects once they have occurred within the accounting system – attributable to producing output that is not within its specification.

Task

As a first step towards the implementation of TQM, a meeting of the senior staff in the management accounting department has been called to discuss the role the department can play in making TQM a success. Jane Greenwood has asked you to prepare a brief background paper for the meeting.

Your paper should do the following.

i) Explain in outline what is meant by Total Quality Management.

ii) Briefly discuss why the current accounting system fails to highlight the cost of quality.

iii) Identify FOUR general categories (or classifications) of Local Engineering's activities where expenditure making up the explicit cost of quality will be found.

iv) Give ONE example of a cost found within each category.

v) Give ONE example of a cost of quality not normally identified by the accounting system.

b) Local Engineering Ltd has capacity to produce no more than 1,000 X4s per month and currently is able to sell all production immediately at a unit selling price of £1,250. A major component of the X4 is a complex circuit board. Spot checks are made on these boards by a team of specialist employees when they are received into stores. In May, 100 units were found to be faulty. Good components are then issued to production along with other material.

Upon completion, each X4 is tested. If there is a fault, this involves further remedial work prior to dispatch to customers. For the month of May, 45 units of the X4 had to be reworked because of subsequent faults discovered in the circuit board. This remedial work cost an additional £13,500 in labour charges.

Should a fault occur after delivery to the customer, Local Engineering is able to call upon a team of self-employed engineers to rectify the fault as part of its customer support function. The cost of the remedial work by the self-employed engineers carried out in May – and the number of times they were used – is shown as contractors under customer support.

quality

Extract from the accounting records of Local Engineering Ltd for the month of May

	Units	£		Units	£
Purchases:			Production:		
Printed circuits	1,000	120,000	Printed circuits	900	108,000
Less returns	(100)	(12,000)	Other material		121,500
Net costs	900	108,000	Labour		193,500
Other material		121,500	Direct prod'n o/hd		450,000
Total purchases issued to production		229,500	Cost of production		873,000
Other direct stores costs:					
Goods received, labour costs and rent		54,000	Customer support:		
Inspection costs		10,000	Direct costs		36,000
Costs of returns	100	4,500	Contractors	54	24,300
Costs of stores		68,500			60,300

Task

As part of the continuing development of Total Quality Management, you are asked by Jane Greenwood to calculate the following:

i) The explicit **cost of quality** for Local Engineering Ltd for the month of May
ii) A further **cost of quality** not reported in the above accounting records.

chapter 8: BUDGETARY CONTROL SYSTEMS

1 a) What is a budget?

    b) How can a budgetary system help management to perform their duties and carry out their responsibilities?

2 a) What is the difference between strategic plans and operational plans?

    b) Explain how the management of a business will set the strategic plans and operational plans for the business.

3 Why is it important to produce a capital budget?

4 Briefly explain what figures would appear in each of the resource budgets that a manufacturing organisation would be likely to prepare and how these figures would be determined.

5 a) What is a key budget factor and why is it important?

    b) Give three examples of possible key budget factors for a manufacturing organisation other than sales demand.

budgetary control systems

6   In each of the following situations suggest what may be the key budget factor:

   i)   A private nursing home with 140 beds. The home is situated in an area which has a large proportion of retired amongst the population and there is little difficulty in recruiting suitable staff.

   ii) A vendor of ice cream in a busy shopping centre. The transportable stall can store a maximum of 50 litres of ice cream.

   iii) A partnership of three skilled craftsmen making carved chess sets from wood and marble for home sales and exports to specific order. Sales demand is high and orders have to be frequently rejected.

   iv) A manufacturer of CD players and hi-fi systems which are similar to those of other manufacturers and who distributes the systems amongst a number of small high street electrical retailers.

7   Briefly explain each of the following terms:

   i)   budget manual
   ii) budget committee
   iii) budget holder
   iv) master budget

8   Explain the procedures that will be followed from the start of the budgeting process through to the completion of the master budget in a participative budgeting system.

9   What is a rolling budget and what benefits does it have?

10 Explain each of the following terms:

   i)   incremental budgeting
   ii) zero based budgeting
   iii) activity based budgeting

budgetary control systems

11 A company is considering its budget for next year and estimates that it will sell 300 units of product J during August and 600 units during September.

Each unit of product J requires eight hours of labour, the labour rate being £8 per hour.

It is company policy to hold stocks of finished goods at the end of each month equal to 50% of the following month's sales demand.

At the end of the production process the products are tested: it is usual for 10% of those tested to be faulty. It is not possible to rectify these faulty units.

Explain clearly, using the data above, how you would construct a spreadsheet to produce the labour requirements budget for August 2006. Include a specimen cell layout diagram containing formulae which would be the basis for the spreadsheet.

chapter 9:
FORECASTING INCOME

1   Forecasting is an important technique for budgeting purposes however it has limitations. Explain the general limitations of forecasting.

2   A business has analysed its historical sales data and has estimated that the trend of its sales figures in units over the last three years has been a 3.5% increase in each quarter. The sales in quarter 1 of 2006 were 122,000 units.

    The time series analysis has also indicated the following seasonal variations:

    | Quarter 1 | +6,000 units |
    | Quarter 2 | −8,000 units |
    | Quarter 3 | +12,000 units |
    | Quarter 4 | −10,000 units |

    Using this information what are the forecast sales in units for the remaining three quarters of 2006?

3   The trend figures for sales in units for a business for the four quarters of 2006 are given below:

    | Quarter 1 | 320,000 |
    | Quarter 2 | 325,000 |
    | Quarter 3 | 330,000 |
    | Quarter 4 | 335,000 |

    The seasonal variations are expressed as follows:

    | Quarter 1 | −18% |
    | Quarter 2 | +21% |
    | Quarter 3 | +7% |
    | Quarter 4 | −10% |

    What are the forecast sales for each of the quarters of 2007?

73

forecasting income

4   The sales data for the last three years have been subject to a time series analysis and the trend is that there is an increase of 2% per quarter in unit sales. The unit sales for quarter 4 of 2006 were 90,000 units.

The time series analysis also shows the following seasonal variations:

Quarter 1	−31%
Quarter 2	−3%
Quarter 3	+23%
Quarter 4	+11%

Forecast the unit sales for each of the four quarters of 2007.

5   The trend figures for sales in units for a business for the four quarters of 2006 and the seasonal variations are estimated as:

	Trend unit sales	Seasonal variations
Quarter 1	160,000 units	+7%
Quarter 2	164,500 units	+9%
Quarter 3	169,000 units	−3%
Quarter 4	173,500 units	−13%

What are the forecast sales in units for each of the quarters of 2007?

6   The sales of a business are considered by the sales director to have a distinct trend and regular seasonal variations. The recent quarterly sales have been as follows:

Units sold each quarter

Year	Quarter 1	Quarter 2	Quarter 3	Quarter 4
2003			1,900	2,300
2004	2,800	3,000	2,400	2,500
2005	3,200	3,400	2,500	2,700
2006	3,500	3,700*		

* estimated figure

You are to:

i)   calculate the centred four quarter moving average trend figures

ii) calculate the seasonal variations using the additive method

iii) forecast the sales volume for quarter 3 of 2006

iv) suggest two reasons why there might be a difference between the forecast figure for sales in quarter 3 of 2006 and the actual figure

forecasting income

7 What are the limitations of using time series analysis to forecast figures?

8 a) Explain the five stages of the product life cycle and how costs and income will alter in each of the five stages.

b) How does knowledge of the product life cycle affect forecasting of future sales?

9 At which stage in the product life cycle is time series analysis likely to produce a fairly accurate figure for future sales?

10 The following spreadsheet is to be used to forecast the sales for the following year in both units and in value.

	A	B	C	D	E
1	Unit sales price - £	150			
2	Annual sales volume - units	180,000			
3	Seasonal variation	-14%	-28%	+20%	+22%
4		Quarter 1	Quarter 2	Quarter 3	Quarter 4
5	Seasonal variation - units				
6	Quarterly volume - units				
7	Quarterly sales - £				

You are to:

i) insert formulae in rows 5, 6 and 7 of the spreadsheet in order to determine the quarterly figures for unit sales and sales value

ii) calculate the quarterly sales in units and in value

11 Star Fuels is a multinational oil company selling oil for industrial and domestic purposes through a network of distributors. Distributors purchase fuel oil from Star Fuels and then sell it on to their own customers.

A regular complaint of the distributors is that they either have to pay for the fuel on delivery to their storage tanks or be charged interest on a daily basis on the amount owed. This problem could be reduced if the distributors were able to forecast their demands more accurately.

You are employed as the Assistant Management Accountant to Northern Fuel Distributors Ltd, a major distributor of Star Fuels's fuel oils. You recently attended a meeting with Mary Lamberton, a member of Star Fuels's central staff. At the meeting, she demonstrated a statistical software package used for estimating demand for fuel oil. The user enters sales volumes per period and the package

forecasting income

then calculates the least-squares regression equation for the data. This is in the form y = a + bx where x is the time period, y is the forecast and a and b are terms derived from the original data. Following further inputs by the user, the package can also estimate seasonal variations. Two forms of seasonal variation are calculated: the first calculates the seasonal variance as an absolute amount, the second as a percentage.

One week after the meeting, your copy of the software arrives at the head office of Northern Fuel Distributors Ltd and you immediately set about testing its capability. Purely for the purpose of testing, you assume seasonal variations occur quarterly. You enter this assumption along with the sales turnover figures for fuel oil for the last 20 quarters. Within moments, the software outputs the following information.

Regression line   y = £2,000,000 + £40,000x

Seasonal variations

Quarter	A	B	C	D
Amount	+£350,000	+£250,000	−£400,000	−£200,000
Percentage	+15%	+10%	−15%	−10%

Quarter A refers to the first quarter of annual data, B to the second quarter, C to the third and D to the fourth. The pattern then repeats itself. In terms of the specific data you input, seasonal variation A refers to quarter 17, B to quarter 18, C to quarter 19 and D to quarter 20.

Actual sales turnover for quarters 17 to 20 was as follows.

Quarter	17	18	19	20
Sales turnover	£3,079,500	£3,002,400	£2,346,500	£2,490,200

Tasks

a) Making use of the formula derived by the software package, calculate the forecast sales turnover for quarters 17 to 20 using:

   i) the absolute seasonal variations;
   ii) the percentage seasonal variations.

b) i) From your answers to task (a), determine which method of calculating seasonal variations gives the best estimate of actual sales turnover.

   ii) Having identified the preferred method, use that method to forecast the sales turnover for quarters 21 to 24.

c) Write a memorandum to your Managing Director. The memorandum should do the following.

   i) Explain what is meant by seasonal variations and seasonally adjusted data. Illustrate your explanation with examples relevant to Northern Fuel Distributors.

   ii) Suggest why your chosen method of seasonal adjustment might be more accurate.

   iii) Show how an understanding of seasonal variations and seasonally adjusted data can help Northern Fuel Distributors be more efficient.

   iv) Identify TWO weaknesses within your approach to forecasting undertaken in Tasks (a) and (b).

chapter 10:
FORECASTING EXPENDITURE

1. A business makes a single product, each unit of which requires 5 kg of raw material. Unfortunately, due to a shortage of suppliers of the raw material, only 129,000 kgs will be available in the coming year. The materials are available on a monthly basis spread evenly over the year.

   How many units of the product can be produced in total and each month?

2. The raw materials requirements for production for the next six months for a business are as follows:

	July	Aug	Sept	Oct	Nov	Dec
Raw materials requirements – kg	4,800	4,300	4,100	4,900	4,200	5,000

   It is only possible to purchase 4,500 kg of the product each month.

   a) What is the maximum shortage of raw materials over the six month period in total if only the amount required each month is purchased, or the maximum amount if demand is greater than 4,500 kgs ?

   b) How many kgs of the material should be purchased each month in order to maximise production and keep stock levels to the minimum possible?

   What is the total shortage of raw materials over the six month period under this policy?

3. How could a business try to alleviate the problem of shortage of materials if:

   a) the shortage is a short-term problem and full supplies will be available after a few months; or

   b) the shortage is a long-term problem?

forecasting expenditure

4   The raw materials requirements for production for Selby Electronics for the next six months are as follows:

	May	June	July	Aug	Sep	Oct
Raw materials requirements – kg	9,500	10,200	10,200	9,300	10,200	10,300

Selby is only able to purchase 10,000 kg of the material in each month.

a) How can the purchases be scheduled in order to ensure the maximum production over the six month period together with the minimum possible stock level?

b) What is the total shortage of materials over the six month period under the purchasing scheme in part a)?

5   A business produces a product which requires 3 hours of a highly skilled grade of labour per unit but the business currently only has 12 employees with the skills required. They normally work a 38 hour week although, by paying an overtime rate of double time, it has been possible to negotiate for each employee to work 8 hours of overtime a week.

a) What is the maximum level of production each week?

b) Suggest ways in which the labour shortage problem could be solved.

6   In week 3 of the next quarter the sales demand for a business's product is expected to be for 1,860 units. Each unit requires 4 hours of direct labour time and the business employs 160 employees each working a 35 hour week. How much overtime would be required in order to meet demand with the current workforce?

7   A manufacturing organisation operates out of one factory with two identical production lines. The factory operates two 7 hour shifts each day for 5 days a week with the production lines working at full capacity. The production line is capable of producing 30 units of product per hour.

a) What is the maximum production for a week?

b) How could the business deal with this capacity problem if sales demand exceeds the maximum production level?

forecasting expenditure

8 The sales and production in units for a business for the next six months are as follows:

	Jan	Feb	Mar	Apr	May	June
Production – units	3,600	2,900	3,200	3,100	3,400	4,000
Sales – units	3,500	3,000	3,000	3,200	3,500	3,800

The variable production costs are £10.50 per unit and the variable selling costs are £3.80 per unit.

What are the forecast figures for variable production and selling costs?

9 The direct materials cost for quarter 1 and quarter 2 of next year have been estimated in terms of current prices at £657,000 and £692,500 respectively. The current price index for these materials is 126.4 and the price index is estimated as 128.4 for quarter 1 of next year and 131.9 for quarter 2.

What are the forecast direct materials costs for quarters 1 and 2 of next year?

10 The production and sales levels for the next six months for a business are estimated as follows:

	Jan	Feb	Mar	Apr	May	June
Production – units	4,200	4,400	4,500	5,100	5,300	4,800
Sales – units	4,100	4,300	4,650	4,700	5,000	5,100

Variable production costs are currently £25.00 per unit and variable selling costs are £8.00 per unit. The price indices for the production costs and selling costs are currently 135.2 and 140.5 respectively.

The anticipated price indices for production and selling costs for the next six months are given below:

	Jan	Feb	Mar	Apr	May	June
Production costs index	137.3	139.0	139.6	140.3	141.2	143.0
Selling costs index	141.5	143.0	143.7	144.4	145.1	146.0

What are the forecast variable production costs and variable selling costs for each of the next six months?

forecasting expenditure

11 A business rents its premises annually from 1 January to 31 December. The rent for the year ending 31 December 2006 was £65,000 but the business has been told by the letting company that there is to be a 5.5% increase for the year ended 31 December 2007.

The company incurred insurance premiums of £15,700 in the year ended 31 December 2006; it is widely thought that insurance premiums are likely to rise by 10% next year.

The power costs for the year ended 31 December 2006 were £84,000 and these normally increase in line with the average RPI each year.

The business is now trying to forecast its costs for the year ending 31 December 2007. The average RPI for 2001 was 166.3 and it is believed that the average RPI for 2002 will be 171.2.

Determine the forecast fixed costs for the year ending 31 December 2007.

12 The costs of a factory maintenance department appear to be partially dependent upon the number of machine hours operated each month. The machine hours and the maintenance department costs for the last six months are given below:

	Machine hours	Maintenance cost £
June	14,200	285,000
July	14,800	293,000
August	15,200	300,000
September	14,500	290,000
October	15,000	298,000
November	14,700	292,000

i) Estimate the variable cost per machine hour.
ii) Estimate the fixed costs of the maintenance department.

13 The activity levels and related production costs for the last six months of 2006 for a business have been as follows:

	Activity level units	Production cost £
July	63,000	608,000
August	70,000	642,000
September	76,000	699,000
October	73,000	677,000
November	71,000	652,000
December	68,000	623,000

i) Estimate the fixed element of the production costs and the variable rate using the hi lo method.

ii) Estimate the production costs if the level of production is expected to be:

    a) 74,000 units
    b) 90,000 units

iii) Comment upon which of the two estimates of production costs calculated in (ii) is likely to be most accurate and why.

14 a) What is the general equation of a straight line?

b) What do the figures a and b stand for in the equation of a straight line?

c) If the equation of a straight line defines a semi-variable cost what do the figures representing a and b in the equation mean?

15 The linear regression equation for production costs for a business is:

$$y = 138{,}000 + 6.4x$$

If production is expected to be 105,000 units in the next quarter what are the anticipated production costs?

16 The linear regression equation for the power costs of a factory is given as follows:

$$y = 80{,}000 + 0.5x$$

where x is the number of machine hours used in a period.

The anticipated machine hours for the next six months are:

	Machine hours
April	380,000
May	400,000
June	395,000
July	405,000
August	410,000
September	420,000

What are the forecasts for the power costs for the next six months?

forecasting expenditure

17 The linear regression equation for the trend of sales in thousands of units per month based upon time series analysis of the figures for the last two years is:

$$y = 3.1 + 0.9x$$

What is the estimated sales trend for each of the first three months of next year?

18 A time series analysis of sales volumes each quarter for the last three years, 2004 to 2006, has identified the trend equation as follows:

$$y = 400 + 105x$$

where y is the sales volume and x is the time period.

The seasonal variations for each quarter have been calculated as:

Quarter 1	−175
Quarter 2	+225
Quarter 3	+150
Quarter 4	−200

Estimate the actual sales volume for each quarter of 2007.

chapter 11:
PREPARING BUDGETS

1. A business has budgeted sales for the following period of 13,800 units of its product. The stocks at the start of the period are 2,100 units and these are to be reduced to 1,500 units at the end of the period. What is the production quantity for the period?

2. A business is preparing its production budget for the next quarter. It is estimated that 200,000 units of the product can be sold in the quarter and the opening stock is currently 35,000 units. The stock level is to be reduced by 30% by the end of the quarter.

    What is the production budget for the quarter?

3. A production process has normal losses of 3% of completed output. If production of 16,200 good units is required how many units must be produced in total?

4. For budgeting purposes a business operates 13 four week periods with five working days in each week.

    The sales forecasts in units for the next four periods is as follows:

Period 4	Period 5	Period 6	Period 7
10,800 units	11,500 units	11,000 units	11,200 units

    It is the business's policy to maintain closing stocks of finished goods at a level which is sufficient to cover 5 days of the next period's sales. The stocks of finished goods at the end of period 3 are 2,700 units.

    The quality control procedures of the organisation have shown that 4% of completed production are found to be defective and are unsaleable.

    a) Produce the production budget for periods 4 to 6.

preparing budgets

b) Complete the following computer spreadsheet in order to determine the production budget for periods 4 to 6.

	A	B	C	D	E
1					
2					
3					
4					
5					
6					

5 A business requires 25,400 units of production in a period and each unit requires 5 kg of raw materials in the finished product. The production process has a normal loss of 10% during the production process. What is the total amount of the raw material required for the period?

6 A business is preparing its material usage budget for the next quarter for one its raw materials used in the production of one of its products. The production budget for the product is 40,000 units in the quarter.

Each unit of product requires 5 kgs of raw material. Opening stock of raw material is budgeted to be 30,000 kg and stock levels are to be reduced by 20% by the end of the quarter.

a) What is the usage budget for the raw material for the quarter?
b) What is the materials purchasing budget for the raw material for the year?

7 For budgeting purposes a business operates 13 four week periods with five working days in each week.

The production budget in units for the next four periods is as follows:

Period 1	Period 2	Period 3	Period 4
32,000 units	35,000 units	40,000 units	48,000 units

Each completed unit of the product requires 8 kgs of raw material; however, the production process has a normal loss of 20% of materials input. Stock levels of raw materials are held in order to be sufficient to cover 5 days of gross production for the following period. The stocks of raw material at the start of period 1 are budgeted to be 64,000 kgs.

The price of each kilogram of raw material is £2.50 currently but is expected to rise by 4% in period 3.

a) You are required to produce for period 1, 2 and 3:

- the materials usage budget in units
- the materials purchasing budget in units
- the materials purchasing budget in pounds

b) Complete the following computer spreadsheet in order to produce the materials purchasing budget in both units and pounds.

	A	B	C	D	E
1		Period 1	Period 2	Period 3	Period 4
2	Production--units	32,000	35,000	40,000	48,000
3					
4					
5					
6					

8   A product requires 18 labour hours for each unit. However 10% of working hours are non-productive. How long must an employee be paid for in order to produce 20 units?

9   A business wishes to produce 120,000 units of its product with a standard labour time of 4 hours per unit. The workforce are currently working at 120% efficiency. How long will it take to produce the units required?

10 For budgeting purposes a business has four quarters made up of 12 weeks each quarter and 5 working days in each week. The budgeted sales in units for quarters 1 and 2 are as follows:

	Quarter 1	Quarter 2
Budgeted sales	102,000 units	115,000 units

The stocks of finished goods at the start of quarter 1 are 17,000 units and it is the business policy to maintain closing finished goods stock levels at 10 days of the following quarter's budgeted sales.

The standard cost card indicates that each unit should take 5.5 labour hours however it is anticipated that during quarter 1, due to technical problems, the workforce will only be working at 95% efficiency.

You are to produce the production budget and the labour usage budget for quarter 1.

preparing budgets

11 A business produces a single product, the Oliver. For budgeting purposes the year is divided into 13 four week periods with 5 working days each week. The forecast sales quantities for the first 5 periods of 2006 are as follows:

Period 1	Period 2	Period 3	Period 4	Period 5
3,000 units	3,400 units	3,900 units	3,500 units	4,000 units

i) The current selling price of the Oliver is £40 although it is anticipated that there will be a 6% price increase in Period 4.

ii) The closing stocks of finished goods are to be enough to cover 4 days of sales demand for the next period.

iii) 3% of production is defective and has to be scrapped with no scrap value.

iv) The stocks of finished goods at the start of period 1 will be 600 units.

v) Each unit of production requires 4 kgs of raw material X and the production process has a normal loss of 10% of the materials input into the process.

vi) It is policy to hold enough raw materials stocks to cover 7 days of the following period's production. The stock level at the start of period 1 is 4,200 kgs of raw material. The material usage for production in Period 5 is budgeted as 16,200 kgs.

vii) The standard time for production of one unit is 2 labour hour however due to necessary break times only 80% of the time worked is productive. The labour force are paid at a rate of £8 per hour but only 8,000 hours can be worked within the normal working hours any hours above 8,000 are overtime hours that are paid at time and a half.

For periods 1 to 4 you are to produce:

a) the sales budget in value
b) the production budget in units
c) the materials usage budget
d) the materials purchases budget in kgs
e) the labour budget in hours
f) the labour budget in value

12 A business produces two products, the Aye and the Bee. Both products use the same material and labour but in different proportions.

The previous policy has been to keep stocks of raw materials and finished goods at constant levels. However it has now been decided that closing stocks of finished goods should be expressed in terms of days' sales of the next quarter and that closing stocks of raw materials should be in terms of days' production for the next quarter.

preparing budgets

The data provided by the sales and production departments are as follows:

	Aye	Bee
Budgeted sales (units) quarter 1	1,500	2,400
Budgeted sales (units) quarter 2	1,500	2,400
Budgeted material per unit (kg)	4	7
Budgeted labour hours per unit	10	7
Opening units of finished stock	160	300
Closing units of finished stock (days' sales next quarter)	5 days	5 days
Failure rate of finished production	2%	2.5%
Finance and other costs of holding a unit in stock per quarter	£6.00	£7.00

The failed units are only discovered after completion of the products and they have no resale value.

Other information available is as follows:

Weeks in each quarter	12 weeks
Days per week	5 days
Hours per week	35 hours
Number of employees	70 employees
Budgeted labour rate per hour	£8.00
Overtime premium for hours worked in excess of 35 hours per week	50%
Budgeted cost of material per kg	£10.00
Opening stock of raw materials	2,800 kgs
Closing stock of raw materials (days' production next quarter)	6 days
Financing and other costs of keeping 1 kg of raw material in stock per quarter	£2.00

a) Calculate the following information for quarter 1:

    i) the number of production days
    ii) the closing finished stock of Aye and Bee in units
    iii) the labour hours available before overtime has to be paid

b) Prepare the following budgets for quarter 1:

    i) the production budget in units for Aye and Bee, including any faulty production
    ii) the materials purchases budget in kgs and value
    iii) the production labour budget in hours and value, including any overtime payments

c) Calculate the savings arising from the change in required stock levels for quarter 1.

preparing budgets

13 a) You have recently been promoted to the post of assistant management accountant with Northern Products Ltd, a company formed four years ago. The company has always used budgets to help plan its production of two products, the Exe and the Wye. Both products use the same material and labour but in different proportions.

You have been asked to prepare the budget for quarter 1, the twelve weeks ending 24 March 2006. In previous budgets, the closing stocks of both raw materials and finished products were the same as opening stocks. You questioned whether or not this was the most efficient policy for the company.

As a result, you have carried out an investigation into the stock levels required to meet the maximum likely sales demand for finished goods and production demand for raw materials. You conclude that closing stocks of finished goods should be expressed in terms of days sales for the next quarter and closing stocks of raw materials in terms of days production for the next quarter.

Your findings are included in the data below, which also shows data provided by the sales and production directors of Northern Products Ltd.

Product data	Exe	Wye
Budgeted sales in units, quarter 1	930 units	1,320 units
Budgeted sales in units, quarter 2	930 units	1,320 units
Budgeted material per unit (litres)	6 litres	9 litres
Budgeted labour hours per unit	12 hours	7 hours
Opening units of finished stock	172 units	257 units
Closing units of finished stock (days sales next quarter)	8 days	9 days
Failure rate of finished production*	2%	3%
Finance and other costs of keeping a unit in stock per quarter	£4.00	£5.00

*Failed products are only discovered on completion of production and have no residual value.

Other accounting data

Weeks in accounting period	12 weeks
Days per week for production and sales	5 days
Hours per week	35 hours
Number of employees	46 employees
Budgeted labour rate per hour	£6.00
Overtime premium for hours worked in excess of 35 hours per week	30%
Budgeted cost of material per litre	£15.00
Opening raw material stocks (litres)	1,878 litres
Closing raw material stocks (days production next quarter)	5 days
Financing and other costs of keeping a litre of raw material in stock per quarter	£1.00

Tasks

i) Calculate the following information for quarter 1, the twelve weeks ending 24 March 2006.

   1) The number of production days
   2) The closing finished stock for Exe and Wye in units
   3) The labour hours available before overtime has to be paid

ii) Prepare the following budgets for quarter 1, the twelve weeks ending 24 March 2006.

   1) The production budget in units for Exe and Wye, including any faulty production
   2) The material purchases budget in litres and value
   3) The production labour budget in hours and value, including any overtime payments

iii) Calculate the savings arising from the change in the required stock levels for the twelve weeks ending 24 March 2006.

b) On completing the budget for quarter 1, the production director of Northern Products Ltd tells you that the company is likely to introduce a third product, the Zed, in the near future. Because of this, he suggests that future budgets should be prepared using a spreadsheet. He explains that the use of spreadsheets to prepare budgets not only saves time but also provides flexibility by allowing the results of changes in the budget to be readily shown. The sales director is not convinced.

The production director suggests you demonstrate the advantages of budgets prepared on spreadsheets by using a template of a spreadsheet and sales data for the planned third product.

He gives you the following sales data he has received from the sales director.

- Estimated annual volume for Zed is 20,000 units.
- Planned unit selling price is £90.00.
- Seasonal variations are as follows.

1	+20%
2	+30%
3	−10%
4	−40%

Tasks

i) Calculate the budgeted volume of Zed for each quarter.

ii) Using the information provided by the sales director and a copy of the suggested spreadsheet template reproduced below, express the data provided by the sales director as formulae which would enable revised sales budgets to be calculated with the minimum of effort if sales price and annual volume were to change. (You may amend the template if desired to suit any spreadsheet with which you are familiar.)

preparing budgets

	A	B	C	D	E	F
1		Unit selling price	£90			
2		Annual volume	20,000			
3		Seasonal variations	20%	30%	– 10%	– 40%
4			Quarter 1	Quarter 2	Quarter 3	Quarter 4
5		Seasonal variations (units)				
6		Quarterly volume				
7		Quarterly turnover				

c) During quarters 1 to 3 of 2006 it became increasingly evident that there were problems with the supply of material. Shortages were so severe during quarter 3 that budgeted production quantities could not be met and closing stocks of both raw material and finished goods were eliminated. The situation did not improve during quarter 4, and the supplier warned that available supplies would be limited to 18,870 litres in quarter 1 of 2007.

During quarter 4 it comes to light that a colleague charged with setting profit-maximising production plans during this period has simply been allocating half the material to production of Exes and the other half to production of Wyes. You have been asked to take over this task and ensure that the limited supply of material is allocated to production of the two products so as to ensure a profit-maximising production budget.

Task

Produce a revised production budget for period 1 of 2007 that maximises profit given that the total variable cost of the Exe is £240 and that of the Wye is £258, budgeted sales for quarter 1 of 2007 are 1,120 units of Exe and 1,480 units of Wye, the selling price of the Exe is £360, that of the Wye £420, and that there will be no opening or closing stocks of raw material or finished goods.

14 (a) Sandwell Ltd makes a single product, the Gamma. You are Sandwell's management accountant and you are responsible for preparing its operating budgets. The accounting year is divided into 13, four-week periods. There are five days in each week.

The sales director of Sandwell has recently completed the following forecast sales volume for the next five periods.

Sales forecast five periods to 18 November 2006					
Period number	1	2	3	4	5
Four weeks ending	29 Jul	26 Aug	23 Sep	21 Oct	18 Nov
Number of Gammas	19,400	21,340	23,280	22,310	22,310

The production director provides you with the following information.

- On completion of production, 3% of the Gammas are found to be faulty and have to be scrapped. The faulty Gammas have no scrap value.
- Opening stocks: period 1, four weeks ending 29 July
    - Finished stock 3,880 Gammas
    - Raw materials 16,500 litres
- Closing stocks at the end of each period
    - Finished stock must equal 4 days' sales volume of Gammas in the next period.
    - Raw materials must equal 5 days' gross production in the next period.
- Each Gamma requires three litres of material costing £8 per litre.
- Each Gamma requires 0.5 hours of labour.
- Sandwell employs 70 production workers who each work a 40 hour week. Each employee is paid a guaranteed wage of £240 per week.
- The cost of any overtime is £9 per hour.

Tasks

Prepare the following budgets for the production director.

i) Gross production budget in Gammas (including faulty production) for each of the first four periods

ii) Material purchases budget in litres for each of the first three periods

iii) Cost of the material purchases for each of the first three periods

iv) Labour budget in hours for each of the first three periods including any overtime required in each period

v) Cost of the labour budget for each of the first three periods, including the cost of any overtime

b) After receiving your budgets, Sandwell's production director raises the following points.

- Overtime payments should only be made if absolutely necessary.
- The faulty Gammas are thought to be caused by poor work practices by some of the production workers although this is not known for certain.
- The 70 production workers work independently of one another in making Gammas.

Task

Write a memo to the production director. In your memo, you should do the following.

i) Explain and quantify the value of any possible overtime savings.

ii) Suggest ONE extra cost which might be necessary to achieve the overtime savings.

iii) Identify TWO advantages of sampling as a way of discovering reasons for the faulty Gammas.

iv) Briefly explain the difference between true (or simple) random sampling, systematic sampling and stratified sampling.

v) State which form of sampling Sandwell should use.

preparing budgets

15 (a) You are employed as an accounting technician by Guildshot Ltd, a company that makes statues. Statues are made in batches. A special powdered rock is added to water and poured into moulds. These moulds are then placed in ovens. Afterwards, the statues are removed from their moulds and inspected before being sold. At this inspection stage, some of the statues are found to be faulty and have to be destroyed. The faulty statues have no residual value.

Guildshot makes two types of statues, the Antelope and the Bear. Both use the same type of material and labour but in different amounts.

One of your duties is to prepare the production, material purchases and labour budgets for each four-week period. You are given the following information for period 8, the four weeks ending 26 July 2006.

	Antelope	Bear
• Sales volume, period 8, four weeks ending 26 July 2006	141,120 units	95,000 units

Product information

	Antelope	Bear
• Opening finished stocks	30,576 units	25,175 units
• Kilograms of powdered rock per statue	0.75 kg	0.50 kg
• Production labour hours per statue	0.10 hours	0.05 hours
• Faulty production	2%	5%

Material information

- Material: opening stock of powdered rock — 30,000 kg
- Material: closing stock of powdered rock — 40,000 kg
- Price per kilogram of powdered rock — £8.00

Labour information

- Number of production employees — 140 employees
- Days per week — 5 days
- Weeks per period — 4 weeks
- Hours per production employee per week — 38 hours
- Guaranteed weekly wage * — £228.00

The guaranteed weekly wage is paid even if hours produced are less than hours worked.

Closing finished stocks

The closing finished stocks are based on the forecast sales volume for period 9, the four weeks ending 23 August 2006.

- Demand for the Antelope in period 9 is forecast to be 50% more than in period 8. The closing finished stock of Antelope statues for period 8 must be equal to four days' sales in period 9.
- Demand for the Bear statue in period 9 is forecast to be 30% more than in period 8. The closing finished stock of Bear statues for period 8 must be equal to five days' sales in period 9.

Other information

- The faulty production is only discovered after the statues have been made.
- For technical reasons, the company can only operate the ovens for five days per week.

Task

Prepare the following information for period 8, the four weeks ending 26 July 2006.

i) Production budget in units for Antelopes and Bears
ii) Material purchases budget in kilograms
iii) Cost of the materials purchases budget
iv) Labour budget in hours
v) Cost of the labour budget

b) Hilary Green is the production director for Guildshot. She tells you that there are likely to be material and labour shortages in period 9. For commercial reasons, the company must fully meet the demand for Bear statues. As a result it will not be able to meet all the demand for Antelope statues.

Hilary suggests it might be possible to meet the demand by producing extra Antelope statues in period 8. She gives you the following information.

- Because of the technology involved, Guildshot cannot increase the number of production employees and the existing employees cannot work any overtime. The maximum hours are limited to the 38 hours per week for each production employee.

- It would be possible to buy up to a maximum 3,000 extra kilograms of powdered rock in period 8.

Tasks

i) Calculate the maximum number of extra fault-free Antelope statues that could be made in period 8.

ii) Prepare a revised purchases budget in kilograms to include the production of the extra fault-free statues.

16 You are employed as an accounting technician in the management accounting department of Dobra Ltd. The company makes several chemicals and one of your jobs is to prepare quarterly budgets for the year ahead for each of the chemicals. There are 12 weeks in each quarter and five working days in each week.

The sales director gives you the following forecast of the number of tins of chemicals A120 to be sold in each quarter.

Sales forecast for tins of chemical A120 to 25 June 2006				
Quarter number	1	2	3	4
12 weeks ending	19/9/2005	12/12/2005	19/3/2006	25/6/2006
Sales volume: number of tins	2,910	3,395	3,880	4,365

preparing budgets

The production director gives you the following information.

- Production and sales volumes in the two quarters following quarter 4 will be the same as in quarter 4.
- Finished stocks:
    - Opening stocks for quarter 1 will be 582 tins.
    - Closing stocks in each quarter must equal 12 days sales volume of the next quarter.
- 3% of finished production is faulty and has to be destroyed. The faulty production has no scrap value.
- Each tin of A120 requires seven kilograms of raw materials.
- Raw material stocks:
    - Opening stocks for quarter 1 will be 2,170 kilograms.
    - Closing stocks in each quarter must equal 6 days gross production in the next quarter.
- The budgeted cost of material is £12.00 per kilogram.
- Each tin of A120 requires three labour hours.
- The company employs 29 production workers to make A120. Each worker is paid a guaranteed wage of £280 per week for a 35-hour week. If a worker works more than 35 hours a week, overtime is payable at £11.00 per hour.

Tasks

a) Prepare the following budgets for EACH of the first four quarters.

   i) Production budget in tins (including faulty production) for A120
   ii) Material purchases budget in kilograms
   iii) Cost of material purchases budget
   iv) Labour budget in hours, including any overtime required
   v) Cost of labour budget, including the cost of any overtime

b) The chief executive of Dobra is Jemma Hughes. After receiving your budgets, she gives you the following information.

   - Overtime should be avoided if possible. The company would be willing to increase the level of finished stocks if this reduced overtime.
   - There would be extra holding costs if finished stocks increased but these should be kept as low as possible.

   She also tells you that the company has been investigating the use of linear regression to help forecast sales. The sales director has plotted the last 24 quarterly actual sales and has calculated the linear regression formula $y = a + bx$ as:

   $y = 1,000 + 100x$

   where y is the forecast sales trend measured in tins of A120, 1,000 is a constant and x is the quarter number. For quarter 1 of the year to 25 June 2006, x would therefore be 25.

   The sales director has also calculated the following seasonal variations based on the 24 observations.

	Seasonal variations			
	Quarter 1	Quarter 2	Quarter 3	Quarter 4
Seasonal variation (tins)	(500)	(300)	300	500

Write a memo to Jemma Hughes. In your memo you should do the following.

i) Prepare a revised budget of labour hours for each quarter to reduce overtime as much as possible.

ii) Prepare a revised production budget in tins for each quarter to take account of your planned reduction in overtime.

iii) Use the formula to forecast the trend for each of the quarters 1 to 4.

iv) Use the seasonal variations to forecast the sales volume for each of the quarters 1 to 4 for the year to 25 June 2006.

v) Identify THREE reasons why linear regression might not give accurate estimates of the demand for tins of A120.

chapter 12:
RECONCILING BUDGETS AND ACTUAL FIGURES

1   Explain what is meant by a fixed budget and a flexed budget and how each is used in the management process.

2   The budget for production supervisors' costs for a period for a business at an activity level of 250,000 units is £15,000. One production supervisor is required for every 100,000 units of production. If actual production is 330,000 units what figure would appear in the flexed budget for production supervisors' costs?

3
	100,000 units £	120,000 units £
Materials cost	240,000	288,000
Labour cost	124,000	144,000
Production overhead	38,000	38,000

How would each cost appear in a budget flexed to an actual activity level of 112,000 units?

4   The budgeted production overhead for a business is £524,000 at an activity level of 60,000 units and £664,000 at an activity level of 80,000 units. If the actual activity level is 72,000 units what is the flexed budget figure for production overhead?

97

reconciling budgets and actual figures

5

	Quarter 4 budget £
Sales (20,000 units)	130,000
Material	(55,000)
Labour	(35,000)
Production overhead	(18,000)
Gross profit	22,000
General expenses	12,000
Operating profit	10,000

The details of the cost behaviour of each of the costs is given below:

Materials — the materials cost is totally variable

Labour — each operative can only produce 2,000 units each quarter – the cost of each operative is £3,500 each quarter

Production overhead — the production overhead is a totally fixed cost

General expenses — the general expenses are made up of a budgeted fixed cost of £6,400 and a variable element

Actual sales and production were in fact only 15,000 units during quarter 4. Prepare a flexed budget for an activity level of 15,000 units.

6

The budget for a manufacturing company for the month of March and the actual results for the month are given below:

	Budget 28,000 units £	Actual 31,500 units £
Sales	406,000	441,000
Materials	165,200	180,400
Labour	100,800	115,600
Production overhead	37,500	39,000
Gross profit	102,500	106,000
General expenses	55,600	68,900
Operating profit	46,900	37,100

The materials and labour costs are variable costs, the production overhead is a fixed cost and the general expenses are a semi-variable cost with a fixed element of £13,600

i) Calculate variances between the fixed budget and the actual results

ii) Prepare a flexed budget for the actual activity level and show the variances for each of the figures

iii) Comment on the differences shown by the two sets of variances

reconciling budgets and actual figures

7   Given below is the original fixed budget for a manufacturing operation for quarter 2. However, as sales and production were subsequently anticipated to be higher than this budget made allowance for, a revised budget was also prepared. The actual results for quarter 2 are also given.

	Original budget 200,000 units		Revised budget 240,000 units		Actual 230,000 units	
	£	£ 680	£	£	£	£ 661
Sales		1,360,000		1,632,000		1,532,000
Materials	690,000		828,000		783,200	
Labour	387,000		449,000		428,600	
Production expenses	162,000		186,000		173,500	
Production cost		1,239,000		1,463,000		1,385,300
Gross profit		121,000		169,000		146,700
General expenses		72,000		72,000		74,700
Operating profit		49,000		97,000		72,000

Prepare a flexed budget to reflect the actual level of activity for the month and calculate the variances from that budget.

8   Given below is the budget for quarter 2 prepared using absorption costing principles. There were no opening stocks.

	Quarter 2 budget	
	£	£
Sales (50,000 units)		400,000
Materials	165,400	
Labour	69,800	
Production overhead	56,000	
Cost of production 56,000 units	291,200	
Less: closing stock	31,200	
Cost of sales		260,000
Gross profit		140,000
General expenses		52,000
Operating profit		88,000

The materials and labour costs are variable with the level of production but the production overhead and general expenses are both fixed costs.

i)   Prepare the budget for quarter 2 using marginal costing principles.

ii) Reconcile the budgeted profit figure using absorption costing to the budgeted profit figure using marginal costing.

reconciling budgets and actual figures

9 A business has an overhead absorption rate of £16.40 per unit produced. The budgeted fixed overhead was £3,034,000

What is the budgeted activity level for the period?

10 A business has the following budgeted and actual figures for a period:

Budgeted fixed overheads	£331,200
Actual fixed overhead	£315,000
Fixed overhead absorption rate	£1.20 per unit

What is the budgeted activity level?

11 The following information is known about a business's budgeted and actual figures:

Budgeted fixed overhead	£84,000
Budgeted activity level	24,000 units
Actual fixed overhead	£93,600
Under-absorption	£3,650

What was the actual activity level during the period?

12 The following information is known about a business's budgeted and actual figures:

Budgeted fixed overhead	£483,000
Budgeted activity level	70,000 units
Actual fixed overhead	£490,000
Over-absorption	£15,080

What was the actual level of activity?

13 Explain what is meant by the following terms:

i) a responsibility centre
ii) responsibility accounting
iii) an expense centre
iv) a profit centre

reconciling budgets and actual figures

14 Why is it important that managerial performance is only judged on the basis of controllable variances?

15 Explain what is meant by feedback and feedforward.

16 Given below is the original fixed budget for a business's operations for the six months ending 31 March 2006 and the actual results for that period.

	Budget		Actual	
Units	30,000		34,000	
	£	£	£	£
Sales		660,000		697,000
Direct costs				
Materials	252,000		299,200	
Labour	180,000		192,600	
Factory power	83,600		88,600	
	515,600		580,400	
Fixed overheads	75,000		79,000	
Cost of sales		590,600		659,400
Operating profit		69,400		37,600

You are also provided with the following information:

i) the budget had assumed that there would be no closing stocks. However the actual production was 40,000 units with actual sales of 34,000 units

ii) the closing stocks of 6,000 units have been valued by including fixed overheads based upon the budgeted fixed overhead absorption rate

iii) the production employees are paid per week irrespective of the production level. The employees that were budgeted for are capable of producing a maximum of 45,000 units in a six month period

iv) the budgeted and actual figures for factory power include a fixed cost element of £20,600

101

reconciling budgets and actual figures

a) Calculate the following figures:
   i) the budgeted selling price per unit
   ii) the budgeted material cost per unit
   iii) the budgeted marginal cost of factory power per unit
   iv) the actual marginal cost of factory power per unit

b) Prepare a flexed budget operating statement for the actual activity level using marginal costing principles. Show variances for the sales and costs figures.

c) Give two reasons why the flexed budget operating statement shows different results from that of the original budget.

d) Give two reasons why the flexed budget operating statement might be a better measure of management performance than the original operating results.

17 a) Rivermede Ltd makes a single product called the Fasta. Last year, Steven Jones, the managing director of Rivermede Ltd, attended a course on budgetary control. As a result, he agreed to revise the way budgets were prepared in the company. Rather than imposing targets for managers, he encouraged participation by senior managers in the preparation of budgets.

An initial budget was prepared but Mike Fisher, the sales director, felt that the budgeted sales volume was set too high. He explained that setting too high a budgeted sales volume would mean that his sales staff would be de-motivated because they would not be able to achieve the sales volume. Steven Jones agreed to use the revised sales volume suggested by Mike Fisher.

Both the initial and revised budgets are reproduced below complete with the actual results for the year ended 31 May 2006.

Rivermede Ltd – budgeted and actual costs for the year ended 31 May 2006

	Original budget	Revised budget	Actual results	Variances from revised budget
Fasta production and sales (units)	24,000	20,000	22,000	2,000 (F)
	£	£	£	£
Variable costs				
Material	216,000	180,000	206,800	26,800 (A)
Labour	288,000	240,000	255,200	15,200 (A)
Semi-variable costs				
Heat, light and power	31,000	27,000	33,400	6,400 (A)
Fixed costs				
Rent, rates and depreciation	40,000	40,000	38,000	2,000 (F)
	575,000	487,000	533,400	46,400 (A)

reconciling budgets and actual figures

Assumptions in the two budgets
1 No change in input prices
2 No change in the quantity of variable inputs per Fasta

As the management accountant at Rivermede Ltd, one of your tasks is to check that invoices have been properly coded. On checking the actual invoices for heat, light and power for the year to 31 May 2006, you find that one invoice for £7,520 had been incorrectly coded. The invoice should have been coded to materials.

Tasks

i) Using the information in the original and revised budgets, identify the following.

1) The variable cost of material and labour per Fasta
2) The fixed and unit variable cost within heat, light and power

ii) Prepare a flexible budget, including variances, for Rivermede Ltd after correcting for the miscoding of the invoice.

b) On receiving your flexible budget statement, Steven Jones states that the total adverse variance is much less than the £46,400 shown in the original statement. He also draws your attention to the actual sales volume being greater than in the revised budget. He believes these results show that a participative approach to budgeting is better for the company and wants to discuss this belief at the next board meeting. Before doing so, Steven Jones asks for your comments.

Task

Write a memo to Steven Jones. Your memo should do the following.

i) **Briefly** explain why the flexible budgeting variances differ from those in the original statement given in the data to task (a).

ii) Give TWO reasons why a favourable cost variance may have arisen other than through the introduction of participative budgeting.

iii) Give TWO reasons why the actual sales volume compared with the revised budget's sales volume may not be a measure of improved motivation following the introduction of participative budgeting.

18 a) HFD plc opened a new division on 1 December 2005. The division, HFD Processes Ltd, produces a special paint finish. Because of the technology, there can never be any work in progress. The original budget was developed on the assumption that there would be a loss in the initial year of operation and that there would be no closing stock of finished goods.

One year later, HFD Processes Ltd prepared its results for its first year of operations. The chief executive of HFD plc was pleased to see that, despite budgeting for an initial loss, the division had actually returned a profit of £74,400. As a result, the directors of HFD Processes were entitled to a substantial bonus. Details of the budget and actual results are reproduced below.

reconciling budgets and actual figures

HFD Processes
Operating results for year ended 30 November 2006

	Budget		Actual	
Volume (units)	20,000		22,000	
	£	£	£	£
Turnover		960,000		1,012,000
Direct costs				
Materials	240,000		261,800	
Production labour	260,000		240,240	
Light, heat and power	68,000		65,560	
	568,000		567,600	
Fixed overheads	400,000		370,000	
Cost of sales		968,000		937,600
Operating profit/(loss)		(8,000)		74,400

You are employed as a management accountant in the head office of HFD plc and have been asked to comment on the performance of HFD Processes Ltd. Attached to the budgeted and actual results were the relevant working papers. A summary of the contents of the working papers is reproduced below.

- The budget assumed no closing finished stocks. Actual production was 25,000 units and actual sales 22,000 units.
- Because of the technology involved, production employees are paid per week, irrespective of production levels. The employees assumed in the budget are capable of producing up to 26,000 units.
- The cost of material varies directly with production.
- The cost of light, heat and power includes a fixed standing charge. In the budget this fixed charge was calculated to be £20,000 per year. However, competition resulted in the supplier reducing the actual charge to £12,000 for the year.
- During the year, HFD Processes Ltd produced 25,000 units. The 3,000 units of closing finished stock were valued on the basis of direct cost plus 'normal' fixed overheads.

The number of units was used to apportion direct costs between the cost of sales and closing finished stock.

The budgeted fixed overhead of £20 per unit was used to calculate the fixed overheads in closing finished stocks.

The detailed composition of the cost of sales and closing stocks using these policies was as follows.

	Closing finished stocks	Cost of sales	Cost of production
Units	3,000	22,000	25,000
	£	£	£
Material	35,700	261,800	297,500
Production labour	32,760	240,240	273,000
Light, heat and power	8,940	65,560	74,500
Fixed overheads	60,000	370,000	430,000
	137,400	937,600	1,075,000

Tasks

i) Calculate the following.

1) The budgeted unit selling price
2) The budgeted material cost per unit
3) The budgeted marginal cost of light, heat and power per unit
4) The actual marginal cost of light, heat and power per unit

ii) Prepare a flexible budget statement for the operating results of HFD Processes Ltd using a **marginal costing** approach, identifying fixed costs for the year and showing any variances.

b) You present your flexible budget statement to the chief executive of HFD plc who is concerned that your findings appear different to those in the original operating results.

Task

You are asked to write a **brief** memo to the chief executive. In your memo, you should do the following.

i) Give TWO reasons why the flexible budget operating statement shows different results from the original operating results.

ii) Give ONE reason why the flexible budget operating statement might be a better measure of management performance than the original operating results.

reconciling budgets and actual figures

19 a) Hall Ltd makes a product called the Omega. The budgeted and actual results for the year ended 30 November 2006 are shown below.

Hall Ltd: Budgeted and actual operating statement
Year ended 30 November 2006

	Budget	Actual
Sales volume (units)	36,000	35,000
	£	£
Turnover	1,440,000	1,365,000
Direct costs		
Material	432,000	500,000
Labour	216,000	232,000
Light, heat and power	92,000	96,000
Fixed overheads		
Depreciation	100,000	70,000
Other fixed overheads	400,000	420,000
Costs of production	1,240,000	1,318,000
less closing stock	–	164,750
Cost of sales	1,240,000	1,153,250
Operating profit	200,000	211,750

Ann Jones, the senior management accountant gives you the following information.

- Material and labour are variable costs.
- The budgeted total cost of light, heat and power includes a fixed element of £20,000.
- The **actual** cost of light, heat and power includes a fixed element of £12,000.
- There were no budgeted or actual opening stocks.
- During the year, actual production was 40,000 Omegas, of which 5,000 were unsold at the year end.
- The closing stock of 5,000 Omegas were valued at their actual direct cost plus an appropriate proportion of fixed overheads.
- The company did not purchase or sell any fixed assets during the year.
- There was no work in progress at any time.

Tasks

i) Calculate the following.

   1) Budgeted selling price per Omega
   2) Budgeted material cost per Omega
   3) Budgeted labour cost per Omega
   4) Budgeted variable cost of light, heat and power per Omega
   5) The percentage of cost of production carried forward in closing stock

6) Total actual variable cost of sales by expenditure type
7) Total actual fixed costs

ii) Prepare a flexible budget statement using variable (or marginal) costing, showing the budgeted and actual results and any variances.

b) The chief executive of Hall Ltd is Harry Easton. On receiving the original budgeted and actual operating statement, he had been very pleased with the performance of Hall Ltd. After reading your revised statement, however, he is concerned about the changes in both the budgeted profits and actual profits and is considering investigating whether or not the managers of Hall Ltd were responsible for the differences. Ann Jones suggests you write a memo to the chief executive.

Task

Write a short memo to Harry Easton, the chief executive. In your memo you should do the following.

i) Briefly explain the main reason for the following.

1) The difference between the original budget and the budget you prepared in task (a)

2) The difference between the original operating profit and the operating profit you prepared in task (a)

ii) Give TWO possible reasons why the actual operating profit shown in task (a) was greater than the budgeted operating profit despite a lower sales volume.

20 KBV Sound Ltd makes a CD player that is fitted to the cars made by KBV Motors.

You have recently been appointed as KBV Sound's assistant management accountant. You are responsible for preparing statements showing actual results against flexible budgets.

You have been given the working papers of the previous assistant management accountant. These contain the following.

- Two draft budgets for the year ended 31 May 2006. The first assumes a production and sales volume of 80,000 CD players. The second assumes a production and sales volume of 100,000 CD players. Any differences between the two budgets arose entirely from the different volumes assumed.
- The actual operating results for the year.
- A note stating there were no opening or closing stocks of any sort.
- A note stating that there were no purchases or sales of fixed assets during the year.

The draft budgets and actual results from the working papers are shown below.

reconciling budgets and actual figures

KBV Sound Ltd: budgets and actual results for the year ended 31 May 2006

	Draft budgets		Draft budgets		Actual results	
CD player production and sales volume		80,000		100,000		140,000
	£'000	£'000	£'000	£'000	£'000	£'000
Conversion costs						
Labour	640		760		972	
Light, heat and power	370		450		586	
Rent, rates and insurance	200		200		200	
Depreciation	150		150		132	
		1,360		1,560		1,890
Bought-in materials		1,600		2,000		3,220
Total expense		2,960		3,560		5,110
Turnover		3,200		4,000		6,440
Operating profit		240		440		1,330

Tasks

a) Calculate the following data.

    i) Budgeted selling price per CD player
    ii) Budgeted bought-in material cost per CD player
    iii) Budgeted variable cost of labour per CD player
    iv) Budgeted total labour fixed cost
    v) Budgeted variable cost of light, heat and power per CD player
    vi) Budgeted total light, heat and power fixed cost

b) Prepare a flexible budget statement showing the budgeted and actual results and any variances.

c) Mike Jones is the personnel manager of KBV Sound. He believes the high profits of £1,330,000 are due to increased effort by the managers following the introduction of performance related pay on 1 June 2005. He explains the scheme to you.

- The bought-in materials for the CD players are purchased from outside suppliers but the conversion costs – those manufacturing costs that transform the raw materials into the finished product – are all provided by KBV Sound.

- The only customer for the CD player is the parent company, KBV Motors. Because of this, there is no market price and so the price has had to be negotiated.

- It was agreed that the price of the CD players sold to KBV Motors should be twice the cost of the bought-in materials.

- Additional performance related payments are based on the following.
    - Exceeding the annual budgeted volume of sales
    - Increasing the actual profit per CD player above the budgeted profit per CD player
- The budgeted sales volume for the year was 100,000 CD players and the budgeted profit per CD player was £4.40.
- The actual sales volume for the year was 140,000 and the actual profit per CD player was £9.50.

Write a memo to Mike Jones. In your memo you should do the following.

i) Use the data in the question to explain THREE reasons why profits might have improved even without the introduction of performance related pay.

(ii) Identify THREE general conditions necessary for performance related pay to lead to improved performance.

UNIT 8

PRACTICE EXAM 1

LNG LTD

These tasks were set by the AAT in December 2005

Time allowed: 3 hours plus 15 minutes reading time

unit 8 – practice exam 1

INSTRUCTIONS

This examination paper is in TWO sections.

You must show competence in BOTH sections.

You should therefore attempt and aim to complete EVERY task in EACH section.

All essential workings should be included within your answers, where appropriate.

Both sections are based on LNG Ltd. Data provided in Section 1 may also be needed for Section 2.

SECTION 1 (Suggested time allowance: 100 minutes)

DATA

You work as an accounting technician at LNG Ltd reporting to the Finance Director. LNG Ltd prints and publishes newspapers. The company operates an integrated standard cost system in which:

- purchases of materials are recorded at standard cost
- direct materials and direct labour costs are both variable costs
- all production overheads are fixed and are absorbed using direct labour hours

The standard cost for printing 1,000 newspaper is as follows.

Product:	Newspaper		
Standard quantity:	1,000		
Inputs	**Quantity**	**Unit Price**	**Total cost**
		£	£
Paper	200 kgs	0.50	100.00
Ink	40 litres	4.00	160.00
Direct labour	10 hours	6.00	60.00
Fixed production overheads	10 hours	12.00	120.00
Standard cost			440.00

Actual and budgeted data for November are as follows.

- 23,200 litres of ink were purchased and used at a cost of £95,120.
- Actual output for the month was 600,000 newspapers.
- The budgeted output for the month was 560,000 newspapers.
- 6,200 direct labour hours were worked at a cot of £38,440.
- Actual fixed production overheads were £70,000.

112

Task 1.1

a) Calculate the following information for November:

   i) actual price of ink per litre
   ii) standard usage of ink for actual production
   iii) actual labour rate per hour
   iv) standard labour hours for actual production
   v) budgeted production overheads

b) Calculate the following variances for November:

   i) price variance for ink
   ii) usage variance for ink
   iii) labour rate variance
   iv) labour efficiency variance
   v) fixed overhead expenditure variance
   vi) fixed overhead volume variance
   vii) fixed overhead capacity variance
   viii) fixed overhead efficiency variance

c) Prepare a statement for November which reconciles the fixed overheads incurred with the fixed overheads absorbed in production.

ADDITIONAL DATA

Paper supplies are imported and invoiced in US dollars. Following investigation, you discover that the standard cost for paper was set in July when the exchange rate between the UK pound and the US dollar was $1.80 = £1.00. In November, the company purchased 130,000 kgs of paper for $110,565 at a sterling cost of £58,500.

Task 1.2

a)   i) Calculate the percentage decrease in the value of the dollar between July and November.

   ii) Calculate the material price variance in UK pounds for paper for November

   iii) Subdivide the material price variance for paper showing which part is due to changes in the dollar exchange rate and which part is due to other factors.

b) Write a note to the Finance Director which considers whether the price variance due to changes in the dollar exchange rate should be included or excluded from the Purchasing Manager's performance report.

unit 8 – practice exam 1

ADDITIONAL DATA

The cost of ink represents the largest component of product cost. Your Managing Director is concerned about the recent increase in the cost of ink. You are given the following data by the Purchasing Manager.

Month	Average monthly ink cost £/litre	Ink Producers' Price Index
July	4.00	107.6
August	4.04	111.0
September	4.05	112.8
October	4.08	115.3
November	4.10	116.2

Task 1.3

a) Calculate the percentage increase in the cost of ink to the company between July and November.

b) Calculate the percentage increase in the Ink Producers' Price Index between July and November.

c) Using your answers from a) and b), comment on your Managing Director's concerns.

SECTION 2 (Suggested time allowance: 80 minutes)

ADDITIONAL DATA

Extracts from the latest operating statements of LNG Ltd and certain performance indicators from its competitor Ads Ltd are shown below.

Profit and loss account extract for the year ended 30 November 2005

	LNG Ltd £'000
Advertising sales	4,200
Less cost of sales:	
Materials	(1,900)
Direct labour	(430)
Fixed production overheads	(880)
Gross profit	990
Sales and distribution costs	(540)
Administration costs	(240)
Operating profit	210

Balance sheet extract at 30 November 2005

	LNG Ltd £'000
Fixed assets	3,265
Debtors	1,050
Cash	85
Creditors	(600)
Net assets	3,800

Other operating data

	LNG Ltd
Newspapers produced	7,500,000
Number of employees	70
Advertising transactions	40,000

Performance indicators for Ads Ltd

Gross profit margin	33.2%
Operating profit margin	10.0%
Return on capital employed	15.4%
Debtor age (in months)	2.0
Average revenue per newspaper	£0.75
Advertising revenue per employee	£88,500.00
Advertising revenue per advertising transaction	£120.00

Task 2.1

a) With reference to the performance indicators for Ads Ltd, briefly explain how benchmarking is used to improve performance.

b) Calculate the following performance indicators for LNG Ltd:

   i) gross profit margin
   ii) operating profit margin
   iii) return on capital employed
   iv) average age of debtors in months
   v) average advertising revenue per newspaper produced
   vi) advertising revenue per employee
   vii) average advertising revenue per advertising transaction

ADDITIONAL DATA

At LNG Ltd, a management meeting was held to discuss the annual results. In a bid to increase profits and be more competitive, the following improvements were identified.

- Average advertising revenue per advertising transaction could be increased by 5%.
- Wastage of paper could be reduced which would result in a saving of 3% in total material costs.
- A credit controller could be employed at an annual cost of £25,000. As a result, debtors would be reduced to £850,000.
- Surplus land could be sold for its book value of £500,000 and the proceeds distributed to the shareholders.

Task 2.2

a) Restate the LNG Ltd profit and loss account for the year ended 30 November 2005, assuming each of the improvements had been implemented on 1 December 2004.

b) In a memo to the Board of Directors, indicate the overall effect of the improvements on EACH of the performance indicators for LNG Ltd calculated in Task 2.1.

UNIT 8

PRACTICE EXAM 2

BELL PLC

These tasks were set by the AAT in June 2005

Time allowed: 3 hours plus 15 minutes reading time

unit 8 – practice exam 2

INSTRUCTIONS

This examination paper is in TWO sections.

You must show competence in BOTH sections.

You should therefore attempt and aim to complete EVERY task in EACH section.

All essential workings should be included within your answers, where appropriate.

SECTION 1 (Suggested time allowance: 100 minutes)

DATA

Bell plc manufactures and sells two types of stove, Model F and Model H. You work as an accounting technician reporting to the Finance Director. The company uses a standard cost stock system in which purchases of materials are recorded at standard cost. Fixed production overheads are absorbed using a budgeted overhead absorption rate per labour hour.

The standard production cost for both models was set in January and is as follows.

	Model F Quantity	Model F Price £	Model F Total £	Model H Quantity	Model H Price £	Model H Total £
Materials	20 kg	2.00	40.00	40 kgs	2.00	80.00
Labour	5 hours	5.00	25.00	8 hours	5.00	40.00
Fixed overheads	5 hours	6.00	30.00	8 hours	6.00	48.00
Standard cost			95.00			168.00

Actual and budgeted data for May are as follows.

- 350,000 kgs of materials were purchased at a cost of £675,500
- Issues from stores for the production of Model F were 210,000 kgs
- 52,000 direct labour hours were worked producing Model F at a cost of £254,800
- Total direct labour hours worked were 58,600
- Budgeted output for Model F was 10,000 and for Model H was 1,000
- 9,800 Model F and 1,000 Model H stoves were produced
- Actual fixed production overheads were £360,000
- The company had 1,000 Model F and 500 Model H stoves in stock on both 1 May and 31 May

Task 1.1

a) Calculate the following information for May:
   i) the actual price of materials per kg
   ii) the standard usage of materials for Model F
   iii) the standard hours for the production of Model F
   iv) the actual direct labour hour rate for producing Model F
   v) the budgeted fixed production overheads

b) Calculate the following variances for May:
   i) the materials price variance
   ii) the fixed overhead expenditure variance
   iii) the fixed overhead volume variance
   iv) the fixed overhead capacity variance
   v) the fixed overhead efficiency variance

c) Calculate for the production of the Model F stove for May:
   i) the materials usage variance
   ii) the labour rate variance
   iii) the labour efficiency variance

ADDITIONAL DATA

The purchasing department has provided the following data for the purchase of materials for January to April.

	Quantity purchased kgs	Price variance £
January	200,000	4,000 (F)
February	250,000	10,000 (F)
March	280,000	11,200 (F)
April	300,000	18,000 (F)

Task 1.2

a) Calculate the actual price of materials per kg for each of the four months to April.

b) Write a memo to the finance director in which you:
   i) identify the movement in material prices over the four months
   ii) explain TWO possible reasons for this movement
   iii) identify ONE effect this movement in material prices might have on the purchasing department and any implications it has for the company

ADDITIONAL DATA

Following a review of production processes, the production director has established that budgeted fixed production overheads can be directly related to either the Model F or Model H stove. The analysis of monthly budgeted overhead costs is as follows.

Production process	Total budgeted cost £'000	Model F £'000	Model H £'000
Material handling	100	80	20
Production set up	85	65	20
Quality inspection	125	85	40
Production supervisor	38	20	18

The budgeted monthly production is for 10,000 Model F and 1,000 Model H stoves.

Task 1.3

a) Calculate the budgeted standard unit overhead cost for Model F and Model H using activity based overhead costs.

b) The Finance Director is considering whether to change the costing system from one which absorbs production overheads using labour hours to an activity based system. In a memo to the Finance Director you are required to:

　i) calculate and comment on the effect on profit for May if the company makes this change in valuing its stock of finished goods at 31 May

　ii) explain how computer software packages could assist in the operation of an activity based costing system.

SECTION 2 (Suggested time allowance: 80 minutes)

DATA

At the May management meeting the following information relating to Models F and H stoves for April was presented.

	Model F Actual	Model F Budget	Model H Actual	Model H Budget
Units sold	10,100	9,800	850	900
Units produced	10,000	10,000	1,000	1,000
Direct labour hours	50,200	50,000	7,800	8,000

	Model F Actual £	Model F Budget £	Model H Actual £	Model H Budget £
Turnover	1,010,000	980,000	187,000	198,000
Standard variable costs	(656,500)	(637,000)	(102,000)	(108,000)
Variable cost variances	(19,500)	-	19,000	-
Contribution	334,000	343,000	104,000	90,000
Fixed prod'n o/heads	(294,000)	(294,000)	(43,200)	(43,200)
Gross profit	40,000	49,000	60,800	46,800

Task 2.1

a) Calculate the following performance indicators for Model F and Model H for April:

   i) budgeted contribution margin
   ii) actual contribution margin
   iii) budgeted gross profit margin
   iv) actual gross profit martin
   v) actual capacity ratio
   vi) actual efficiency ratio

b) Using these indicators and other available data, write a memo to the Managing Director. You should:

   i) suggest THREE ways to improve the actual gross profit margin for Model F and indicate the feasibility of each

   ii) identify and explain TWO limitations of using the gross profit margin indicator for decision making purposes.

ADDITIONAL DATA

At the same May management meeting, the managing director presented a proposal from Chime Ltd to sub-contract the manufacture of Model H.

It was proposed that Chime Ltd would produce the Model H stove for a cost of £180 per stove and would employ all staff currently involved in its production. Chime Ltd would also guarantee next day delivery so that Bell plc could eliminate holding all finished goods stocks of Model H.

This proposal was considered and the following opinions were expressed.

Production director

'We should reject this proposal because the sub-contract cost is £12 greater than our standard cost.'

Managing director

'Estimates show that we can eliminate all the material handling, production set up and production supervision overheads plus half of the quality inspection overheads that relate to Model H. This will save the company £78,000 each month.'

Finance director

'There would be additional annual savings in costs of £12,000 which result from not holding stocks of Model H.'

Task 2.2

Using the financial and other information from the May management meeting, write a report to the Board on whether to proceed with the proposal to sub-contract the manufacture of the Model H stove. You should assume that the actual unit variable costs achieved for April will continue to apply in the future.

UNIT 8

PRACTICE EXAM 3

BLOSSOM LTD

These tasks were set by the AAT in December 2004

Time allowed: 3 hours plus 15 minutes reading time

unit 8 – practice exam 3

INSTRUCTIONS

This examination paper is in TWO sections.

You must show competence in BOTH sections.

You should therefore attempt and aim to complete EVERY task in BOTH sections.

You should spend about 100 minutes on Section 1 and 80 minutes on Section 2.

Include all essential workings within your answers, where appropriate.

SECTION 1 (Suggested time allowance: 100 minutes)

DATA

Blossom Ltd manufactures and sells garden statues. You work as an accounting technician reporting to the Finance Director. The company uses a standard cost stock system.

The actual and budgeted results for the production department for November are as follows:

Production Department: Actual and Budgeted Results for November

		Actual		Budget
Production		6,500 units		7,500 units
		£		£
Materials	20,800 kgs	91,520	22,500 kgs	90,000
Labour	7,150 hours	44,330	7,500 hours	45,000
Fixed overheads		15,850		15,000
Total production cost		151,700		150,000

Fixed production overheads are absorbed using a budgeted overhead absorption rate per labour hour.

Task 1.1

a) Calculate the following information for November:

  i)   standard price of materials per kg
  ii) actual price of materials per kg
  iii) standard usage of materials for actual production
  iv) standard labour rate per hour
  v)   actual labour rate per hour
  vi) standard labour hours for actual production
  vii) budgeted overhead absorption rate

b) Calculate the following variances for November:

   i) the material price variance
   ii) the material usage variance
   iii) the labour rate variance
   iv) the labour efficiency variance
   v) the fixed overhead expenditure variance
   vi) the fixed overhead volume variance
   vii) the fixed overhead capacity variance
   viii) the fixed overhead efficiency variance

c) Using the variances you have calculated in Task 1.1 (b), prepare an operating statement for November which reconciles the standard absorption cost of total actual production with the actual absorption cost of total actual production.

ADDITIONAL DATA

At a meeting of senior management, the validity of the November variance data was questioned. Particular comments were as follows:

Purchasing Manager

'I don't think it's fair to measure my performance against the standard materials cost. This was set in January when the price index for materials was 110. In November, the same price index was 123.2.'

Production Manager

'I have a point to make. One batch of 500 kgs of materials was inferior in quality and had to be scrapped. As a result, we lost 150 labour hours of production whilst the mixing machines were washed down.'

Personnel Manager

'We have had real difficulties recruiting production labour and we're seeing the result in overtime working.'

Managing Director

'If we've got all these problems with financial variances, then perhaps we should monitor performance with physical measures of output.'

Task 1.2

Using the senior managers' comments and your answers from Task 1.1, write a report to the Managing Director. Your report should include:

a) A response to the comments of each of the three managers outlining whether they fully account for the labour and material variances you have calculated in Task 1.1. You should use calculations to support your findings.

b) A response to the Managing Director explaining why there might be a problem with financial variances and listing THREE possible measures of physical output.

SECTION 2 (Suggested time allowance: 80 minutes)

DATA

Duo Ltd owns two factories, A and B, which make and sell furniture to customers' orders. Each factory has its own general manager who is responsible for sales policy, pricing and purchasing. The forecasts for both factories for the year ending 31 December 2007 are shown below.

Profit and loss account extract for the year ending 31 December 2007

	Factory A £'000	Factory B £'000
Turnover	2,200	2,850
Materials	660	784
Direct labour	440	448
Fixed production overheads	220	420
Cost of sales	1,320	1,652
Gross profit	880	1,198
Sales and distribution costs	(520)	(640)
Administration costs	(210)	(250)
Operating profit	150	308

Balance sheet extract at 31 December 2007

	£'000	£'000
Fixed assets	1,255	7,410
Stocks	120	142
Debtors	183	238
Cash	2	10
Creditors	(60)	(100)
Net assets	1,500	7,700

Other data

Units produced and sold	22,000	30,000
Budgeted labour hours	75,000	85,000

The following information is also relevant:

- Stocks comprise raw materials for both factories.
- Stocks will remain unchanged throughout the year.
- The amount for trade creditors relates only to purchases of stocks.
- Factory A has a capacity of 70,000 labour hours and Factory B 140,000 labour hours.
- Sales and distribution costs are variable with turnover from each factory.
- Administration costs are fixed.

Task 2.1

Using the forecast financial information, calculate the following performance indicators, to one decimal place, for both factories:

a) gross profit margin
b) operating profit margin
c) return on capital employed
d) stock turnover in months. Note that stock value is based on materials cost only.
e) age of creditors in months
f) age of debtors in months
g) labour capacity ratio

ADDITIONAL DATA

When she received the performance indicators, your Managing Director called a meeting to discuss future manufacturing strategy. Several changes were proposed including the following.

From the Managing Director

'I propose that we close Factory A and transfer its business to Factory B.'

From the General Manager of Factory A

'I estimate that 60% of Factory A's output is sold locally. If we close Factory A, this business will be lost. Also, the closure costs will be £250,000. Surely, the General Manager of Factory B should be looking to increase sales from his facility.'

From the General Manager of Factory B

'Given the current poor economic climate, I think it would be wrong to plan an increase in our sales. Taking on 40% of Factory A's sales would lead to an increase in our fixed production overheads and administration costs. I estimate that production overheads would increase by £100,000 and administration costs by £60,000. In addition, all sales and distribution costs will rise in line with turnover.'

From the Finance Director

'If we close Factory A, we will centralise purchasing. I have carried out some research and we can move to just-in-time manufacture. If we rationalise our supplier base, we can save 5% in our total material costs and remove the need to hold raw material stocks.'

Task 2.2

Prepare a revised profit and loss account for Factory B, assuming Factory A is closed.

Task 2.3

Using appropriate financial data and performance indicators calculated above, write a memo to the Board of Directors on whether to proceed with the closure of Factory A.

As the basis for your decision, your memo should include:

a) a brief comparison of the performance of Factory B before and after closure of Factory A
b) a brief comparison of the company's performance before and after closure of Factory A

UNIT 8

PRACTICE EXAM 4

BROWN LTD

These tasks were set by the AAT in June 2004

Time allowed: 3 hours plus 15 minutes reading time

unit 8 – practice exam 4

INSTRUCTIONS

This examination paper is in TWO sections.

You must show competence in BOTH sections.

You should therefore attempt and aim to complete EVERY task in BOTH sections.

You should spend about 90 minutes on Section 1 and 90 minutes on Section 2.

Include all essential workings within your answers, where appropriate.

Both sections are based on Brown Ltd. Data provided in Section 1 may also be needed for Section 2.

SECTION 1 (Suggested time allowance: 90 minutes)

DATA

Brown Ltd manufactures and sells office furniture. The company operates an integrated standard cost system in which:

- purchases of materials are recorded at standard cost
- finished goods are recorded at standard cost
- direct materials and direct labour costs are both variable costs
- fixed production overheads are absorbed using direct labour hours.

You are an accounting technician at Brown Ltd. You report to Sam Thomas, the Finance Director.

The company's most popular product is an executive desk. Its standard cost is as follows:

Product: Executive Desk

Inputs	Quantity	Unit Price £	Total Cost £
Direct materials	30 kgs	5.00	150.00
Direct labour	5 hours	6.00	30.00
Fixed production overheads	5 hours	4.00	20.00
Standard cost			200.00

Actual and budgeted data for the manufacture of executive desks for May 2006 are shown below.

- 27,500 kgs of direct materials were purchased for £143,000.
- Issues from stores to production totalled 27,500 kgs.
- The actual output for the month was 900 desks.
- The budgeted output for the month was 1,000 desks.
- 4,200 direct labour hours were worked at a cost of £26,040.
- Actual fixed production overheads were £23,000.

unit 8 – practice exam 4

Task 1.1

a) Calculate the following information for May:

   i) actual price of materials per kg
   ii) standard usage of materials for actual production
   iii) actual labour rate per hour
   iv) standard labour hours for actual production
   v) budgeted production overheads

b) Calculate the following variances for the production of executive desks for May:

   i) the material price variance
   ii) the material usage variance
   iii) the labour rate variance
   iv) the labour efficiency variance
   v) the fixed overhead expenditure variance
   vi) the fixed overhead volume variance
   vii) the fixed overhead capacity variance
   viii) the fixed overhead efficiency variance

c) Prepare an operating statement for May which reconciles the standard absorption cost of total actual production with the actual absorption cost of total actual production.

d) Write a memo for Sam Thomas to present to the Board of Directors. Your memo should comment on the usefulness, or otherwise, of the statement you have prepared in your answer to (c) above.

DATA

Sam Thomas is concerned about the rise in prices of direct materials and has asked you to investigate.

The prices per kg of direct materials charged by suppliers for the period January 2006 to May 2006 are as follows.

	£
January	5.05
February	5.02
March	5.08
April	5.11
May	5.20

Task 1.2

a) Calculate the moving average of monthly direct material prices over a period of three months.

b) Write a memo to Sam Thomas to:

   i) explain what the trend in direct material prices, based on the moving average series, shows
   ii) suggest ONE possible use of the trend in setting the standard cost of direct materials for 2006
   iii) give TWO more pieces of information needed to set the standard cost of direct materials for 2006

SECTION 2 (Suggested time allowance: 90 minutes)

DATA

The actual and budgeted operating results for the sale and production of executive desks for the year to May 2006 are set out below.

	Actual £	Budget £
Sales	2,750,000	3,000,000
Cost of sales		
Opening finished goods stock	200,000	200,000
Cost of production	2,329,600	2,400,000
Closing finished goods stock	(240,000)	(200,000)
Cost of sales	2,289,600	2,400,000
Gross profit	460,400	600,000
Distribution and administration costs	345,000	360,000
Operating profit	115,400	240,000

Other data for the production and sale of executive desks for the year to May 2006 is as follows.

	Actual	Budget
Number of desks sold	11,000	12,000
Number of desks produced	11,200	12,000
Direct labour hours	58,200	60,000
Net assets employed	£1,075,400	£1,200,000

Task 2.1

a) Calculate the following actual and budgeted performance indicators:

   i) gross profit margin
   ii) operating profit margin
   iii) return on capital employed
   iv) stock turnover in months
   v) labour capacity ratio
   vi) labour efficiency ratio

   Note. All performance indicators - except (iv) - should be expressed as percentages.

b) Write a memo to Sam Thomas. Your memo should include ONE course of action the company could take to improve EACH performance indicator.

DATA

Sam Thomas has been on a course on product management. He was particularly interested in the concept of value engineering or value analysis. This was explained to be a process which involves different specialists to evaluate a product's design. The objective of the process is to identify how a product may be redesigned to improve its value.

Task 2.2

Write a brief memo to Sam Thomas. Your memo should describe how value engineering or value analysis may be used to reduce the production cost of an item such as an executive desk.

UNIT 8

PRACTICE EXAM 5

ECONAIR LTD

These tasks were set by the AAT in December 2003

Time allowed: 3 hours plus 15 minutes reading time

unit 8 – practice exam 5

INSTRUCTIONS

This examination paper is in TWO sections.

You must show competence in BOTH sections.

You should therefore attempt and aim to complete EVERY task in BOTH sections.

You should spend about 100 minutes on Section 1 and 80 minutes on Section 2.

Include all essential workings within your answers, where appropriate.

SECTION 1 (Suggested time allowance: 100 minutes)

DATA

You are an accounting technician employed by Garforth Cookridge and Co, a firm of accountants and registered auditors. A new client is Econair Ltd. Econair is a small airline that operates two routes from its home airport.

One of your tasks is to prepare standard costing variances for Econair. To help you, the airline provides you with the following information for the 28 days ended 30 November for the route between the home airport and Alpha City.

Budgeted and actual operating results 28 days ended 30 November

Operating data	Budget		Actual	
Number of flights	168		160	
Number of flying hours	672		768	

Expenses	Quantity	£	Quantity	£
Fuel	33,600 gallons	50,400	38,400 gallons	61,440
Pilots' remuneration	1,322 pilot hours	67,200	1,536 pilot hours	79,872
Aircraft fixed overheads	672 flying hours	75,600	768 flying hours	76,200
Cost of operations		193,200		217,512

Other information

- Pilot hours are the same as labour hours for a manufacturer.
- Flying hours are the same as machine hours for a manufacturer.
- The number of flights is the same as production volume for a manufacturer.
- Fuel and pilots' remuneration are treated as variable costs.
- Fixed overheads are charged to operations on the basis of flying hours.

Task 1.1

a) Use the budgeted data to calculate the following information:

   i) standard price of fuel per gallon
   ii) standard fuel usage for 160 flights
   iii) standard hourly rate for pilots
   iv) standard pilot hours per flight
   v) standard pilot hours for 160 flights
   vi) standard fixed overhead cost per budgeted flying hour
   vii) standard flying hours per flight
   viii) standard flying hours for 160 flights
   ix) standard fixed overhead absorbed by the 160 flights
   x) standard cost of actual operations

(b) Using the data given and your answers to part (a), calculate the following:

   i) fuel price variance
   ii) fuel usage variance
   iii) pilots' labour rate variance
   iv) pilots' labour efficiency variance
   v) fixed overhead expenditure variance
   vi) fixed overhead volume variance
   vii) fixed overhead capacity variance
   viii) fixed overhead efficiency variance

(c) Prepare a statement for the 28 days ended 30 November reconciling the standard cost of actual operations to the actual cost of actual operations. standard cost of actual operations.

DATA

The Chief Executive of Econair, Lisa Margoli, is given a copy of the standard costing reconciliation statement you prepared. Lisa tells you she is concerned about the fixed overhead variances and gives you the following information.

- **Flight and passenger data:** During the 28 days to 30 November, the actual number of flights to Alpha City was 8 less than budgeted. Although the budget assumed 70 passengers per flight, the actual number of passengers per flight was 80.

- **Current policy for apportioning and charging fixed overheads:** The second route operated by Econair is from the home airport to another country, Betaland. Econair's current practice is to apportion budgeted and actual fixed overheads between the two routes based on the number of aircraft. The apportioned fixed overheads are then charged to operations using flying hours.

unit 8 – practice exam 5

- **Budgeted operating data for the 28 days to 30 November**

Route	Alpha City	Betaland	Total
Number of aircraft	2	4	6
Number of flights per 28 days	168	448	616
Number of flying hours per 28 days	672	2,240	2912
Insurance value of each aircraft	£10m	£20m	
Total aircraft insurance value per route	£20m	£80m	£100m

- **Analysis of total budgeted fixed overhead expenses for both routes for the 28 days to 30 November**

	£
Aircraft maintenance	116,480
Insurance	98,020
Luggage handling and in-flight facilities *	12,300
Budgeted fixed overheads	226,800

  * Luggage handling and in-flight facilities only apply to the route to Betaland.

  Budgeted fixed overheads per aircraft (£226,800/6 aircraft) = £37,800

  Budgeted fixed overheads apportioned to Alpha City route (£37,800 × 2 aircraft) = £75,600

Task 1.2

Write a memo to Lisa Margoli. In your memo you should:

a) identify a more appropriate method than flying hours for charging standard fixed overheads

b) **briefly** explain why your chosen method for charging standard fixed overheads would give different fixed overhead capacity and efficiency variances to those calculated in Task 1.1

c) use the analysis of budgeted fixed overhead expenses and the operating data to reallocate the budgeted fixed overheads apportioned to the Alpha City route

SECTION 2 (Suggested time allowance: 80 minutes)

DATA

You are employed as an accounting technician by Aspex Technologies Ltd. One of your duties is to prepare performance indicators and other information for Stuart Morgan, the Financial Director.

Aspex Technologies make a single product, the Zeta. In the year to 30 November 2006, the company has had problems with the quality of the material used to make Zetas and Stuart would like to know what the *cost of quality* has been for the year.

The *cost of quality* is defined as the total of all costs incurred in preventing faults plus those costs involved in correcting faults once they have occurred. It is a single figure measuring all the explicit costs of quality – that is, those costs collected within the accounting system.

Stuart provides you with the following financial statements and data.

Operating statement – year ended 30 November 2006

	Units	£'000	£'000
Turnover	360,000		14,400
Purchases	400,000	6,400	
Less: returns	(40,000)	(640)	
Net purchases	360,000	5,760	
Add: opening stocks	90,000	1,440	
Less: closing stocks	(90,000)	(1,440)	
Material issued to production	360,000	5,760	
Production labour		3,600	
Variable cost of production and sales			9,360
Contribution			5,040
Heat, light and power		720	
Depreciation		1,000	
Inspection cost		80	
Production overhead		2,000	
Reworking of faulty production		40	
Customer support		200	
Marketing and administrative expenses		424	
Total fixed overheads			4,464
Operating profit			576

unit 8 – practice exam 5

Balance sheet at 30 November 2006

	£'000	£'000
Fixed assets at cost		8,000
Cumulative depreciation		2,000
Net book value		6,000
Stock of materials	1,440	
Debtors	2,400	
Cash	960	
Creditors	(1,200)	
Net current assets		3,600
		9,600
Financed by:		
Debt		6,000
Equity		3,600
		9,600

- The number of production employees in the company is 180.
- Production labour is a variable expense.
- The demand for Zetas in the year to 30 November 2006 was 390,000 but not all could be produced and sold due to poor quality materials. Any orders not completed this year can be completed next year.
- The only reason for the reworking of faulty production and customer support expenses was the poor quality of the materials.
- Material and heat, light and power are the only bought-in expenses.
- Creditors relate entirely to material purchases.
- There are no stocks of finished goods or work in progress.
- Depreciation is based on the straight-line method.

Task 2.1

Prepare the following information for Stuart Morgan:

a) selling price per Zeta
b) material cost per Zeta
c) labour cost per Zeta
d) contribution per Zeta
e) contribution percentage
f) net profit (or sales) margin
g) return on capital employed
h) asset turnover

i)   average age of debtors in months
j)   average age of stock in months
k)   average age of creditors in months
l)   added value per employee
m)   average delay in completing an order in months
n)   cost of quality

DATA

Stuart Morgan tells you that the Directors of Aspex Technologies have agreed an action plan for the year to 30 November 2007. The plan involves:

- using market research to forecast likely sales volume and prices
- implementing total quality management and just-in-time stock control
- greater working capital control.

Stuart provides you with the following information.

Market research

- Indices for this year and next year

	Selling price Index	Sales volume Index
Indices for year ended 30 November 2006	180	70
Forecast indices for year ending 30 November 2007	171	84

- The total forecast sales volume for the year ending 30 November 2007 is made up of two elements:
    - a revised volume from applying the sales volume indices to the 360,000 Zetas sold in the year to 30 November 2006
    - an additional volume from completing orders placed in the year to 30 November 2006 but not made in that year because of the poor quality materials
- The forecast selling price applies to the total forecast sales volume using the selling price indices.

Total quality management and just-in-time stock control

- The material supplier has agreed to take back the existing closing stock and replace it with fault-free materials.
- The supplier has also agreed to guarantee all material will be fault-free next year and improve the speed and reliability of deliveries. In exchange, Aspex has agreed that the unit cost of material will remain the same as last year.
- Aspex will no longer keep stocks of material.
- The costs making up the *cost of quality* will be saved.

Working capital control and other matters

- The unit cost of production labour will remain the same and there will be no change in the remaining fixed overheads.
- The average age of debtors will be 2 months.
- Aspex has agreed that the average age of creditors will be 1 month.
- The cash balance will remain the same. Any surplus cash will be used to pay off the existing loans.
- No fixed assets will be bought or sold during the year to 30 November 2007.

Task 2.2

Prepare the following estimates for the year to 30 November 2007 for Stuart Morgan:

a) sales volume
b) purchases
c) cost of purchases
d) selling price per Zeta
e) turnover
f) total contribution
g) fixed costs
h) operating profit
i) net assets at 30 November 2007
j) net profit (or sales) margin
k) return on capital employed

UNIT 9

PRACTICE EXAM 6

MERANO LTD

These tasks were set by the AAT in December 2005

Time allowed: 3 hours plus 15 minutes reading time

unit 9 – practice exam 6

INSTRUCTIONS

This examination paper is in TWO sections.

You must show competence in BOTH sections.

You should therefore attempt and aim to complete EVERY task in EACH section.

You should spend about 90 minutes on Section 1 and 90 minutes on Section 2.

Include all essential workings within your answers, where appropriate.

SECTION 1 (Suggested time allowance: 90 minutes)

DATA

You are employed as a management accountant by Merano Ltd and report to Louise Owen, the Finance Director. The company uses marginal (or variable) costing when preparing management accounts and divides the year into 20-day periods for both production and sales. One subsidiary, Solden Ltd, makes two products, the Exe and the Wye.

Louise Owen asks you to prepare Solden's budgets for period 1, the 20 days ending 27 January.

Louise Owen gives you the following information.

Sales data

	Units of Exe	Units of Wye
■ Budgeted sales for period 1, 20 days ending 27 January	3,200	2,344
■ Budgeted sales for period 2, 20 days ending 24 February	3,000	2,500

Stock data

- The opening finished stocks for period 1 will be 140 Exes and 184 Wyes.
- Closing finished stocks of Exe for period 1 must equal 2 days' sales in period 2.
- Closing finished stocks of Wye for period 1 must equal 4 days' sales in period 2.
- There is no stock of work-in-progress at any time.

Faulty production

- 4% of Exe finished production and 5% of Wye finished production is faulty and has to be destroyed. This faulty production has no value.

Task 1.1

Prepare a production budget for period 1, the 20 days ending 27 January, showing the number of Exes and the number of Wyes to be produced, including any faulty production, to meet the budgeted sales in period 1.

DATA

After you prepared the production budget, Louise Owen tells you that:

- Exe and Wye use the same material.
- Each Exe requires 6 kgs of material.
- Each Wye requires 8 kgs of material.
- The material costs £20 per kg.
- The stock of material at the beginning of period 1 will be 2,000 kgs.
- The stock of material at the end of period 1 will be 2,400 kgs.

Task 1.2

Prepare the following budgets for period 1:

a) material purchases budget in kgs
b) cost of materials budget

DATA

Louise Owen gives you the following additional information.

- Exe and Wye use the same type of labour.
- Each Exe requires 8 labour hours.
- Each Wye requires 5 labour hours.
- In any 20-day period, the workforce can work up to 40,000 labour hours before overtime.
- The normal labour rate is £6 per hour.
- The maximum overtime the employees in Solden can work is 4,000 labour hours.
- If any overtime is worked, the labour rate is £9 per hour.

Task 1.3

Prepare the following budgets for period 1:

a) labour hours budget, including any idle time or overtime to be worked
b) cost of labour budget including any overtime to be paid

unit 9 – practice exam 6

DATA

Louise Owen has to discuss the budgeted results of Solden with her other directors and asks for your help in preparing the information. She gives you the following information.

- Solden uses marginal (or variable) costing when preparing reports for directors.
- Any idle time or overtime is charged to fixed overheads.
- The budgeted selling price of each Exe is £200.
- The budgeted selling price of each Wye is £250.
- The opening stocks of 140 Exes, 184 Wyes and 2,000 kgs of materials have the same unit costs as in period 1.

Task 1.4

Prepare the following statements for period 1:

a) the budgeted marginal (or variable) cost of production for each product

b) the unit cost of fault-free production for each product

c) a budgeted operating statement showing for each product the total turnover, total expenses and total contribution.

DATA

After preparing the budgets, Louise Owen tells you that:

- Solden now believes it can sell an extra 220 Exes in period 1.
- total overtime cannot be more than the hours given in Task 1.3 and labour hours cannot be increased in any other way
- the maximum extra material available for period 1 is 1,200 kgs.

Task 1.5

Calculate:

a) the maximum extra production of fault-free units of Exe possible if labour hours were the only constraint

b) the maximum extra production of fault-free units of Exe possible if material were the only constraint

c) the revised fault-free production of Exes in period 1.

SECTION 2 (Suggested time allowance: 90 minutes)

DATA

Merano bought a new subsidiary, Otzal Ltd, 12 months ago. Otzal makes one product, the Kat. Otzal Ltd has recently completed the management accounting operating statement for the 12 months ended 30 November. This is shown below.

Otzal Ltd Operating statement 12 months ended 30 November

	Budget	Actual	Variance
Sales volume (Kats)	1,100	1,000	
Production volume (Kats)	1,100	1,200	
	£	£	£
Turnover	990,000	897,000	93,000 (A)
Materials	264,000	291,600	27,600 (A)
Labour	132,000	147,600	15,600 (A)
Electricity	260,000	279,600	19,600 (A)
Depreciation	40,000	36,000	4,000 (F)
Rates	70,000	69,000	1,000 (F)
Property expenses	80,000	78,000	2,000 (F)
Cost of production	846,000	901,800	
Less closing finished stock		150,300	
Cost of sales	846,000	751,500	94,500 (F)
Operating profit	144,000	145,500	1,500 (F)

Notes to the operating statement

- All Kats were sold for the same price.
- Material and labour are variable costs.
- Electricity is a semi-variable cost.
    - The budgeted fixed cost of electricity was £40,000
    - The actual marginal (or variable) cost of electricity per Kat was £198.
- All other costs are fixed costs.
- No assets were bought or sold during the year.
- There were no stocks of work-in-progress at any time and no opening finished stocks.

Louise Owen asks you to prepare a revised operating statement using marginal (or variable) costing.,

unit 9 – practice exam 6

Task 2.1

a) Calculate the following budgeted data per Kat:

   i)   selling price
   ii) material cost
   iii) labour cost
   iv) variable cost of electricity

b) Calculate the folllowing actual data per Kat:

   i)   selling price
   ii) material cost
   iii) labour cost

c) Calculate the fixed cost part of the actual cost of electricity.

d) Prepare a revised operating statement using marginal (or variable) costing. Your statement should include:

   i)   a flexible budget showing the budgeted turnover, the budgeted marginal (or variable) costs of that turnover, the budgeted contribution and the budgeted operating profit for the year

   ii) the actual turnover, the marginal (or variable) costs of that turnover, the actual contribution and the actual operating profit for the year

   iii) any variances between the budgeted and actual results.

DATA

Louise Owen gives your revised operating statement to Winston Smith, Merano's Marketing Director. Winston sends you an e-mail raising the following queries.

- Why is your revised budget different from the one prepared by Otzal Ltd?

- Why is the actual profit in your revised operating statement different from the actual profit prepared by Otzal Ltd?

- Which statement is of more help in controlling costs, the original operating statement or your revised one?

Task 2.2

Write an email to Winston Smith. In your email, you should:

a) explain why there is a difference between:

　i) the two budgets
　ii) the two actual profits

b) identify which operating statement is of more help in controlling costs, the one given in the task data or the one you prepared in Task 2.1 (d).

c) give ONE reason why your preferred operating statement is of more help to managers.

UNIT 9

PRACTICE EXAM 7

ARUSHA LTD

These tasks were set by the AAT in June 2005

Time allowed: 3 hours plus 15 minutes reading time

unit 9 – practice exam 7

INSTRUCTIONS

This examination paper is in TWO sections.

You must show competence in BOTH sections.

You should therefore attempt and aim to complete EVERY task in EACH section.

You should spend about 90 minutes on Section 1 and 90 minutes on Section 2.

Include all essential workings within your answers, where appropriate.

SECTION 1 (Suggested time allowance: 90 minutes)

DATA

You are employed as a management accountant by Arusha Ltd. Arusha makes several products, two of which are the Aston and the Brum. Both products use the same type of labour, but different materials. The Aston uses material A1 and the Brum, material B2.

Arusha uses absorption costing for reporting budgeted and actual results, and the first-in-first-out (FIFO) method for valuing closing stocks. The company operates a seven-day week for both production and sales, and its budgets are divided into four-week periods.

Budgeted data for period 7, the four-weeks commencing 4 July, together with budgeted sales data for period 8, the four-weeks commencing 1 August, is shown below.

Sales information

	Aston	Brum
■ Sales (units): period 7	1,840	2,625
■ Sales (units): period 8	2,520	3,000
■ Budged selling prices all periods	£100	£140

Stocks

	Aston	Brum
■ Opening finished stocks: units	200	875
■ Opening finished stocks: FIFO value	£16,000	£96,250

■ Closing finished costs must equal 4 days' sales in period 8 for the Aston and 7 days' sales for the Brum.

■ There are no stocks of raw materials or work in progress at any time.

152

Materials

	Aston	Brum
■ Name of material used	A1	B2
■ Litres required per unit produced	6	12
■ Evaporation before issued to production	4%	0%
■ Material cost per litre	£8	£7

Labour

	Aston	Brum
■ Labour hours per unit	2	3

- There are 75 employees who work a 35-hour week.
- The basic hourly rate is £8 and any overtime is paid at £12 per hour.

Overheads

- Fixed overheads are charged to production at a rate of £4 per labour hour.
- Any overtime premium is charged to fixed overheads.

Task 1.1

Prepare the following information for Arusha for period 7, the four weeks commencing 4 July:

a) production budget for Astons and Brums

b) material purchases budget in litres for A1 and B2

c) cost of material purchases budget for A1 and B2

d) labour hours budget, including any overtime for the company

e) cost of labour budget for the company

f) cost of overheads budget for Astons and Brums

g) absorption cost of production budget for Astons and Brums

h) unit absorption cost of production for Astons and Brums

i) budgeted operating statement for Astons and Brums, showing budgeted turnover, budgeted expenses and budgeted operating profit.

DATA

Arusha employs 200 workers making another product called the Guard. Each Guard is made by an individual employee.

Mark Jones is Arusha's Production director. At a management meeting, he tells you that some of the Guards sold are returned as faulty and have to be scrapped. He believes these faults arise from poor work practices by some of the employees making Guards. He suggests a sample of Guards are tested before being sold. Any Guard tested, however, could not be sold and would have to be scrapped.

He asks you to prepare a note for the next management meeting to show whether sampling of Guards' production would help identify those employees responsible for the faulty production.

unit 9 – practice exam 7

Task 1.2

Prepare notes for the next management meeting. Your notes should:

a) give TWO advantages of sampling as a way of identifying who is responsible for the faulty production

b) briefly explain the difference between true (or simple) random sampling, systematic sampling and stratified sampling

c) briefly explain which form of sampling Arusha should use.

SECTION 2 (Suggested time allowance: 90 minutes)

DATA

You are employed as a management accountant by CityEng Ltd and you report to Tara Williams, CityEng's Finance Director. CityEng makes a single product, the M9, which it sells to only one customer, Car Makers plc. The M9 is a precision product and Car Makers demands high levels of quality control.

When preparing the budgets for the year ending 31 May, it was not certain what the demand would be for the M9. Because of that CityEng developed two possible plans. The fist plan, Plan A, assumed demand for the M9 would be 300,000 units; the second plan, Plan B, assumed demand would be 400,000 units.

Both plans are shown below, together with the actual operating results of CityEng for the year ended 31 May.

CityEng Ltd: planned and actual operating results year ended 31 May

	Plan A	Plan B	Actual results
Volume	300,000	400,000	380,000
	£'000	£'000	£'000
Turnover	6,900	9,200	8,626
Material	2,400	3,200	3,116
Labour	1,500	2,000	1,938
Semi-variable cost: electricity	1,400	1,800	1,624
Stepped cost: quality control	360	480	358
Fixed cost: rent and rates	200	200	200
Fixed cost: depreciation	400	400	100
Operating profit	640	1,120	1,290

Notes to the planned operating results

- Both plans assumed the same unit selling price, the same unit variable (or marginal) costs and the same fixed costs.

- Both material and labour are variable (or marginal) costs.

- Quality control includes supervision. It is a stepped cost. The cost increases by the same amount for every 100,000 - or part of 100,000 - M9s produced.

Notes to the actual operating results

- Car Makers needed 420,000 M9s during the year.

- For technical reasons, the same amount of electricity is required for each M9 and no economies are possible.

- There is only one possible electricity supplier for CityEng Ltd. For the year to 31 May, the electricity supplier reduced both its fixed charge and its variable charge per unit of electricity.

Task 2.1

a) Calculate the budgeted selling price per M9.

b) Calculate the budgeted variable cost per M9 of:
   i) material
   ii) labour
   iii) electricity

c) Calculate the budgeted fixed cost of electricity.

d) Prepare a statement showing the flexible budget, the actual results and any variances.

DATA

Tara Williams tells you that the company introduced performance-related pay in June for its senior managers. She believed this could be the reason why the actual profit was greater than forecast under Plan B.

Task 2.2

Write a memo to Tara Williams. In your memo you should identify:

a) THREE reasons, other than performance-related pay, to explain why CityEng's actual profit for the year was greater than planned

b) FOUR general conditions necessary for performance-related pay to successfully lead to improved performance in organisations.

UNIT 9

PRACTICE EXAM 8

JORVIK LTD

These tasks were set by the AAT in December 2004

Time allowed: 3 hours plus 15 minutes reading time

unit 9 – practice exam 8

INSTRUCTIONS

This examination paper is in TWO sections.

You must show competence in BOTH sections.

You should therefore attempt and aim to complete EVERY task in BOTH sections.

You should spend about 100 minutes on Section 1 and 80 minutes on Section 2.

Include all essential workings within your answers, where appropriate.

SECTION 1 (Suggested time allowance: 100 minutes)

DATA

You are employed as an accounting technician by Jorvik Ltd, a company that makes several products including one called the Delta. The company operates a five-day week for both production and sales, and budgets for the Delta are divided into four-weekly periods. Jorvik has prepared a sales forecast for Deltas for the next five periods. This is shown below.

Period	1	2	3	4	5
Twenty days ending	28 January	25 February	25 March	22 April	21 May
Sales of Deltas	19,200	23,040	28,800	34,560	30,720

Anne Morris is Jorvik's production director. She gives you the following information.

Stocks

- There are no stocks of raw materials or work in progress at the end of any period.
- There are 7,680 Deltas in stock at the beginning of period 1.
- Closing stocks of Deltas must equal 8 days sales volume of the next period.

Production data

- 4% of finished Delta production is found to be faulty on completion.
- Faulty production has no value and has to be destroyed.
- Each Delta requires 2 litres of material.
- Material has to be used in the period it is purchased.

Task 1.1

Prepare the following budgets for EACH of the first four periods:

a) production budget showing the numbers of Deltas to be made to achieve the sales forecasts
b) material purchases budget in litres

158

DATA

After you prepared your production and material budgets, Anne Morris tells you that:

- the maximum material available in any four-week period will be 60,000 litres
- Jorvik will allow finished stocks to be greater than 8 days over the first four periods if necessary
- any increase in the amount of stock should be kept to a minimum because of financing costs.

Task 1.2

For each of the first four periods, prepare the following:

a) A statement showing any shortages or surpluses of materials in each period.

b) A statement that reschedules any shortages while allowing the sales forecasts to be met and financing costs to be minimised.

c) A revised material purchases budget in litres.

d) A revised production budget in units based on the revised material purchases and showing production before and after allowing for the faulty Deltas.

DATA

You give Anne Morris your revised production and material budgets. She gives you the following additional information.

Materials

- Material costs £2.10 per litre.

Labour

- Five Deltas can be made per labour hour.
- Jorvik employs 40 production employees who each work a guaranteed 35 hours per five-day week.
- The hourly rate per employee is £6.00 and, if overtime is required, the premium is 50%.

Factory overheads

- Factory overheads are 150% of the labour cost of production.
- Any overtime premium is charged to factory overheads.
- Idle time is also charged to factory overheads.

Task 1.3

Using the revised production budget prepare the following for each of the first four periods:

unit 9 – practice exam 8

a) Cost of material purchases budget.

b) Labour budget in hours.

c) Cost of labour budget broken down into labour charged to production and labour charged to factory overheads.

d) Cost of production budget, including factory overheads.

DATA

Jorvik makes another product called the Omega. One of your tasks is to develop quarterley sales forecasts for the Omega. Quarter 1 represents the three months ending 31 March; quarter 2, the three months ending 30 June; quarter 3, the three months ending 30 September; and quarter 4, the three months ending 31 December.

Jorvik uses the linear regression formula $y = a + bx$ to forecast Omega sales volumes in each quarter. In the formula, y represents the trend, a is a constant and b is the slope of the regression line. The regression formula is based on data for the last nine years and so the value of x for the fourth quarter of 2006, the three months ending 31 December 2006, is 36.

The values used for forecasting Omega sales volumes are:

- $a = 10,000$
- $b = 400$
- $x =$ the quarter number

Your manager suggests you should build a spreadsheet model to forecast sales volumes. She tells you that the seasonal variation for the first quarter of 2007, the three months ending 31 March 2007, is +500 and the seasonal variation for the second quarter, the three months ending 30 June 2007, is –1,000.

Task 1.4

Enter the formulae for the trend and sales volume forecasts for the first two quarters of 2006 in cells B7 to C8.

	A	B	C
1	a	10,000	
2	b	400	
3	x at 31 December 2004	36	
4	Period	3 months to 31 March 2006	3 months to 30 June 2006
5	Quarter	1	2
6	Seasonal variation		–1,000
7	Trend = y	+500	
8	Forecast		

: unit 9 – practice exam 8

SECTION 2 (Suggested time allowance: 80 minutes)

DATA

Eboracum Limited is a small engineering company that makes one product, the Yorker. Eboracum recently computerised its accounting system. The accounting software automatically prepares a management report showing budgeted and actual performance, together with variances, whenever a profit and loss account is prepared. A copy of the statement for the year ended 30 November 2006 is shown below.

Budgeted and actual operating statement: one year ended 30 November 2006

	Budget		Actual		Variance
Volume (Yorkers)	70,000		85,000		
	£'000	£'000	£'000	£'000	£'000
Turnover		1,680		1,955	275 (F)
Material	350		442		92 (A)
Labour	420		493		73 (A)
Electricity	230		230		0
Maintenance	140		160		20 (A)
Rent and rates	400		420		20 (A)
Administration	100		95		5 (F)
Total expenses		1,640		1,840	
Operating profit		40		115	75 (F)

You have recently started working as the accountant for Eboracum and you are given the working papers showing the assumptions made when preparing the original budget.

Assumptions made when preparing the original budget

- Both material and labour are variable costs.

- Electricity is a semi-variable cost. The budgeted fixed cost of electricity is £20,000.

- Maintenance is a stepped cost. For every £20,000 spent on maintenance, Eboracum can produce up to 10,000 Yorkers.

- All other expenses are fixed.

unit 9 – practice exam 8

Task 2.1

a) Calculate the budgeted selling price per Yorker.

b) Calculate the budgeted variable cost per Yorker of:
   i) material
   ii) labour
   iii) electricity

c) Calculate the budgeted maintenance cost per 10,000 Yorkers.

d) Prepare a statement showing Eboracum's actual results, the flexible budget and any variances.

DATA

Carol Brown, the Managing Director of Eboracum Ltd, is currently visiting customers in another country. You have emailed her the statement prepared in Task 2.1. She responds with three queries:

- Why are there two budgets?

- Do businesses have to investigate all variances?

- Which variances are best for cost control, the variances prepared by the accounting software or those prepared by you in Task 2.1?

Task 2.2

Prepare an email to send to Carol Brown. In the email, you should briefly:

a) explain the purpose of the original budget and the one you prepared in Task 2.1

b) suggest THREE general factors that should be considered before any business investigates variances

c) explain whether the original variances or the ones you prepared in Task 2.1 are better for cost control

UNIT 9

PRACTICE EXAM 9

NEWMARKET LTD

These tasks were set by the AAT in June 2004, and have been slightly amended

Time allowed: 3 hours plus 15 minutes reading time

unit 9 – practice exam 9

INSTRUCTIONS

This examination paper is in TWO sections.

You must show competence in BOTH sections.

You should therefore attempt and aim to complete EVERY task in BOTH sections.

You should spend about 100 minutes on Section 1 and 80 minutes on Section 2.

Include all essential workings within your answers, where appropriate.

SECTION 1 (Suggested time allowance: 100 minutes)

DATA

You are employed as a management accountant by Newmarket Ltd. Newmarket makes two similar products, the Alpha and the Beta, and operates a five-day week for both production and sales. Both products use the same material and labour, but the Beta requires more labour and materials than the Alpha.

The company divides its year into five-week periods for budgetary purposes. One of your responsibilities is to prepare budgets for the Alpha and the Beta.

You are given the following information to help you prepare the production and resource budgets for period 8, the five weeks ending 30 July 2006.

Forecast sales volumes (units)	Days in period	Alpha	Beta
Period 8: 5 weeks to 30 July 2006	25	8,460	9,025
Period 9: 5 weeks to 3 September 2006	25	10,575	12,635

Finished stocks

- There will be 1,692 Alphas and 3,610 Betas in finished stock at the beginning of period 8.

- The closing stock of both Alphas and Betas depends on the forecast sales in period 9.

    - Period 8's closing finished stocks of Alphas must equal 5 days sales of Alphas in period 9.

    - Period 8's closing finished stocks of Betas must equal 10 days sales of Betas in period 9.

    - The first-in-first-out stock valuation method is used to value closing finished stocks.

Production failure rates

- 10% of Alpha finished production and 5% of Beta finished production is faulty and has to be destroyed. This faulty production has no value.
- The faulty production arises from the production technology and is only discovered on completion. The cost of the faulty production is part of the cost of producing fault-free Alphas and Betas.

Materials

- Each Alpha produced requires 20 kilograms of materials and each Beta produced requires 40 kilograms of materials.
- The opening stock of materials at the beginning of period 8 is 64,800 kilograms.
- The closing stock of materials at the end of period 8 is 52,600 kilograms.
- The material costs 50p per kilogram.

Labour

- Each Alpha produced requires two labour hours and each Beta produced requires three labour hours.
- Newmarket employs 300 production employees who work 35 hours per five-day week. The hourly rate per employee is £7 and if any overtime is required the overtime premium is £3 per employee per hour of overtime.
- Any overtime premium is charged to factory overheads and not to the cost of production.

Factory overheads

- Budgeted factory overheads are charged to production on the basis of labour hours.
- For Alpha, the budgeted factory overheads are £62 per labour hour. For Beta, they are £58 per labour hour.

Task 1.1

Prepare the following information for period 8, the 25 working days ending 30 July 2006:

a) production budgets in units for Alpha and Beta

b) material purchases budget in kilograms

c) cost of materials budget

d) budgeted labour hours to be worked, including any overtime

e) cost of labour budget

f) total absorption cost of production budget for Alpha and Beta

g) absorption cost of good production per unit for Alpha and Beta

h) value of closing finished stocks of Alpha and Beta using the unit absorption costs calculated in (g)

DATA

The Chief Executive of Newmarket Ltd is Bob Scott. He developed the sales forecasts used in your budget statements without consulting Newmarket's sales staff. The sales staff have now told Bob that Alpha sales in period 8 will be 2,000 more than he originally forecast.

Bob gives you the following information.

- Newmarket's production employees can work up to a maximum of 5,000 overtime hours in any five-week period.

- The material used in Alpha and Beta production can only be made by one company and Newmarket is the only user of the material. Currently, there is a shortage of the material and the maximum additional material the company can produce in period 8 is 34,000 kilograms.

- The demand for the Beta in period 8 will remain at 9,025 units.

- There will be no change in the level of *finished stocks* or the failure rate.

Task 1.2

Write a memo to Bob Scott. In your memo you should:

a) i) prepare calculations to show whether it is the material or labour hours that limits extra production of Alphas in period 8

 ii) prepare a revised production budget in units for Alphas in period 8

 iii) calculate any shortfall in the planned extra sales of 2,000 Alphas arising from the limit to extra production

 (iv) suggest ONE way to overcome any shortfall

b) give TWO reasons why a budget might be imposed on staff without consultation.

SECTION 2 (Suggested time allowance: 80 minutes)

DATA

You are employed as an accounting technician with a large firm of accountants and registered auditors. One of your firm's clients is Judith Myers. Judith is the major shareholder in Cheltenham Ltd. Last year she appointed a manager to run the company on her behalf.

The company makes a single product, the Zylo, and the manager has prepared the following operating statement for the year ended 31 May 2006.

unit 9 – practice exam 9

Cheltenham Ltd: Budgeted and actual operating statement for the year ended 31 May 2006

	Budget	Actual
Sales volume, Zylos	9,000	8,800
Production volume, Zylos	9,000	10,000
	£	£
Turnover	630,000	616,000
Materials	45,000	52,000
Labour	55,800	65,000
Electricity	38,000	42,000
Depreciation	70,000	65,000
Rent and rates	24,000	25,000
Other fixed overheads	40,000	42,000
Cost of production	272,800	291,000
Less: closing stock		34,920
Cost of sales	272,800	256,080
Operating profit	357,200	359,920

Judith cannot understand why the actual profit is greater than the budgeted profit despite selling less Zylos during the year. The manager gives you the following information.

- All Zylos are sold for the same price.

- Material and labour are variable costs.

- Electricity is a semi-variable cost. The budgeted fixed cost element was £20,000 and the actual fixed cost element was £21,000.

- All other costs are fixed costs.

- The actual closing stocks were valued at their actual variable cost plus an appropriate proportion of production overheads.

- Cheltenham did not buy or sell any fixed assets during the year.

- There was no work in progress at any time and no opening finished stocks.

Task 2.1

a) Calculate the following data per Zylo:
   i) budgeted selling price
   ii) budgeted material cost
   iii) budgeted labour cost
   iv) budgeted variable cost of electricity
   v) actual selling price
   vi) actual material cost
   vii) actual labour cost
   viii) actual variable cost of electricity

unit 9 – practice exam 9

b) Prepare a revised operating statement using marginal (or variable) costing to show the flexible budget, the actual results and any variances.

c) Add a note to your statement to explain why your actual profit is different from the actual profit prepared by the manager.

DATA

The Oxbridge District Council has recently asked your firm to investigate possible improvements to the Council's financial reports.

You report to Mike Town, the partner carrying out the investigation. He gives you a copy of a monthly report prepared for the General Manager of Oxbridge's leisure centre.

The leisure centre has a swimming pool, a gymnasium, a sauna and a sports hall. Mike tells you that the leisure centre's financial year starts on 1 March and that each month managers receive a similar report. A copy of the monthly report is shown below.

Oxbridge District Council Management Report

Cost centre: Leisure complexPeriod: Three months to 31 May 2006

	Total budget for the year £'000	Budget to date £'000	Cash expenditure to date £'000	Under/ over spend £'000	Budget remaining £'000
Management staff	240	90	60	30 Cr	150
Operations staff	680	150	170	20 Dr	530
Administrative staff	40	12	10	2 Cr	28
Cleaning staff	28	5	7	2 Dr	23
Repairs and maintenance	44	2	11	9 Dr	42
Lighting and heating	36	3	9	6 Dr	33
Fixed (non-current) assets	240	0	60	60 Dr	240
Sundry expenses	12	5	3	2 Cr	7
Central services recharge	120	120	30	90 Cr	0
Total	1,440	387	360	27 Cr	1,053

Task 2.2

Prepare notes for Mike Town. Your notes should identify SIX weaknesses of the current report.

UNIT 9

PRACTICE EXAM 10

TIPTON LTD

These tasks were set by the AAT in December 2003

Time allowed: 3 hours plus 15 minutes reading time

unit 9 – practice exam 10

INSTRUCTIONS

This examination paper is in TWO sections.

You have to show competence in BOTH sections.

You should therefore attempt and aim to complete EVERY task in BOTH sections.

You are advised to spend about 90 minutes on Section 1 and 90 minutes on Section 2.

Include all essential workings within your answers, where appropriate.

SECTION 1 (Suggested time allowance: 90 minutes)

DATA

Tipton Ltd makes two types of container for the chemical industry, the Exe and the Wye. Both containers use the same type of material and labour but in different amounts.

You are the Management Accountant and you are responsible for preparing the production and resource budgets for both products. The company operates a five-day week for both production and sales and prepares production and resource budgets every twenty working days.

You are given the following information relating to period 1, the twenty working days ending 30 January 2006.

Forecast sales volumes

	Exe	Wye
■ Period 1: 20 days to 30 January 2006	8,820 units	5,800 units
■ Period 2: percentage increase over period 1	20%	30%

Finished Stocks

At the beginning of period 1, there will be 4,410 Exes and 2,320 Wyes in finished stock.

- The finished stock of Exes at the end of period 1 must be equal to 10 working days sales of Exes in period 2.

- The finished stock of Wyes at the end of period 1 must be equal to 8 working days sales of Wyes in period 2.

Materials

- Each Exe requires 5 square metres and each Wye requires 7 square metres of materials.

- The cost of material is £2.00 per square metre. There has been no change in the price of materials for several months.

- 2% of material issued to production is lost through wastage.

- At the beginning of period 1, the opening material stock will be 16,950 square metres.
- At the end of period 1, the closing material stock will be 18,000 square metres.

Labour

- Tipton produces 6 Exes *per labour hour* and 4 Wyes *per labour hour*.
- The company employs 22 production employees who work a 35-hour, five-day week.
- The labour rate per hour is £8.00 and any overtime is at a premium of 50% per hour.
- Any overtime premium is charged to the production overhead account and not directly to production.

Production overheads

- Overheads are charged to production at the rate of £12.00 per labour hour.

Task 1.1

Prepare the following information for period 1, the 20 working days ending 30 January 2006:

a) production budgets in units for the Exe and the Wye
b) material purchase budget in square metres
c) cost of materials purchases budget
d) budgeted labour hours to be worked, including any overtime
e) cost of labour budget
f) cost of production budgets for the Exe and the Wye

DATA

Susan Fellows is the Production Director of Tipton Ltd. She tells you that there will not be sufficient factory capacity in period 2 to meet the likely demand for the Exe and the Wye. One way of overcoming the capacity constraint in period 2 is to increase production of Exe in period 1 as Exe requires less material and labour than Wye. She tells you that:

- the surplus capacity of the factory in period 1 is equivalent to 88 labour hours and the production employees would be willing to work these extra hours.
- Tipton can obtain up to 2,000 square metres of extra material for period 1.

Task 1.2

Write a memo to Susan Fellows. In your memo you should:

a) identify whether it is the material or labour constraints that limit extra Exe production
b) prepare a revised production budget in units after allowing for the increased production of Exes
c) *briefly* identify TWO other short-term ways of overcoming the capacity constraint in period 2

SECTION 2 (Suggested time allowance: 90 minutes)

DATA

You are an accounting technician employed by Telford plc. Telford has a subsidiary, Shifnal Ltd that makes one product, the Omega. Barry Jones, the Finance Director of Telford, has asked you to prepare a statement analysing the performance of Shifnal Ltd. He gives you a copy of the company's latest operating statement and tells you the assumptions made about costs when preparing the statement.

Shifnal Ltd: Operating statement – 12 months ended 30 November 2006

	Budget	Actual
Number of Omegas produced and sold	120,000	95,000
	£'000	£'000
Turnover	4,800	3,990
Variable expenses		
Material A	480	456
Material B	840	665
Material C	360	266
Semi-variable expenses		
Light, heat and power	290	249
Water	212	182
Stepped expenses		
Labour	200	168
Maintenance	60	54
Fixed expenses		
Rent and rates	360	355
Distribution expenses	600	620
Administrative expenses	300	280
Operating profit	1,098	695

Assumptions made

- Budgeted semi-variable expenses
    - The variable cost of light, heat and power was £2.00 per Omega.
    - The fixed cost of water was £20,000 per year.

- Budgeted stepped expenses
    - For every £5,000 spent on labour, Shifnal could produce up to 3,000 Omegas.
    - For every £10,000 spent on maintenance, Shifnal could produce up to 20,000 Omegas.

- The budgeted selling price per Omega was the same throughout the year.

- There were no stocks of any kind.

Task 2.1

a) Calculate the budgeted selling price per Omega.

b) Calculate the budgeted variable cost per Omega of:

   i) material A
   ii) material B
   iii) material C

c) Calculate the:

   i) budgeted fixed cost of light, heat and power
   ii) budgeted variable cost of water per Omega

d) Prepare a statement showing Shifnal's actual results, the flexible budget and any variances.

DATA

Telford plc has another subsidiary, Ironbridge Ltd. This was formed on 1 January 2002. Ironbridge makes a single product, the Delta. The directors of Ironbridge are considering using time series to improve sales forecasting.

The company has collected quarterly turnover data for its first 19 quarters of trading. Quarter 1 was the first three months of 2002; quarter 2 the second three months of 2002; quarter 5 the first three months of 2003; and quarter 19 the three months ended 30 September 2006.

Two models have been suggested.

Model A

This uses the linear regression formula of $y = a + bx$ to describe the trend. The term y represents the forecast trend (or seasonally adjusted) turnover, a is a constant and x represents the quarter number being forecast. Applying the 19 quarters' data resulted in the development of the following formula:

$$y = £200,000 + £58,000x$$

For quarter 19, the three months ended 30 September 2006, x would be 19. The effect of this formula is for the forecast trend to increase by a constant £58,000 per quarter.

Model B

The formula for model B is $y = a + z(1+g)^x$. In this model, a is a constant, x is the quarter number being forecast and g is a constant growth percentage. Applying the 19 quarters' data produced the following formula:

$$y = £1,000,000 + £60,000(1.1)^x$$

Barry Jones explained how the formula for model B worked. The first term, the £1,000,000, is a constant. However, the value of the second term, $£60,000(1.1)^x$, increases quarterly by 10% over the previous quarter's figure.

unit 9 – practice exam 10

To demonstrate this, Barry explained that the value of the second term for quarter 16 was £275,698, and so the value for quarter 17 would be 10% more, £303,268. Similarly, the value of the second term for quarter 18 would be 10% more than the value for quarter 17, a total of £333,595.

Barry gives you the actual seasonally adjusted data for the first three quarters of 2006.

Seasonally adjusted actual data Three months ended	Quarter 17 31 March 2006 £1,300,000	Quarter 18 30 June 2006 £1,350,000	Quarter 19 30 September 2006 £1,390,000

Task 2.2

a) Calculate the forecast turnover for quarters 17, 18 and 19 using both models.

b) Identify the model that gives the better estimate of the seasonally adjusted actual data. Give ONE reason for your answer.

c) Write a memo to Barry Jones. In your memo, you should:

   i) use the model that gives the better estimate to forecast the seasonally adjusted turnover for quarter 20, the three months ending 31 December 2006

   ii) identify TWO limitations to using that model as a forecasting technique

ANSWERS

answers to chapter 1: INTRODUCTION TO MANAGEMENT ACCOUNTING

1 Financial accounting is predominantly concerned with the collection and classification of historic data in order to prepare the annual, or sometimes six monthly, financial statements of the business. These statements include a profit and loss account, balance sheet and a cash flow statement. These financial statements are prepared for users outside of the business such as:

- the current shareholders
- prospective investors
- providers of loan capital
- debtors and creditors
- the government

The aim of the financial statements is that they can be used by those external to the organisation to judge the performance of the management as a whole and in particular how successfully the directors of a company have carried out their stewardship function.

The financial statements must be prepared according to both legal requirements and the extensive requirements of accounting standards and must be presented in statutory formats. If the organisation is a company the financial statements must generally also be audited by an external auditor.

Management accounting, however, is all about providing the management of an organisation with the information that it needs to carry out its functions properly. The three main functions of management are planning, control and decision making. Therefore the purpose of management accounting information is to provide information that is relevant to these three functions.

This will require the provision of both historic information and estimates of future figures in a format which is useful to the relevant members of the management team. Most importantly the information must be provided regularly and on a timely basis, particularly for the purposes of control. Management accounting information can also take the form of one-off reports or information for decision making purposes.

introduction to management accounting: answers

2 i) The three main purposes of management accounting are planning, control and decision making.

ii) If production levels decrease then total variable costs will decrease.

iii) The stores department in a manufacturing organisation is an example of a service cost centre.

iv) Costs which cannot be directly attributed to a unit of production are known as indirect costs.

v) When service cost centre costs are divided between the production cost centres this is known as apportionment of costs.

vi) The range of activity levels over which a fixed cost is anticipated to remain fixed is known as the relevant range.

3   **True/false**

i)	Management accounts must be audited by an external auditor	False
ii)	As production levels fall fixed costs per unit will rise	True
iii)	A semi-variable cost is one which is fixed for a certain range of activity and then increases and is fixed again for a further range of activity	False
iv)	As production levels rise the variable costs per unit will remain constant	True
v)	The salary of the production manager is an indirect cost	True
vi)	Absorption of overheads is the process of allocating overheads to relevant cost centres	False

4

	Activity level	
	16,000 units	22,000 units
Total cost	£54,400	£68,200
Cost per unit	£3.40	£3.10

Therefore this is not a variable cost – if it were a true variable cost then the cost per unit would be the same at each activity level.

5 Cost I   Variable cost
    Cost II   Semi-variable or stepped cost
    Cost III   Fixed cost
    Cost IV   Variable cost

6

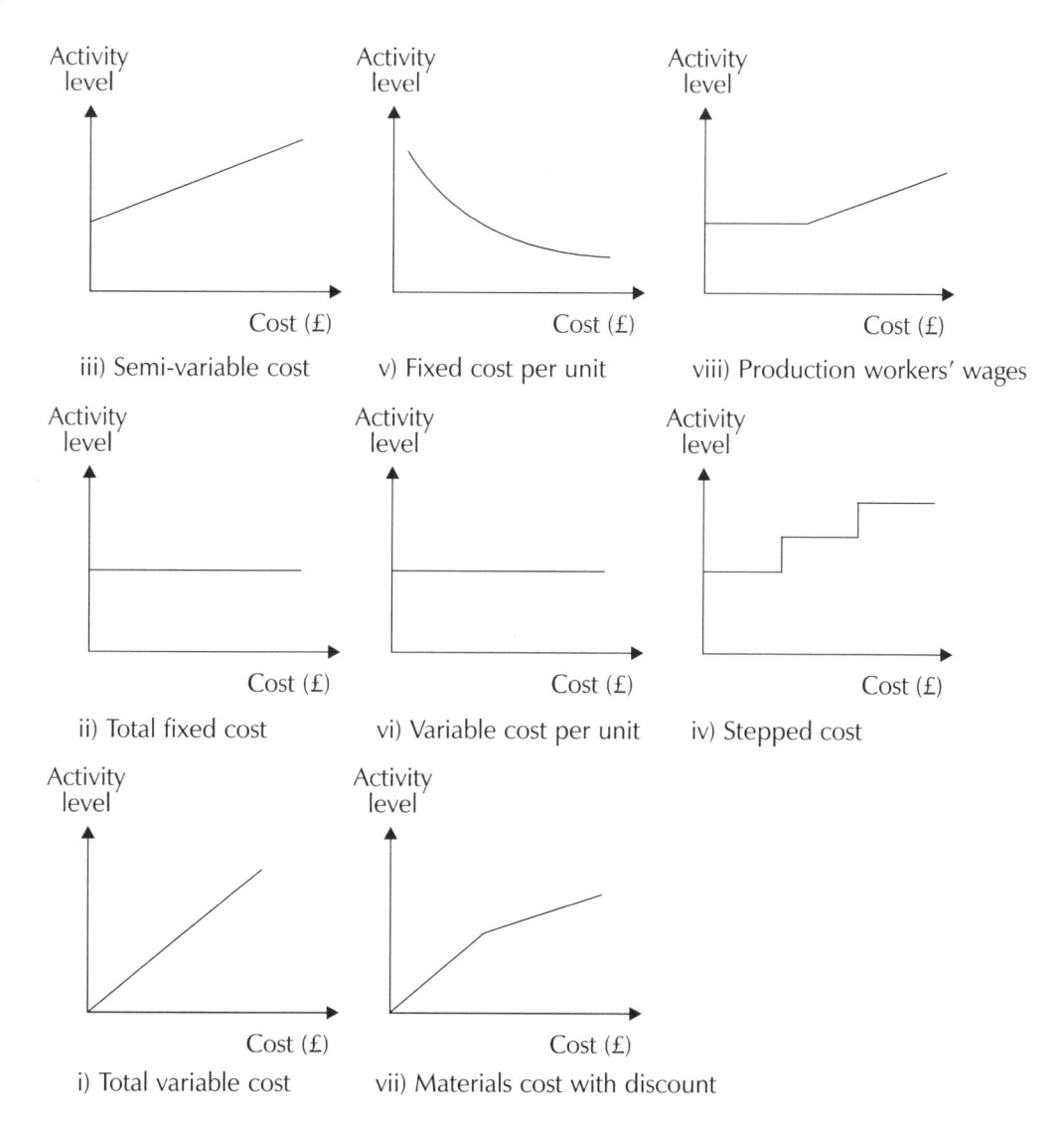

(rising line from y-intercept)	iii) Semi-variable cost
(decreasing curve)	v) Fixed cost per unit
(horizontal then rising)	viii) Production workers' wages
(horizontal line)	ii) Total fixed cost
(horizontal line)	vi) Variable cost per unit
(step function rising)	iv) Stepped cost
(straight line from origin)	i) Total variable cost
(steep line then shallower)	vii) Materials cost with discount

Each graph has Activity level on the vertical axis and Cost (£) on the horizontal axis.

Note: the graphs for ii) and vi) are interchangeable.

introduction to management accounting: answers

7

	Activity level		
	8,000 units £	12,000 units £	15,000 units £
Variable costs			
£32,000/10,000 x 8,000	25,600		
£32,000/10,000 x 12,000		38,400	
£32,000/10,000 x 15,000			48,000
Fixed costs	25,000	25,000	25,000
	50,600	63,400	73,000
Cost per unit	£6.325	£5.283	£4.867

8

		Cost behaviour
i)	Maintenance department costs which are made up of £25,000 of salaries and an average of £500 cost per call out	Semi-variable
ii)	Machinery depreciation based upon machine hours used	Variable
iii)	Salary costs of nursery school teachers where one teacher is required for every six children in the nursery	Stepped
iv)	Rent for a building that houses the factory, stores and maintenance departments	Fixed

9 i)

	Activity level		
	1,000 units £	1,500 units £	2,000 units £
Direct materials			
6kgs x £4.80 x units	28,800	43,200	57,600
Direct labour			
4 hours x £7.00 x units	28,000	42,000	56,000
Building costs – fixed	18,000	18,000	18,000
Leased machines	1,200	1,800	2,400
Stores costs			
£3,000 + £3.00 x units	6,000	7,500	9,000
	82,000	112,500	143,000
Cost per unit	£82.00	£75.00	£71.50

ii) The cost per unit is decreasing as production quantities increase. This is due to the fact that not all of the costs are variable. The buildings costs are fixed and part of the stores (inventories) costs are also fixed. For these elements of total cost as the production quantity increases so the cost per unit decreases. This in turn reduces the total overall unit cost as the quantity increases.

10 i) Absorption costing

Apportionment of overheads

	Cutting £	Finishing £	Stores £
Allocated overhead	380,000	280,000	120,000
Stores overhead apportioned 80:20	96,000	24,000	(120,000)
Overhead absorption rate	476,000	304,000	–
	476,000	304,000	
Hours worked 50,000 x 3	150,000		
50,000 x 2		100,000	
Overhead absorption rate	476,000 / 150,000	304,000 / 100,000	
	£3.17 per labour hour	£3.04 per labour hour	

Unit cost – absorption costing

	£
Direct materials	16.00
Labour – cutting 3 hours x £7.50	22.50
finishing 2 hours x £6.80	13.60
Overheads – cutting 3 hours x £3.17	9.51
finishing 2 hours x £3.04	6.08
Unit cost	67.69

ii) Marginal costing

Unit cost – marginal costing

	£
Direct materials	16.00
Labour – cutting 3 hours x £7.50	22.50
finishing 2 hours x £6.80	13.60
Cutting £380,000 x 60%/50,000	4.56
Finishing £280,000 x 60%/50,000	3.36
Stores £120,000 x 60%/50,000	1.44
Unit cost	61.46

introduction to management accounting: answers

11 a) i) The fixed production overhead absorbed by the products would be 16,500 units produced × £2.50 (W1) = £41,250.

ii) Budgeted annual fixed production overhead = £150,000

Actual quarterly fixed production o/hd = budgeted quarterly prod'n o/hd	37,500
Production o/hd absorbed into production (see (i) above)	41,250
Over absorption of fixed production o/hd	3,750

iii) Profit for the quarter, using absorption costing

	£	£	£
Sales (13,500 × £12)			162,000
Costs of production (no opening stocks)			
Value of stocks produced (16,500 × £8.50)(W2)		140,250	
Less value of closing stocks			
(3,000 units × full production cost of £8.50)(W2)		(25,500)	
		114,750	
Sales etc costs			
Variable (13,500 × £1)(W1)	13,500		
Fixed (¼ of £90,000)	22,500		
		36,000	
Total cost of sales		150,750	
Less over-absorbed production overhead		3,750	
			147,000
Profit			15,000

b) Profit statement using marginal costing

	£	£
Sales		162,000
Variable costs of production (16,500 × £6)(W1)	99,000	
Less value of closing stocks (3,000 × £6)(W1)	18,000	
Variable production cost of sales	81,000	
Variable sales etc costs (13,500 × £1)(W1)	13,500	
Total variable cost of sales (13,500 × £7)		94,500
Contribution (13,500 × £5)		67,500
Fixed costs: production	37,500	
sales etc	22,500	
		60,000
Profit		7,500

Workings

Working 1

	Production costs £	Sales etc costs £
Total costs of 60,000 units (fixed plus variable)	510,000	150,000
Total costs of 36,000 units (fixed plus variable)	366,000	126,000
Difference = variable costs of 24,000 units	144,000	24,000
Variable costs per unit	£6	£1

	Production costs £	Sales etc costs £
Total costs of 60,000 units	510,000	150,000
Variable costs of 60,000 units	360,000	60,000
Fixed costs	150,000	90,000

Working 2

The rate of absorption of fixed production overheads will therefore be:

$$\frac{£150,000}{60,000} = £2.50 \text{ per unit}$$

Total absorption costing production cost = £(6 + 2.50) = £8.50

12

a)

	£
Actual overheads incurred	496,500
Over-absorbed overheads	64,375
Overheads absorbed	560,875

Overhead absorption rate = £560,875/22,435 = £25 per hour

b) Change in stock = (8,500 − 6,750) litres = decrease of 1,750 litres

There was a reduction in stock during the period and so more overhead was charged against profit via opening stock than carried forward via closing stock. Marginal costing therefore shows the higher profit.

Absorption costing profit = marginal costing profit − (overhead absorbed in change in stock)

= £(27,400 − (1,750 × £2)) = £23,900

c) Overhead absorption rate = budgeted overheads/budgeted activity level

Budgeted number of machine hours = budgeted overheads ÷ overhead absorption rate
= £475,200/£32 = 14,850

introduction to management accounting: answers

13 a)

	HMG/012 £	CFG/013 £
Equipment cost	175,000	120,000
Direct labour cost	130,000	66,000
Total direct cost	305,000	186,000
Gross profit percentage	50%	50%
Price	£457,500	£279,000

b) **Calculation of cost per unit of cost driver**

Activity	Budgeted cost pool £	Cost driver	Cost driver units pa	Cost per unit of cost driver £
Design department	675,000	Design hours	25,000	27.00
Site engineers	370,000	Miles travelled	185,000	2.00
Purchasing department	105,000	Items purchased	15,000	7.00
Payroll department	75,000	Direct hours	300,000	0.25
Site management	750,000	Direct hours	300,000	2.50
Post-installation inspection	80,000	Items purchased	20,000	4.00

Schedule of activity-based overhead costs

Activity	Cost per unit of cost driver £	HMG/012 Cost driver units	HMG/012 ABC cost £	CFG/013 Cost driver units	CFG/013 ABC cost £
Design department	27.00	1,280	34,560	620	16,740
Site engineers	2.00	9,600*	19,200	900*	1,800
Purchasing department	7.00	650	4,550	410	2,870
Payroll department	0.25	10,000	2,500	6,000	1,500
Site management	2.50	10,000	25,000	6,000	15,000
Post installation inspection	4.00	650	2,600	410	1,640
Activity-based overhead			88,410		39,550

* Miles travelled = distance × visits

introduction to management accounting: answers

c) **Memo**

To: Alice Devereaux
From: Accounts assistant
Cc: Mark Langton
Date: xx/xx/xx
Subject: **Profitability of jobs HMG/012 and CFG/013**

As requested, I have investigated jobs HMG/012 and CFG/013. Set out below is a statement which contains the projected profit for those two jobs.

	HMG/012 £	CFG/013 £
Price	457,500	279,000
Equipment cost	175,000	120,000
Direct labour cost	130,000	66,000
Total direct cost	305,000	186,000
Gross profit	152,500	93,000
Activity-based overhead	88,410	39,550
Projected profit	64,090	53,450
Profit as a % of selling price	14.0%	19.2%
Profit as a % of total cost	16.3%	23.7%

Both jobs would be profitable at the suggested prices. The government contract is less profitable than the furniture store, however, because it is carrying a higher overhead cost. This higher overhead cost is caused by the extra complexity of the government contract and the distance of the government offices from our offices. It may therefore be necessary to increase the quoted price for the government contract to provide an adequate level of profit.

Please contact me if you require further information.

14 File note

To: Drampton's finance director
From: Financial analyst
Date: xx/xx/xx
Subject: **Little Ltd – treatment of fixed overheads**

Following our recent discussions, I set out below calculations showing the reclassification of fixed overheads between the two units manufactured by Little Ltd, using activity based costing.

introduction to management accounting: answers

a) **Reallocation of Little Ltd's budgeted total fixed annual overheads between server and PC production**

Step 1. Calculation of cost per cost driver

	Budgeted total annual overheads £	Cost driver	Number of cost drivers	Cost per cost driver £
Set-up costs	10,000	Number of set-ups	5	2,000.00
Rent and power (production area)	120,000	Number of wks' production	50	2,400.00
Rent (stores area)	50,000	Floor area of stores (m²)	800	62.50
Salaries of store issue staff	40,000	No of issues of stock	10,000	4.00
	220,000			

Step 2. Reallocation of overheads based on costs per cost driver

Server

	(i) Number of cost drivers	(ii) Cost per cost driver £	(i) × (ii) Allocated overheads
Set-up costs	5	2,000.00	10,000.00
Rent & power (production area)	10	2,400.00	24,000.00
Rent (stores area)	400	62.50	25,000.00
Salaries of store issue staff	2,000	4.00	8,000.00
			67,000.00

PC

	(i) Number of cost drivers	(ii) Cost per cost driver £	(i) × (ii) Allocated overheads
Set-up costs	0	2,000.00	–
Rent and power (production area)	40	2,400.00	96,000
Rent (stores area)	400	62.50	25,000
Salaries of store issue staff	8,000	4.00	32,000
			153,000

b) **Revised unit fixed overheads for each of the two types of computer**

Type of computer	Allocated overheads £'000	Annual budgeted volume Units	Unit fixed overheads £
Server	67	5	13,400.00
PC	153	5,000	30.60

187

answers to chapter 2: COLLECTION OF DATA

1   **Primary/secondary**

i)	Retail Price Index	Secondary
ii)	Stock Exchange share price listings	Secondary
iii)	Analysis of sales of a company by product	Primary
iv)	Trade Association inter-firm comparisons	Secondary
v)	A company's aged debtor listing	Primary

2
- i) The Retail Price Index is an indication of the level of **inflation** in the UK.
- ii) Quantitative data can be either **financial** or **non-financial** data.
- iii) The National Statistics are published in 13 separate **themes**.
- iv) A good alternative to pure random sampling are **quasi-random** sampling methods.
- v) When sampling the name given to all items that are to be considered is the **population**.

3   **True/false**

i)	An analysis of purchase invoices to determine the average trade terms from suppliers is an example of secondary data	False
ii)	The number of days holiday taken per year by qualified staff in a firm of solicitors is non-financial quantitative data	True
iii)	A survey showing favourite holiday destinations is an example of qualitative data	True
iv)	Quota sampling is an example of random sampling	False

collection of data: answers

4 The quantitative information that can be found from the purchase invoices of a business include:

- unit costs for materials
- cost of services
- trade and settlement discounts offered
- quantity of goods purchased
- payment terms

Such information can be used for a variety of purposes:

- valuing stock
- valuing the unit cost of production
- producing profit figures
- determining the amount of creditors
- comparison to budgeted costs
- estimating future costs
- choosing suppliers
- negotiating credit terms

5

		Source
i)	Local planning applications	Local council offices
ii)	The previous year's financial statements for a company	Companies House
iii)	Previous month's discounts allowed	Internal accounting records
iv)	Industry average profit margin	Trade association
v)	Information about a competitor's success	Financial press
vi)	Average sick days of employees per month	Personnel department

6 The government appreciates the importance of statistics regarding the state of the nation both for its own purposes and for those of businesses and the public and thus launched the new National Statistics in June 2000. A Statistics Commission was established together with the appointment of a National Statistician who has overall responsibility for all National Statistics output.

The statistics available are divided into 13 separate themes covering distinct areas of national life. The themes are:

- agriculture, fishing and forestry
- commerce, energy and industry
- crime and justice
- economy
- education and training
- health and care
- labour market
- natural and built environment
- population and migration

- social and welfare
- transport, travel and tourism

Each of these themes can be accessed via the internet or by registering with the National Statistics office.

No business can operate in a vacuum and on many occasions it is likely that information about the economy, the population, social trends etc will be required. For example if a private health care organisation were considering investing in a new private hospital in an area they might wish to access information under the following themes:

- economy – the state of the economy in general and in this particular area
- health and care – information concerning health care in general in that area
- labour market – for potential staff in the area
- population and migration – moves into or out of the area
- social and welfare – information about the population in the area

7 i) **Random sampling** is the method of sampling that will give the best results as it is completely free from bias as to the items included in the sample. The entire population must be known and each item of the population is assigned a sequential number. The items to be sampled are then chosen using random number tables or a random number generator.

In order for random sampling to be used every item of the population must be known and numbered. An example where this could be used is if a check was to be made on the accuracy of calculations on sales invoices for the quarter from January to March. Each sales invoice has a sequential number therefore the first invoice sent out in January would be assigned the number 01, the second invoice sent out 02 etc. The invoices to be checked would then be chosen by random numbers.

ii) **Systematic sampling** is an approximation to random sampling where the first item in the sample is chosen by generating a random number and thereafter every nth item is chosen.

This method could be used for the invoice check considered above. The first invoice would be chosen by a random number and this may be invoice number 054131. Thereafter it is decided to check every 20th invoice so the next to be checked is invoice number 054151, then 054171 etc.

iii) **Stratified sampling** can be used where the population is split into a number of different groups. The size of the population in each group is determined and the size of sample from each group is then based upon the proportionate size of the group to the whole population.

For example if the sales invoices to be checked for accuracy had been prepared by three different divisions of the company the number of invoices sent out in the quarter by each division would determine the relative sizes of the samples taken from each division. Once the sizes of the divisional sample were determined, they would each then be chosen using random or systematic sampling.

collection of data: answers

8 i) As the entire population will be known, being all the purchase invoices processed in the period, and can be sequentially numbered, then the most appropriate method of sampling would be either random sampling or systematic sampling.

ii) In the case of the train customer sample it would not be possible to carry out random sampling as the entire population cannot be known or numbered.

As the types of passengers that travel on the railway are likely to be fairly diverse, in order to canvas the views of all types of commuter quota sampling may be most appropriate. For example the sample might be required to include a set number of business commuters, non-business commuters, men, women, commuters under 30, commuters between 30 and 60, commuters over 60 etc in order to gain a wide range of views.

iii) A sample of batches from production over a period needs to be tested to ascertain the number of defectives in each batch. As it will not necessarily be known in advance how many batches will be produced in the period, a pure random method may not be possible. Thus a form of systematic sampling may be used such that every, say, 3rd batch produced over the period is tested.

9 a) i) **Simple random sampling**

A simple random sample is one in which every member of the population has an equal chance of being included. A sampling frame of the entire adult population of the Northern sales territory would have to be drawn up if this method were to be used. Such a sampling frame would probably be constructed by combining the electoral registers for the areas in question. Each person on the electoral register would then need to be allocated a number and a sample of 10,000 (500,000 x 2%) would be selected using random number tables or a random number generator on a computer.

ii) **Cluster sampling**

Cluster sampling involves selecting one definable subsection of the population as the sample, that subsection is taken to be representative of the population in question. In the Northern sales territory, where a sample of 10,000 is required, the regions might be split into groups (or clusters) of size 10,000 each. Northia would, for instance, contain 9 clusters while Wester would contain only one. In total there would be 50 clusters from which one would be selected randomly by numbering them and using random number tables as in (i). Every member of the selected cluster would then be surveyed. A more representative cluster sample could be obtained at greater cost by dividing the population into 500 geographic groups of 1,000 people each and then randomly selecting ten groups to be surveyed.

iii) **Stratified sampling**

It is possible that people's responses to the survey will depend on the region in which they live and so, in order to obtain a representative sample, it is important to ensure that all regions contribute to the sample in proportion to their population sizes. This is achieved by dividing the total population into strata (the regions in this case), sampling separately in the six strata (regions) and then pooling the samples. Regional samples must be proportional to regional sizes so, for instance, Northia's population of 90,000 would require a sample of 2% of 90,000 which is 1,800 people. The members of this sample would be selected randomly from the population of Northia by numbering and using random numbers as outlined in (i). The other sample sizes required would be as follows.

Wester	2% of 10,000 =	200
Southam	2% of 140,000 =	2,800
Eastis	2% of 40,000 =	800
Midshire	2% of 120,000 =	2,400
Centrasia	2% of 100,000 =	2,000

The total of the six smaller samples is 10,000.

iv) **Systematic sampling**

This method selects the sample by choosing every nth person from a list of the population, having first made a random start at some point between 0 and fifty on the list (we require a sample of 2% of the population so every fiftieth (500,000 / 2% of 500,000) name will be chosen). Assuming that the territory does not have a single list of the adult population but does have electoral registers spanning the entire area, these could constitute a single list provided agreement could be reached on the order they were to be taken. A computer could randomly select one number between 0 and 50 and the person on the list in that position could be the random start. Thereafter every fiftieth person would be selected, with counting running on from one electoral list to the next until the total sample of 10,000 was selected.

b) The method likely to give the most representative sample is stratified sampling since this method deliberately selects from the different groups in the population in a representative fashion. The groups used in this case would be geographic, however, and it may be that people's characteristics regarding sales intentions do not vary according to the region in which they live. It may be that the sample would be more representative were it stratified by age or by gender. It would be very difficult, perhaps impossible, to stratify in such a way, however. With the caveat therefore that the basis of stratification needs to be relevant to the subject of the survey, stratification can be expected to give the most representative sample. Its disadvantages are that both the initial division of the sampling frame into strata and the process of numbering all population members, generating the required random numbers and identifying the corresponding people are difficult and time-consuming and therefore very costly.

The disadvantage of simple random sampling is that it is theoretically possible, although unlikely, to select highly unrepresentative samples. For example, every single sample member could live in Northia. Additional problems are that a sampling frame for the entire sales territory could be difficult to construct and, as for stratified sampling, the method of numbering and selecting by random numbers is cumbersome and costly.

In general, systematic sampling is just as likely to give unrepresentative samples as simple random sampling, but it has the added problems of bias if the sampling frame contains any cyclical patterns which correspond to the cycle of selection, such as every fiftieth person being elderly. The method we have suggested above would at least remove the danger of geographic imbalance, however. The combination of electoral registers into a single sampling frame would also be difficult.

collection of data: answers

Cluster sampling, although a relatively simple and cheap process by comparison with the other methods, is very open to bias. Indeed it would be surprising if one single geographic group could possibly be representative of the entire population. Even the selection of ten groups could easily prove to be very unrepresentative. There would also be some difficulty in dividing the population into clusters of exactly 10,000 each.

10 a) The major advantage of using personal interviews is that they are associated with high response rates. Other advantages are as follows.

  i) The interviewer can clarify what the questions mean.

  ii) The interviewer completes the questionnaire so it doesn't need to look especially attractive, responses can start being coded straight away and the questionnaire will be completed accurately and professionally.

  iii) Answers may be entered immediately into a hand-held computer.

  iv) Depending on the answers given to various questions, the interviewer need not bother the respondent with certain groups of questions.

There are however a number of disadvantages in using personal interviews. The main ones are that the method is costly and slow and is therefore associated with relatively small sample sizes. Other disadvantages are as follows.

  i) People may be tempted to 'show off' or to try to give the responses that they think the interviewer favours.

  ii) The interviewer may introduce bias by unintentionally letting his opinions show. This can be dealt with by training interviewers but this will only exacerbate the cost and time problem.

  iii) In a personal interview, people may be reluctant to answer questions of an intimate nature.

  iv) Generally speaking, it is not possible to schedule personal interviews at a time to suit the respondent. The respondent may be out or busy when the interviewer calls.

  v) It is often impractical to use personal interviews if the survey covers a wide geographic area.

  vi) The respondent may need time to reflect on certain questions or to look for information. The time available to the respondent and the interviewer is often too brief to allow this.

b) Postal surveys have more or less opposite advantages and disadvantages to personal interviews, and so will be dealt with next.

The major advantages of the use of postal questionnaires are that they are very easy, quick and cheap and hence relatively large samples can be used. Other advantages are as follows.

  i) There is no possibility of interviewer bias and people are less inclined to give what they perceive to be the desired responses.

ii) People are less reluctant to answer questions of an intimate nature.

iii) The respondent can complete the questionnaire at a convenient time and can take as long to reflect on questions or to find information as he needs, subject to sending the questionnaire back in time.

iv) There are fewer problems in locating respondents than there are when using personal interviews.

v) The survey can spread over an area of any size provided that it is covered by the postal service.

The disadvantages of using postal surveys tend to mirror the advantages of personal interviews. The main disadvantage is that low response rates are very common and it is not possible to know whether the views of non-respondents are similar to those of respondents. There are consequently great difficulties in judging the reliability of these surveys. Other disadvantages are as follows.

i) A great deal of thought and effort goes into making the questionnaire look attractive and approachable.

ii) Ideally the questionnaire should be short and simple but it will often have to involve complex formulations like 'if "yes", answer questions 8 and 9, otherwise go straight to question 10'. Interviewers are capable of dealing with these types of question more easily than are postal questionnaires.

iii) Questions should be short and simple but, since there is no possibility of clarifying them, they often have to be long and complicated in order to be as clear as possible.

iv) Postal questionnaires are often filled in very badly and many respondents give up and fail to complete them.

v) Respondents who do not walk past post boxes in their day-to-day routine need to make an effort to go out of their way to return the form.

c) The advantages of telephone surveys fall somewhere between those of personal interviews and postal surveys. For example, telephone surveys will generally achieve higher response rates than postal surveys but lower response rates than personal interviews. They are not as cheap or as quick as postal surveys but they are quite a bit cheaper and easier than personal interviews. Their advantages are as follows.

i) They have reasonable response rates.

ii) The interviewer can clarify questions and can omit any irrelevant questions.

iii) The appearance of the questionnaire does not matter. Responses can be coded immediately. This type of survey is the best method for immediate data entry into a computer.

iv) There is less interviewer bias than there is with personal interviews.

v) They are reasonably quick and cheap to carry out provided the questionnaire is kept short. They are therefore associated with larger samples than personal interviews but smaller samples than postal surveys.

collection of data: answers

vi) The survey can encompass any area provided that it is covered by the telephone network.

The main disadvantage is that there are still quite a lot of people who do not have telephones and this can lead to unrepresentative samples being selected. Other disadvantages are as follows.

i) As with personal interviews, there can be a tendency to 'show off', intimate questions can cause problems, the respondent cannot generally select a convenient time for the interview and the respondent does not have time to reflect or to gather information.

ii) If the respondent is not at home, this is less of a problem than it is with personal interviews since it is simple enough to phone again.

iii) It is not possible to show any forms of identification to the respondent. This is thought to contribute to the response level for this type of survey being lower than that of personal interviews.

answers to chapter 3: TIME SERIES ANALYSIS AND INDEXATION

1 i) The trend of a set of figures in a time series analysis is the underlying movement of the figures over time. For example sales may be erratic each month but in general terms are gradually rising therefore the trend would be a steady increase in sales.

ii) Cyclical variations are due to the fact that most economies will tend to have periods of growth and periods of recession. It is considered that such economic cycles typically take place over a seven to nine year period. Such long term economic cycles will cause alterations in the pattern of sales and costs and this is reflected in the cyclical variations. If the economy is growing then sales are likely to be increasing more rapidly but if the economy is in recession then sales growth may slow down or even reverse.

iii) Seasonal variations stem from the fact the many businesses will experience some sort of regular growth reduction pattern due to the seasonality of their business (not necessarily relating to the actual seasons, summer, winter etc). For example a restaurant that is open 7 nights a week may generally experience peak numbers of customers on Friday and Saturday nights with lows on Monday and Tuesday.

iv) Random variations are the other unforseeable factors over which management have no control which will affect their sales or their production costs. For example in a manufacturing business if 30% of the workforce are affected by flu over a two week period then production will probably drop. These random variations are totally unpredictable.

2

	£	3 month moving total £	3 month moving average £
March	104,500		
April	110,300	327,600	109,200
May	112,800	332,500	110,833
June	109,400	339,800	113,267
July	117,600	343,000	114,333
August	116,000	352,800	117,600
September	119,200	357,500	119,167
October	122,300	362,000	120,667
November	120,500	362,100	120,700
December	119,300		

time series analysis and indexation: answers

3 i)

			5 day moving average TREND	Seasonal variation (actual – trend)
		£	£	£
Week 1	Day 1	600		
	Day 2	700		
	Day 3	1,000	1,000	–
	Day 4	1,200	1,016	+184
	Day 5	1,500	1,026	+474
Week 2	Day 1	680	1,076	–396
	Day 2	750	1,116	–366
	Day 3	1,250	1,188	+ 62
	Day 4	1,400	1,216	+184
	Day 5	1,860	1,272	+588
Week 3	Day 1	820	1,410	–590
	Day 2	1,030	1,550	–520
	Day 3	1,940	1,678	+262
	Day 4	2,100	1,714	+386
	Day 5	2,500	1,772	+728
Week 4	Day 1	1,000	1,696	–696
	Day 2	1,320	1,734	–414
	Day 3	1,560	1,768	–208
	Day 4	2,290		
	Day 5	2,670		

ii) Seasonal variations

	Day 1 £	Day 2 £	Day 3 £	Day 4 £	Day 5 £
Week 1			–	+184	+474
Week 2	–396	–366	+62	+184	+588
Week 3	–590	–520	+262	+386	+728
Week 4	–696	–414	–208		
	–1,682	–1,300	+116	+754	+1,790
	3	3	4	3	3
Average /3. Add those up = 117/5 -234	–561	–433	+29	+251	+597
Difference 117/5	+24	+23	+23	+23	+24
	–537	–410	+52	+274	+621

(Note that day 3 has 4 figures even though the seasonal variation in week 1 was zero therefore it must be averaged over 4 figures).

time series analysis and indexation: answers

iii) The trend shows how the daily takings have increased each day over the four week period and the seasonal variations show how the takings on some days of the week are generally lower or higher than on other days of the week. As the restaurant has only just opened and the time series figures are for the first four weeks of operations the trend figure may not be a good indication of the future trend of the business. The takings appear to be increasing rapidly but this may be due to the fact that the restaurant is new and that customers are trying it out. Only if this trend continues in the longer term will it be a reliable basis for future predictions.

The same criticism of the daily seasonal variation can also be made. However, this does at least appear on the whole to be showing the same pattern each week, other than on day 3 when out of the four figures the variation is zero in the first week, negative for two weeks and then positive in week 4.

In general in order to be able to use the trend of figures and seasonal variations a more stable and longer term set of results is necessary.

4 i)

			Four quarter moving average £	Centred moving average TREND £	Seasonal variations £
2003	Quarter 3		50,600		
	Quarter 4		52,800		
				51,900	
2004	Quarter 1		55,600		51,975	+3,625
				52,050	
	Quarter 2		48,600		52,188	−3,588
				52,325	
	Quarter 3		51,200		52,625	−1,425
				52,925	
	Quarter 4		53,900		53,075	+825
				53,225	
2005	Quarter 1		58,000		53,450	+4,550
				53,675	
	Quarter 2		49,800		53,763	−3,963
				53,850	
	Quarter 3		53,000		54,113	−1,113
				54,375	
	Quarter 4		54,600		54,488	+112
				54,600	
2006	Quarter 1		60,100		54,750	+5,350
				54,900	
	Quarter 2		50,700		54,975	−4,275
				55,050	
	Quarter 3		54,200			
	Quarter 4		55,200			

199

time series analysis and indexation: answers

ii) Seasonal variations

	Quarter 1 £	Quarter 2 £	Quarter 3 £	Quarter 4 £
2004	+3,625	−3,588	−1,425	+825
2005	+4,550	−3,963	−1,113	+112
2006	+5,350	−4,275		
	+13,525	−11,826	−2,538	+937
Average	+4,508	−3,942	−1,269	+469
Difference 234/4	+59	+59	+58	+58
	+4,567	−3,883	−1,211	+527

234/2 =
/4 =
58.50

iii)

	A	B	C	D	E
1	2003	Q3	50,600		
2					
3		Q4	52,800		
4				=(C1+C3+C5+C7)/4	
5	2004	Q1	55,600		=(D4+D6)/2
6				=(C3+C5+C7+C9)/4	
7		Q2	48,600		=(D6+D8)/2
8				=(C5+C7+C9+C11)/4	
9		Q3	51,200		=(D8+D10)/2
10				=(C7+C9+C11+C13)/4	
11		Q4	53,900		=(D10+D12)/2
12				=(C9+C11+C13+C15)/4	
13	2005	Q1	58,000		=(D12+D14)/2
14				=(C11+C13+C15+C17)/	
15		Q2	49,800		=(D14+D16)/2
16				=(C13+C15+C17+C19)/	
17		Q3	53,000		=(D16+D18)/2
18				=(C15+C17+C19+C21)/	
19		Q4	54,600		=(D18+D20)/2
20				=(C17+C19+C21+C23)/	
21	2006	Q1	60,100		=(D20+D22)/2
22				=(C19+C21+C23+C25)/	

time series analysis and indexation: answers

5 Predicted sales

		£
Quarter 1	£418,500 + £21,500	440,000
Quarter 2	£420,400 + £30,400	450,800
Quarter 3	£422,500 – £16,700	405,800
Quarter 4	£423,800 – £35,200	388,600

6 i)

	Actual costs £	RPI		Costs at January prices £
January	129,600	171.1	129,600	129,600
February	129,700	172.0	129,700 x 171.1/172.0	129,021
March	130,400	172.2	130,400 x 171.1/172.2	129,567 ✓
April	131,600	173.0	131,600 x 171.1/173.0	130,155
May	130,500	174.1	130,500 x 171.1/174.1	128,251
June	131,600	174.3	131,600 x 171.1/174.3	129,184

ii) The unadjusted figures show that costs are generally increasing each month. However when adjusted to January prices using the RPI it can be seen that, other than in April, costs are in fact below the January level.

iii)

	£	RPI		June prices £
January	129,600	171.1	129,600 x 174.3/171.1	132,024
February	129,700	172.0	129,700 x 174.3/172.0	131,434
March	130,400	172.2	130,400 x 174.3/172.2	131,990
April	131,600	173.0	131,600 x 174.3/173.0	132,589
May	130,500	174.1	130,500 x 174.3/174.1	130,650
June	131,600	174.3	131,600 x 174.3/174.3	131,600

iv) The price adjusted figures show that costs have fallen in real terms over the six month period.

v) Yes

time series analysis and indexation: answers

7 i)

			Sales £		Index
	2005	Quarter 1	126,500		100.0
		Quarter 2	130,500	130,500/126,500 x 100	103.2
		Quarter 3	131,400	131,400/126,500 x 100	103.9
		Quarter 4	132,500	132,500/126,500 x 100	104.7
	2006	Quarter 1	133,100	133,100/126,500 x 100	105.2
		Quarter 2	135,600	135,600/126,500 x 100	107.2
		Quarter 3	136,500	136,500/126,500 x 100	107.9
		Quarter 4	137,100	137,100/126,500 x 100	108.4

ii) The index shows that sales are growing at a steady rate each quarter.

iii)

			Sales £		Sales at 2006 Quarter 4 prices £
	2005	Quarter 1	126,500	126,500 x 149.1/135.4	139,299
		Quarter 2	130,500	130,500 x 149.1/138.2	140,793
		Quarter 3	131,400	131,400 x 149.1/141.7	138,262
		Quarter 4	132,500	132,500 x 149.1/142.3	138,832
	2006	Quarter 1	133,100	133,100 x 149.1/144.4	137,432
		Quarter 2	135,600	135,600 x 149.1/146.2	138,290
		Quarter 3	136,500	136,500 x 149.1/147.5	137,981
		Quarter 4	137,100		137,100

iv)

			Sales at 2006 Quarter 4 prices £		Index
	2005	Quarter 1	139,299		100.0
		Quarter 2	140,793	140,793/139,299 x 100	101.1
		Quarter 3	138,262	138,262/139,299 x 100	99.3
		Quarter 4	138,832	138,832/139,299 x 100	99.7
	2006	Quarter 1	137,432	137,432/139,299 x 100	98.7
		Quarter 2	138,290	138,290/139,299 x 100	99.3
		Quarter 3	137,981	137,981/139,299 x 100	99.1
		Quarter 4	137,100	137,100/139,299 x 100	98.4

v) The index based upon the price-adjusted figures shows that other than in Quarter 2 2005 the real sales have actually fallen below the 2005 Quarter 1 figures. This is in contrast to the index in (ii) based upon the unadjusted sales figures which showed fairly significant increases in sales in each quarter.

8 a) Updated standard cost = £3.50 x 145/115 = £4.41

b) Planned cost = 100,000/10 = £10,000
Actual cost = 100,000/11.2 = £8,929
Difference = £1,071

time series analysis and indexation: answers

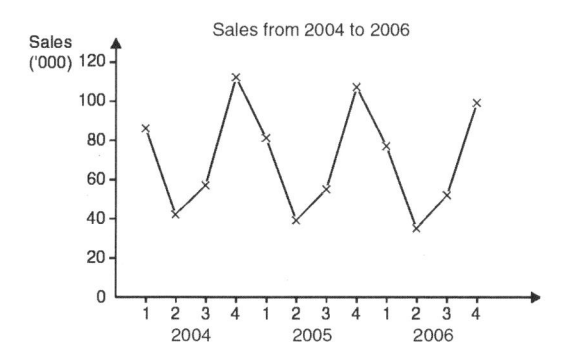

9 (a)

Sales from 2004 to 2006

There are very marked seasonal fluctuations, with the fourth quarter of each year showing the highest sales and the second quarter the lowest sales. There does appear to be a steadily falling trend, with each peak and each trough slightly lower than the previous one.

b)

Year	Quarter	Data £'000	4-quarter total £'000	Moving average of 4-quarter total £'000	Trend £'000
2004	1	86			
	2	42			
			297	74.25	
	3	57			73.625
			292	73.00	
	4	112			72.625
			289	72.25	
2005	1	81			72.000
			287	71.75	
	2	39			71.125
			282	70.50	
	3	55			70.000
			278	69.50	
	4	107			69.000
			274	68.50	
2006	1	77			68.125
			271	67.75	
	2	35			66.750
			263	65.75	
	3	52			
	4	99			

c) **2006**

Quarter	Data £'000	Adjustment £'000	Adjusted data £'000
1	77	−9	68
2	35	+32	67
3	52	+16	68
4	99	−39	60

time series analysis and indexation: answers

d) We can forecast sales by extrapolating the trend and then making seasonal adjustments.

Over the period from 2004, quarter 3 to 2006, quarter 2 (a duration of seven quarters, not eight) the trend fell by 73.625 − 66.75 = 6.875, giving an average fall per quarter of 6.875/7 = 0.982.

Forecasts can then be prepared as follows, extrapolating the trend at this rate from the value for 2006, quarter 2. Forecasts have been rounded to avoid giving a false impression of great precision.

2007

Quarter	Trend £'000	Adjustment £'000	Forecast £'000
1	*63.804	+9	73
2	62.822	−32	31
3	61.840	−16	46
4	60.858	+39	100

* 66.750 − (3 × 0.982)

These forecasts should **not be assumed to be reliable**. Although the decline in the trend has been steady, and the pattern of seasonal variations consistent, from 2004 to 2006, it is always dangerous to extrapolate into the future. The trend or seasonal patterns may break down, or random variations may have a substantial effect.

10 a)

Year	Revenue	Sales	Moving total of 4-quarters' sales	Moving average of 4-quarters' sales	Mid-point of two moving averages Trend	Variation
2004	1	200				
	2	110				
	3	320	870	217.5	219	+101
	4	240	884	221.0	222	+18
2005	1	214	892	223.0	225	−11
	2	118	906	226.5	229	−111
	3	334	926	231.5	232	+102
	4	260	932	233.0	234	+26
2006	1	220	938	234.5	235	−15
	2	124	944	236.0	238	−114
	3	340	962	240.5		
	4	278				

204

b)

Year	Quarter 1	2	3	4	Total
2004			+101	+18	
2005	−11	−111	+102	+26	
2006	−15	−114			
	−26	−225	+203	+44	−4
Unadjusted average	−13.0	−112.5	+101.5	+22.0	−2
Adjustment	+0.5	+0.5	+0.5	+0.5	+2
Adjusted average	−12.5	−112.0	+102.0	+22.5	0

answers to chapter 4: STANDARD COSTING

1 i) Total materials cost variance

	£
Standard cost of actual production 2,800 units x 5 kg x £4.00	56,000
Actual cost	60,480
Total cost variance	4,480 Adv

ii) Materials price variance

	£
Actual quantity at standard cost 14,400 kg x £4.00	57,600
Actual cost	60,480
Price variance	2,880 Adv

iii) Materials usage variance

	£
Standard quantity at standard cost 2,800 units x 5 kg x £4.00	56,000
Actual quantity at standard cost 14,400 kg x £4.00	57,600
Usage variance	1,600 Adv

2 i) Total materials cost variance

	£
Standard cost for actual production 11,400 units x 4 kg x £3	136,800
Actual cost	150,480
Total cost variance	13,680 Adv

ii) Materials price variance

	£
Actual quantity at standard cost 44,800 kg x £3	134,400
Actual cost	150,480
Price variance	16,080 Adv

iii) Materials usage variance

	£
Standard quantity at standard cost 11,400 units x 4kg x £3	136,800
Actual quantity at standard cost 44,800 kg x £3	134,400
Usage variance	2,400 Fav

standard costing: answers

3   i)   Total labour cost variance

	£
Standard cost for actual production 12,100 units x 4.5 hours x £7.30	397,485
Actual cost	410,200
Total cost variance	12,715 Adv

     ii)   Labour rate variance

	£
Actual hours at standard rate 54,900 x £7.30	400,770
Actual hours at actual cost	410,200
Rate variance	9,430 Adv

     iii)   Labour efficiency variance

	£
Standard hours at standard rate 12,100 units x 4.5 hours x £7.30	397,485
Actual hours at standard rate 54,900 x £7.30	400,770
Efficiency variance	3,285 Adv

4   i)   Total labour cost variance

	£
Standard cost for actual production 11,400 x 3 hours x £9	307,800
Actual cost	316,400
Total variance	8,600 Adv

     ii)   Labour rate variance

	£
Actual hours at standard rate 34,700 hours x £9	312,300
Actual cost	316,400
Rate variance	4,100 Adv

     iii)   Labour efficiency variance

	£
Standard hours at standard rate 11,400 units x 3 hours x £9	307,800
Actual hours at standard rate 34,700 hours x £9	312,300
Efficiency variance	4,500 Adv

standard costing: answers

5 i) Fixed overhead expenditure variance

	£
Budgeted overhead £7 x 10,000 units	70,000
Actual overhead	75,000
Expenditure variance	5,000 Adv

ii) Fixed overhead volume variance

	£
Actual production @ OAR 11,500 x £7	80,500
Budgeted production @ OAR 10,000 x £7	70,000
Volume variance	10,500 Fav

6 i) a) Fixed overhead expenditure variance

	£
Budgeted fixed overhead 50,000 units x 6 hours x £7.60	2,280,000
Actual fixed overhead	2,200,000
Expenditure variance	80,000 Adv

b) Fixed overhead volume variance

	£
Standard hours for actual production @ OAR 52,000 units x 6 hours x £7.60	2,371,200
Standard hours for budgeted production @ OAR 50,000 units x 6 hours x £7.60	2,280,000
Volume variance	91,200 Fav

ii) Fixed overhead efficiency variance

	£
Standard hours for actual production @ OAR 52,000 x 6 hours x £7.60	2,371,200
Actual hours @ OAR 310,000 x £7.60	2,356,000
Efficiency variance	15,200 Fav

Fixed overhead capacity variance

	£
Actual hours @ OAR 310,000 x £7.60	2,356,000
Budgeted hours @ OAR 50,000 x 6 x £7.60	2,280,000
Capacity variance	76,000 Fav

standard costing: answers

7 i)   £

Budgeted fixed overhead
14,000 units x 4 hours x £3.60   201,600

ii) Fixed overhead expenditure variance

	£
Budgeted fixed overhead	201,600
Actual fixed overhead	203,000
Expenditure variance	1,400 Adv

iii) Fixed overhead volume variance

	£
Standard hours for actual production @ OAR	
13,200 units x 4 hours x £3.60	190,080
Standard hours for budgeted production @ OAR	
14,000 units x 4 hours x £3.60	201,600
Volume variance	11,520 Adv

iv) Fixed overhead efficiency variance

	£
Standard hours for actual production @ OAR	
13,200 x 4 hours x £3.60	190,080
Actual hours @ OAR 50,000 x £3.60	180,000
Efficiency variance	10,080 Fav

v) Fixed overhead capacity variance

	£
Actual hours @ OAR 50,000 x £3.60	180,000
Budgeted hours @ OAR 14,000 x 4 x £3.60	201,600
Capacity variance	21,600 Adv

standard costing: answers

8 **i)** Materials price variance

	£
Actual quantity at standard cost 5,800 x £2.80	16,240
Actual cost	17,100
	860 Adv

Materials usage variance

	£
Standard quantity at standard cost 1,240 x 4.8 x £2.80	16,666
Actual quantity at standard cost 5,800 x £2.80	16,240
	426 Fav

ii) Labour rate variance

	£
Actual hours at standard cost 3,280 x £8.50	27,880
Actual cost	27,060
	820 Fav

Labour efficiency variance

	£
Standard hours at standard cost 1,240 x 2.5 x £8.50	26,350
Actual hours at standard cost 3,280 x £8.50	27,880
	1,530 Adv

iii) Fixed overhead expenditure variance

	£
Budgeted fixed overhead 1,100 x 2.5 x £1.60	4,400
Actual fixed overhead	4,650
	250 Adv

Fixed overhead efficiency variance

	£
Standard hours for actual production @ OAR 1,240 x 2.5 x £1.60	4,960
Actual hours @ OAR 3,280 x £1.60	5,248
	288 Adv

Fixed overhead capacity variance

	£
Actual hours @ OAR 3,280 x £1.60	5,248
Budgeted hours @ OAR 1,100 x 2.5 x £1.60	4,400
	848 Fav

standard costing: answers

iv) Reconciliation of standard cost of actual production to actual cost

	Variances Adverse £	Favourable £	£
Standard cost of actual production 1,240 x £38.69			47,976
Variances:			
Materials price	860		
Materials usage		426	
Labour rate		820	
Labour efficiency	1,530		
Fixed overhead expenditure	250		
Fixed overhead efficiency	288		
Fixed overhead capacity		848	
	2,928	2,094	
Add: adverse variances			2,928
Less: favourable variances			(2,094)
Actual cost of production (17,100 + 27,060 + 4,650)			48,810

9 a) Standard cost per unit

	£	£
Materials		
A 1.2 kg × £11 =	13.20	
B 4.7 kg × £6 =	28.20	
		41.40
Labour		
1.5 hours × £8		12.00
Prime cost		53.40
Overheads		
1.5 hours × £30		45.00
Standard cost per unit		98.40

b)

215,000 hrs should cost (× £8)	1,720,000	
but did cost	1,700,000	
Labour rate variance	20,000	(F)
126,000 units should take (×1.5 hrs)	189,000	hrs
but did take	215,000	hrs
	26,000	hrs (A)
× standard rate per hour	× £8	
Labour efficiency variance	£208,000	(A)

c) **Material A**

	£	
150,000 kg should cost (× £11)	1,650,000	
but did cost	1,650,000	
Price variance	0	
126,000 units should use (× 1.2 kgs)	151,200	kgs
but did use	150,000	kgs
	1,200	kgs (F)
× standard cost per kg	× £11	
Usage variance	£13,200	(F)

Material B

	£	
590,000 kgs should cost (×£6)	3,540,000	
but did cost	3,600,000	
Price variance	60,000	(A)
126,000 units should use (× 4.7 kgs)	592,200	kgs
but did use	590,000	kgs
	2,200	kgs (F)
× standard cost per kg	× £6	
Usage variance	£13,200	(F)

10 a) Budgeted fixed overhead absorption rate = £22,260 ÷ 8,400 hours = £2.65 per labour hour

Standard labour hours per unit of component RYX = 8,400 hours ÷ 1,200 units = 7 hours per unit

Standard fixed overhead absorbed per unit = 7 hours x £2.65 per hour = £18.55

	£
Fixed production overhead incurred	25,536
Fixed production overhead absorbed (1,100 × £18.55)	20,405
Fixed production overhead cost variance	5,131 (A)

i)
	£
Budgeted expenditure	22,260
Actual expenditure	25,536
Fixed production overhead expenditure variance	3,276 (A)

ii)
1,100 units should have taken (× 7 hrs)	7,700	hrs
but did take	7,980	hrs
	280	hrs (A)
× standard rate per hour	× £2.65	
Fixed production overhead volume efficiency variance	£742	(A)

standard costing: answers

iii)	Budgeted hours of work		8,400 hrs
	Actual hours of work		7,980 hrs
			420 hrs (A)
	× standard rate per hour		× £2.65
	Fixed production overhead volume capacity variance		£1,113 (A)

b) **Reconciliation of fixed overhead variances**

	£
Expenditure variance	3,276 (A)
Volume efficiency variance	742 (A)
Volume capacity variance	1,113 (A)
Cost variance	5,131 (A)

11 a)

			£
i)	Budgeted fixed overhead expenditure (4,100 × 40 × £12.50)		2,050,000
	Actual fixed overhead expenditure		2,195,000
	Fixed overhead **expenditure variance**		145,000 (A)
			£
ii)	Actual production at standard rate (3,850 × 40 × £12.50)		1,925,000
	Budgeted production at standard rate (4,100 × 40 × £12.50)		2,050,000
	Fixed overhead **volume variance**		125,000 (A)
iii)	Budgeted hours (4,100 × 40)		164,000 hrs
	Actual hours		159,000 hrs
	Fixed overhead capacity variance in hours		5,000 hrs (A)
	× standard rate per hour		× £12.50
	Fixed overhead **capacity variance**		£62,500 (A)
iv)	3,850 units should have taken (× 40 hrs)		154,000 hrs
	but did take		159,000 hrs
	Fixed overhead efficiency variance in hours		5,000 hrs (A)
	× standard rate per hour		× £12.50
	Fixed overhead **efficiency variance**		£62,500 (A)

b) **REPORT**

To: Production Director
From: Assistant Management Accountant
Date: xx/xx/xx
Subject: **Performance of Division Omega** – 4 weeks ended 1 April

Set out below is a **reconciliation of the standard cost of production to the actual cost of production** in Division Omega for the four-week period ended 1 April.

	(F) £	(A) £	£
Standard cost of production (3,850 units × £975)			3,753,750
Variances			
Material price		45,000	
Material usage		76,250	
Labour rate		32,500	
Labour efficiency		37,500	
Fixed overhead expenditure		145,000	
Fixed overhead capacity		62,500	
Fixed overhead efficiency		62,500	
	–	461,250	461,250 (A)
Actual cost of production (W)			4,215,000

Working

	£
Materials	795,000
Labour	1,225,000
Fixed overheads	2,195,000
Actual cost of production	4,215,000

c) MEMORANDUM

To: Production Director
From: Assistant Management Accountant
Date: xx/xx/xx
Subject: **Fixed overhead variances**

This memorandum provides information on fixed overhead variances. In particular it covers the similarities between fixed overhead variances and other cost variances, the meaning of the various fixed overhead variances and the ways in which such variances can be of assistance in the planning and the controlling of the division.

Similarities between fixed overhead variances and other variances

The fixed overhead expenditure variance is the difference between the budgeted fixed overhead expenditure and actual fixed overhead expenditure. It is therefore similar to the material price and labour rate variances in that it shows the effect on costs and hence profit of paying more or less than anticipated for resources used.

Material usage and labour efficiency variances show the effect on costs and hence profit of having used more or less resource than should have been used for the actual volume of production. Fixed overheads should remain constant within the relevant range of production, however; they should not change simply because budgeted and actual production volumes differ. Fixed overhead variances similar to material usage and labour efficiency variances (reflecting the difference between the actual fixed overhead expenditure and the fixed overhead expenditure which should have been incurred at the actual volume of production) cannot therefore occur.

The meaning of fixed overhead variances

Whereas labour and material total variances show the effect on costs and hence profit of the difference between what the actual production volume should have cost and what it did cost (in terms of labour or material), if an organisation uses standard absorption costing (as we do), the fixed overhead total variance is the difference between actual fixed overhead expenditure and the fixed overhead absorbed (the under- or over-absorbed overhead).

The total under or over absorption is made up of the fixed overhead expenditure variance and the fixed overhead volume variance. The volume variance shows that part of the under- or over-absorbed overhead which is due to any difference between budgeted production volume and actual production volume.

The volume variance can be further broken down into an efficiency variance and a capacity variance. The capacity variance shows how much of the under- or over-absorbed overhead is due to working the labour force or plant more or less than planned whereas the efficiency variance shows the effect of the efficiency of the labour force or plant.

The volume variance and its two subdivisions, the efficiency variance and the capacity variance, measure the extent of under or over absorption due to production volume being different to that planned. Material usage and labour efficiency variances, on the other hand, measure the effect of usage being different from that expected for the actual volume achieved.

Fixed overhead variances and planning and control

The fixed overhead volume variance and its subdivisions are perhaps misleading as variances for management control, because unlike expenditure variances or variable cost efficiency variances, they are not a true reflection of the extra or lower cash spending by an organisation as a result of the variance occurring. However, the fixed overhead efficiency and capacity variances are of some relevance for planning and control. They provide some measure of the difference between budgeted production volume and actual production volume, and management should obviously be interested in whether budgeted output was achieved, and if not, why not. A favourable efficiency variance might indicate an efficient workforce whereas an unfavourable capacity variance might indicate plant breakdowns or strikes. The existence of a fixed overhead volume variance can therefore be important; it is only the monetary value given to it that can be misleading.

The fixed overhead expenditure variance highlights the effect on costs and hence profit of changes to the level of overheads. For overhead expenditure variances to have any practical value as a planning or control measure, the variance for each overhead cost centre needs to be calculated, and reported to the manager responsible. Within each overhead cost centre, the manager should be able to analyse the total variance into indirect material cost variances, indirect labour cost variances and excess or favourable spending on other items, such as depreciation, postage, telephone charges and so on. Managers can then, for example, consider other suppliers, reconsider pricing structures of products and the like.

answers to chapter 5: STANDARD COSTING – FURTHER ASPECTS

1   The standard cost of the direct labour for a product will be made up of:

- the amount of time being spent on each unit of the product
- the hourly wage rate for the employees working on the product

Factors that should be taken into account when setting the standard for the amount of labour time include:

- the level of skill or training of the labour used on the product
- any anticipated changes in the grade of labour used on the product
- any anticipated changes in work methods or productivity levels
- the effect on productivity of any bonus scheme to be introduced

The hourly rate for the direct labour used on the product can be found from the payroll records. However consideration should be given to:

- anticipated pay rises
- any anticipated changes in the grade of labour to be used
- the effect of any bonus scheme on the labour rate
- whether any overtime is anticipated and should be built into the hourly rate

2   There are two main problems with using ideal standards in business:

Planning – if ideal standards are used for planning purposes it is likely that the results will be inaccurate as the standard does not reflect the reality of the working conditions. Therefore if a labour cost standard is set with no allowance for any inefficiency or idle time in the operations the reality is that the operations will take longer or will require more employees than planned for.

Control – if ideal standards are compared to actual costs then this will always result in adverse variances as the reality is that there will be some inefficiencies and wastage. This can be demotivational to managers and employees who will feel that in reality these standards can never be met and therefore they may stop trying to meet them. A further problem with these adverse variances is that they will be viewed as the norm and be ignored meaning that any corrective action that might be required is not taken.

standard costing – further aspects: answers

3 i) A favourable materials price variance may be caused by:

- negotiation of a better price from a supplier
- negotiation of a trade or bulk purchase discount from a supplier
- purchase of a lower grade of materials

ii) A favourable materials usage variance may be caused by:

- use of a higher grade of material which led to less wastage
- use of more skilled labour leading to less wastage than normal
- new machinery which provides greater efficiency

iii) An adverse labour rate variance may be caused by:

- unexpected increase in labour costs
- use of a higher grade of labour than anticipated
- unexpectedly high levels of overtime

iv) An adverse labour efficiency variance may be caused by:

- use of a less skilled grade of labour
- use of a lower grade of material which takes longer to work on
- more idle time than budgeted for
- poor supervision of the workforce
- problems with machinery

4 i) The fixed overhead volume variance will occur when the actual production level is different from the budgeted production level. If actual production is greater than budget, then the volume variance will be favourable. The volume variance is caused by the absorption of the fixed overheads – therefore this variance only appears in absorption costing systems and not in marginal costing systems. If the absorption is done on the basis of labour hours then the variance will be caused by the standard labour hours worked for the actual level of production being different from the standard labour hours for budgeted production. Analysis of the volume variance into the efficiency and capacity variances can help to find reasons for the volume variance.

ii) The fixed overhead efficiency variance is caused by the efficiency of the workforce, if the absorption basis is that of labour hours. Therefore whatever caused the labour efficiency variance will also be the cause of the fixed overhead efficiency variance.

If the absorption basis is that of machine hours then the fixed overhead efficiency variance will reflect how efficiently the machinery has been used to produce the cost units

iii) The fixed overhead capacity variance, if the absorption basis is that of labour hours, measures whether more or less hours were worked than were budgeted. Therefore the cause of the capacity variance will be the underlying reason for more or less hours than budgeted being worked.

Similarly if the absorption basis is that of machine hours the capacity variance measures whether more or less machine hours were operated than were budgeted.

standard costing – further aspects: answers

5 i)
- Favourable labour rate variance
- Adverse labour efficiency variance
- Adverse materials usage variance

ii)
- Adverse labour efficiency variance
- Adverse fixed overhead expenditure variance (due to additional costs of mending the machine)
- Adverse fixed overhead volume variance
- Adverse fixed overhead efficiency variance
- Adverse fixed overhead capacity variance

6 **New warehouse** – this will have the effect of simply reducing the fixed overhead expense (assuming the rent saved exceeds any new depreciation charge) and therefore is part of the favourable fixed overhead expenditure variance. The standard fixed overhead cost should be adjusted to reflect the rental saving.

New machines – the new machines use less power than the old ones therefore reducing the power costs element of the fixed overhead. The additional depreciation charge however will increase the fixed overhead expense. Once the reduction in power costs and increase in depreciation charge are known then the standard fixed overhead should be adjusted.

Price increase – the price increase will be a cause of the adverse materials price variance. The price increase appears to be a permanent one as all suppliers have increased their prices so the standard materials cost should be altered.

Skilled labour – the use of the higher skilled labour will have been part of the cause of the favourable labour efficiency variance and the favourable materials efficiency variance. If the fixed overheads are absorbed on a labour hour basis then the efficiency of the skilled labour will also be a cause of the favourable fixed overhead efficiency variance. The additional expense of the skilled labour and the overtime that has been worked will have been causes of the adverse labour rate variance. The overtime may also have led to the favourable capacity variance as actual hours exceeded the budgeted hours. Unless the use of this grade of labour is likely to be a permanent policy then there should be no change to the standard labour rate or hours.

7 i) Total materials price variance

	£
Standard cost for actual quantity 45,100 x £8	360,800
Actual cost	397,400
	36,600 Adv

ii) Planning variance caused by price increase

	£
Standard cost for actual quantity 45,100 x £8	360,800
Adjusted cost for actual quantity 45,100 x £8.50	383,350
	22,550 Adv

standard costing – further aspects: answers

Control variance caused by other factors

	£
Adjusted cost for actual quantity 45,100 x £8.50	383,350
Actual cost	397,400
	14,050 Adv

iii) The purchasing manager should not be held responsible for the entire price variance of £36,600 as the element caused by the price increase is not within his control. However the control element caused by other factors, the adverse variance of £14,050, is controllable by the purchasing manager and he should therefore be held responsible.

8 i) Total materials price variance

	£
Standard cost of actual quantity 10,600 x £6.50	68,900
Actual cost	73,140
	4,240 Adv

Planning variance due to price increase

	£
Standard cost of actual quantity 10,600 x £6.50	68,900
Price adjusted cost of actual quantity 10,600 x £7.00	74,200
	5,300 Adv

Control variance due to other factors

	£
Price adjusted cost of actual quantity 10,600 x £7.00	74,200
Actual cost	73,140
	1,060 Fav

ii) The total materials cost variance is £4,240 adverse. However all of this is due to the price increase as the adverse variance caused by the price increase is higher at £5,300. The purchasing manager, instead of being blamed for this portion of the variance, should in fact be praised for the favourable variance caused by other factors.

standard costing – further aspects: answers

9 Total materials price variance

	£
Standard cost of actual quantity 92,000 x £7.00	644,000
Actual cost	631,200
	12,800 Fav

Planning variance due to season

	£
Standard cost of actual quantity 92,000 x £7.00	644,000
Seasonally adjusted price 92,000 x £7.00 x 0.94	605,360
	38,640 Fav

Control variance due to other factors

	£
Seasonally adjusted price 92,000 x £7.00 x 0.94	605,360
Actual cost	631,200
	25,840 Adv

10 Total materials cost variance

	£
Standard cost of actual quantity 42,300 x £4.00	169,200
Actual cost	194,580
	25,380 Adv

Planning variance due to season

	£
Standard cost of actual quantity 42,300 x £4.00	169,200
Seasonally adjusted cost 42,300 x £4.00 x 1.18	199,656
	30,456 Adv

Control variance due to other factors

	£
Seasonally adjusted cost 42,300 x £4.00 x 1.18	199,656
Actual cost	194,580
	5,076 Fav

standard costing – further aspects: answers

11 a) i)

1) Standard marginal cost of a unit of Alpha

	£
Material (36,000m ÷ 12,000) 3m × (£432,000 ÷ 36,000) £12 per m	36.00
Labour (72,000 hrs ÷ 12,000) 6 hrs × (£450,000 ÷ 72,000) £6.25 per hr	37.50
	73.50

2) Standard cost of producing 10,000 units of Alpha

	£
Material (£36 × 10,000)	360,000
Labour (£37.50 × 10,000)	375,000
Fixed overheads	396,000
	1,131,000

ii)

1)

	£
32,000 m should have cost (× £12)	384,000
but did cost	377,600
Material price variance	6,400 (F)

2)

10,000 units should have used (× 3 m)	30,000 m
but did use	32,000 m
Material usage variance in metres	2,000 m (A)
× standard cost per metre	× £12
Material usage variance in £	£24,000 (A)

3)

	£
70,000 hrs should have cost (× £6.25)	437,500
but did cost	422,800
Labour rate variance	14,700 (F)

4)

10,000 units should have taken (× 6 hrs)	60,000 hrs
but did take	70,000 hrs
Efficiency variance in hours	10,000 hrs (A)
× standard rate per hour	× £6.25
Labour efficiency variance in £	£62,500 (A)

5)

	£
Budgeted fixed overhead expenditure	396,000
Actual fixed overhead expenditure (£(330,000 + 75,000))	405,000
Fixed overhead expenditure variance	9,000 (A)

iii) **Report**

To: Managing Director
From: Assistant Management Accountant
Date: xx/xx/xx
Subject: The use of standard marginal costing at Finchley Ltd

As discussed at our earlier meetings, because all companies within the Hampstead Group use standard marginal costing, Finchley Ltd will need to adopt the system from 1 August 20X8. This report is intended to demonstrate and describe the use of standard marginal costing in your company.

1) Set out below is a statement reconciling the standard cost of production for the three months ended 31 May 2006 with the actual cost of production for that period.

	(A) £	(F) £	£
Standard cost of output ((see (a)(i)(2)))			1,131,000
Variances			
Material price		6,400	
Material usage	24,000		
Labour rate		14,700	
Labour efficiency	62,500		
Fixed overhead expenditure	9,000		
	95,500	21,100	74,400 (A)
Actual cost of output			1,205,400

2) The total labour variance in the statement above (£47,800 (A)) differs from that in your absorption costing management report for the three months ended 31 May 2006 because the original report compares the actual cost of producing 10,000 units and the budgeted cost of producing 12,000 units. It therefore fails to compare like with like. The report above, however, compares actual costs of producing 10,000 units and what costs should have been given the actual output of 10,000 units. The total material variances in the two reports differ for this reason. There is very little point comparing a budgeted cost with an actual cost if the production level upon which the budgeted cost was based is not achieved.

The fixed overhead expenditure variance in the statement above also differs from the fixed overhead variance reported in the absorption costing statement. This is because the absorption costing statement compares overhead absorbed whereas the marginal costing statement compares overhead expenditure.

3) There are other reasons why the marginal costing statement provides improved management information.

   i) It separates total variances into their components and so you will be able to determine whether, for example, the total material variance is the responsibility of the purchasing manager (price variance) or the production manager (usage variance).

standard costing – further aspects: answers

ii) It avoids the use of under-or over-absorbed overhead, which is simply a bookkeeping exercise and does not reflect higher or lower cash spending.

iii) It allows management by exception.

iv) The original statement conveys the wrong message (that the overall variance was favourable).

I hope this information has proved useful. If I can be of further assistance or you have any questions, please do not hesitate to contact me.

b)

		(A) £	(F) £	£
Standard cost of output				1,131,000
Variances				
Labour rate due to machine breakdown (W1)			2,520	
Labour rate due to normal working (W1)			12,180	
Labour efficiency due to machine breakdown (W2)		75,000		
Labour efficiency due to normal working (W2)			12,500	
Material price due to change in price index (W3)			38,400	
Material price due to other reasons (W3)		32,000		
Material usage		24,000		
Fixed overhead expenditure		9,000		
		140,000	65,600	74,400 (A)
Actual cost of output				1,205,400

Workings

1

	£
Total labour rate variance	14,700 (F)
Labour rate variance due to machine breakdown (12,000 × £14,700/70,000)	2,520 (F)
Labour rate variance due to normal working (balance)	12,180 (F)

2

	£
Total labour efficiency variance	62,500 (A)
Labour efficiency variance due to machine breakdown (12,000 hrs × £6.25)	75,000 (A)
Labour efficiency variance due to normal production	12,500 (F)

standard costing – further aspects: answers

		£	£
3	Total material price variance		6,400 (F)
	Variance due to price index change		
	32,000 m should have cost (× £12 × 420.03/466.70)	345,600	
	but should originally have cost (× £12)	384,000	
			38,400 (F)
	Variance due to other reasons		32,000 (A)

12 a) MEMO

To: Richard Jones, Managing Director
From: Accounting Technician
Date: xx/xx/xx
Subject: **Variations in kit prices**

i) 1) **UK cost per kit at the time the contract was agreed**

$54,243 ÷ $9.80 = £5,535

2) **UK cost of kits delivered**

	September	October	November
Kits delivered	2,000	2,100	2,050
Contract cost in $ (× $54,243)	$108,486,000	$113,910,300	$111,198,150
Exchange rate	$9.00	$10.00	$10.25
Contract cost in £($ cost/exchange rate)	£12,054,000	£11,391,030	£10,848,600

3) **Price variance due to exchange rate differences**

	September £	October £	November £
Contract cost of kits delivered should have been (from (2) ÷ $9.8)	11,070,000	11,623,500	11,346,750
but cost of kits delivered was (from (2))	12,054,000	11,391,030	10,848,600
Variance	984,000 (A)	232,470 (F)	498,150 (F)

4) Total variance = price variance + usage variance

If price variance is as in (3) above, usage variance is total variance minus price variance in (3).

225

standard costing – further aspects: answers

Usage variance

	September £	October £	November £
Kits delivered should have cost (see (3))	11,070,000	11,623,500	11,346,750
but did cost (given)	12,059,535	11,385,495	10,848,600
	989,535 (A)	238,005 (F)	498,150 (F)
less: price variance (see (3))	984,000 (A)	232,470 (F)	498,150 (F)
	5,535 (A)	5,535 (F)	Nil

ii) The price variances due to exchange rate differences should be excluded from any standard costing report prepared for the production manager of Pronto Ltd because they are not controllable by him and so he can do nothing to influence their occurrence. They do need to be recognised and monitored, however.

b) i) 1) Budgeted overheads per machine (or track) hour = £840,000 ÷ 140 = £6,000 per hour

2) Budgeted number of cars produced per machine (or track) hour = 560/140 = 4 per hour

3) Standard hours of actual production = 500 cars ÷ 4 per hour = 125 hours

ii) 1) **Fixed overhead expenditure variance**

	£
Budgeted expenditure	840,000
Actual expenditure	842,000
	2,000 (A)

2) Fixed overhead absorption rate per unit = £6,000/4 = £1,500

Fixed overhead volume variance

Budgeted production at standard rate (560 × £1,500)	840,000
Actual production at standard rate (500 × £1,500)	750,000
	90,000 (A)

3) **Fixed overhead efficiency variance**

500 cars should have taken (from b)i)3))	125 hrs
but did take	126 hrs
Variance in hours	1 hr (A)
× standard absorption rate per hour	× £6,000
	£6,000 (A)

standard costing – further aspects: answers

   4) **Fixed overhead capacity variance**

Budgeted hours of work	140 hrs
Actual hours of work	126 hrs
	14 hrs (A)
× standard absorption rate per hour	× £6,000
	£84,000 (A)

iii) **Reconciliation of fixed overheads incurred to fixed overheads absorbed**

	£	£	£
Fixed overheads incurred			842,000
Variances			
Expenditure		2,000 (A)	
Volume efficiency	6,000 (A)		
Volume capacity	84,000 (A)		
Volume		90,000 (A)	
			92,000 (A)
Fixed overheads absorbed (125 hrs × £6,000)			750,000

---

13 a) i) 1) Standard price of fuel = £497,664/1,244,160 litres = £0.40 per litre.

   2) Standard litres of fuel per crossing = 1,244,160/6,480 = 192 litres
      Standard litres of fuel for 5,760 crossings = 192 × 5,760 = 1,105,920 litres

   3) Standard labour rate per hr = £699,840/93,312 hrs = £7.50 per hr

   4) Standard labour hours per crossing = 93,312/6,480 = 14.4 hours
      Std labour hrs for 5,760 crossings = 14.4 × 5,760 = 82,944 hrs

   5) Standard fixed overhead cost per budgeted operating hour = £466,560/7,776 = £60 per hour

   6) Standard operating hours per crossing = 7,776/6,480 = 1.2 hours
      Std operating hrs for 5,760 crossings = 1.2 × 5,760 = 6,912 hrs

   7) Standard fixed overhead cost absorbed by 5,760 crossings = 6,912 hours (vi) × £60 per hour (from (5)) = £414,720

   ii)
   1)
	£
1,232,800 litres should cost (× £0.40 a)i)1))	493,120
but did cost	567,088
Material price variance for fuel	73,968 (A)

standard costing – further aspects: answers

2)
5,760 crossings should have used (a)i)2))	1,105,920 litres
but did use	1,232,800 litres
Usage variance in litres	126,880 litres (A)
× standard price per litre ((a)(i)(1))	× £0.40
Material usage variance for fuel	£50,752 (A)

3)
	£
89,856 hours should have cost (× £7.50 a)i)3))	673,920
but did cost	696,384
Labour rate variance	22,464 (A)

4)
5,760 crossings should take (a)i)4))	82,944 hours
but did take	89,856 hours
Efficiency variance in hours	6,912 hours (A)
× standard rate per hour (a)i)3))	× £7.50
Labour efficiency variance	£51,840 (A)

5)
	£
Budgeted fixed overhead expenditure	466,560
Actual fixed overhead expenditure	472,440
Fixed overhead expenditure variance	5,880 (A)

6)
	£
Actual number of crossings (5,760) at standard rate (a)i)7))	414,720
Budgeted number of crossings at standard rate	466,560
Fixed overhead volume variance	51,840 (A)

7)
Budgeted operating hours	7,776
Actual operating hours	7,488
Capacity variance in hours	288 (A)
× std fixed o/hd cost per operating hour (a)i)5))	× £60
Fixed overhead capacity variance	£17,280 (A)

8)
5,760 crossings should take (a)i)6))	6,912	operating hours
but did take	7,488	operating hours
Efficiency variance in operating hours	576	operating hours (A)
× std fixed o/hd cost per op hr (a)i)5))	× £60	
Fixed overhead efficiency variance	£34,560	(A)

standard costing – further aspects: answers

iii) **Statement reconciling the actual cost of operations to the standard cost of operations for year ended 30 November 2006**

Number of ferry crossings 5,760

	£	£
Actual cost of operations		1,735,912
Cost variances	Adverse	
Material price for fuel	73,968	
Material usage for fuel	50,752	
Labour rate	22,464	
Labour efficiency	51,840	
Fixed overhead expenditure	5,880	
Fixed overhead capacity	17,280	
Fixed overhead efficiency	34,560	
		256,744 (A)
Standard cost of operations		1,479,168*

* Check. 5,760/6,480 × £1,664,064 = £1,479,168

b) **MEMO**

To: Chief executive
From: Management accountant
Date: xx/xx/xx
Subject: Variances for the year ended 30 November 2006

This memo addresses some of your concerns about the large number of adverse variances arising during the year.

i) **Subdivision of the material price variance for fuel**

Standard price of fuel per litre (a)i)1)) = £0.40
Actual market price of fuel per litre = £0.40 × 1.2 = £0.48

	£	£
1,232,800 litres at standard price would have cost (× £0.40 (a)(i))		493,120
1,232,800 litres at actual market price would have cost (× £0.48)		591,744
Price variance due to difference between standard price and market price (part (1))		98,624 (A)
1,232,800 litres at actual market price should have cost (× £0.48)	591,744	
but did cost	567,088	
Price variance due to other reasons (part (2))		24,656 (F)
Total material price variance		73,968 (A)

ii) The fixed overhead efficiency variance is not controllable. This variance is caused by the difference between the standard and actual operating hours for the 5,760 crossings. Since this difference arose entirely because of weather conditions, the corresponding variance is not controllable.

229

standard costing – further aspects: answers

iii) The part of the material price variance due to reasons other than the difference between the standard price and the market price for fuel is controllable. This amount was calculated in (i) as £24,656 favourable. The adverse variance of £98,624 calculated in (i) is non-controllable, but the remainder of the price variance has arisen due to controllable factors, since the price paid was different to the prevailing market price.

The labour rate variance is also controllable. It is not affected by the uncontrollable factors of the change in the market price for fuel and the adverse weather conditions.

14 a) i) 1) Actual number of meals served = 4 meals × 7 days × 648 guests
= 18,144 meals

2) Standard number of meals
for actual number of guests = 3 meals × 7 days × 648 guests
= 13,608 meals

3) Actual hourly rate of pay = $5,280 ÷ 1,200 hours
= $ 4.40 per hour

4) Standard hours allowed for
actual number of guests = (648 guests × 3 meals × 7 days)
÷ 12 meals per hour
= 1,134 hours

5) Standard fixed overhead per guest = budgeted overheads ÷
budgeted number of guests
= $38,340 ÷ 540 = $71 per guest

6) **Total standard cost for actual number of guests**

	$
Meal costs (13,608 meals × $3 per meal)	40,824
Catering staff costs (1,134 hours × $4 per hour)	4,536
Fixed overhead costs (648 × $71 per guest)	46,008
Total standard cost	91,368

ii) 1)
	$
18,144 meals should cost (× $3)	54,432
but did cost	49,896
Material price variance for meals served	4,536 (F)

2)
648 guests should have used (a)i)2))	13,608 meals
but did use (a)i)1))	18,144 meals
Usage variance in meals	4,536 meals (A)
× standard cost per meal	× $3
Material usage variance for meals served	$13,608 (A)

standard costing – further aspects: answers

3)
		$
1,200 hrs worked should have cost (× $4/hr)		4,800
but did cost		5,280
Labour rate variance for catering staff		480 (A)

4)
Meals for 648 guests should have taken (a)i)4))	1,134 hours
but did take	1,200 hours
Labour efficiency variance in hours	66 hours (A)
× standard rate per hour	× $4
Labour efficiency variance for catering staff	$264 (A)

5)
	$
Budgeted fixed overhead expenditure	38,340
Actual fixed overhead expenditure	37,800
Fixed overhead expenditure variance	540 (F)

6)
Actual number of guests	648
Budgeted number of guests	540
Volume variance – number of guests	108 (F)
× standard fixed overhead per guest (a)i)5))	× $71
Fixed overhead volume variance	$7,668 (F)

ii) **Bare Foot Hotel complex**

Standard cost reconciliation for seven days ended 27 November 2006

Budgeted number of guests	540
Actual number of guests	648

	$		$	
Standard cost for 648 guests (a)i)6))			91,368	
Cost variances				
Material price variance (a)ii)1))	4,536	(F)		
Material usage variance (a)ii)2))	13,608	(A)		
			9,072	(A)
Catering labour rate variance (a)ii)3))	480	(A)		
Catering labour efficiency variance (a)ii)4))	264	(A)		
			744	(A)
Fixed overhead expenditure variance (a)ii)5))	540	(F)		
Fixed overhead volume variance (a)ii)6))	7,668	(F)		
			8,208	(F)
Actual cost for 648 guests			92,976	

Note. (A) denotes adverse variance, (F) denotes favourable variance.

standard costing – further aspects: answers

b) **Memorandum**

To: Alice Groves, general manager
From: Assistant management accountant
Date: xx.xx.xx
Subject: **Performance report** for seven days ended 27 November 2006

This memorandum deals with a number of issues arising from the standard cost reconciliation statement prepared for the seven days ended 27 November 2006.

i) **Subdivision of the catering labour efficiency variance**

The adverse catering labour efficiency variance of $264 can be divided into that part due to guests taking more meals than planned and that part due to other efficiency reasons.

Standard hours allowed for 648 guests taking 3 meals ((a)(i)(4))	1,134 hours
Standard hours allowed for 648 guests taking 4 meals	
= (648 guests × 4 meals × 7 days) ÷ 12 meals per hour	1,512 hours
Excess hours due to guests taking more meals than planned	378 hours (A)
× standard rate per hour	× $4
Efficiency variance due to guests taking more meals than planned	**$1,512 (A)**
Standard hours allowed for 648 guests taking 4 meals (from above)	1,512 hours
Actual hours worked	1,200 hours
Efficiency variance due to other reasons (in hours)	312 hours (F)
× standard rate per hour	× $4
Catering labour efficiency variance due to other reasons	**$1,248 (F)**

ii) **The meaning of the fixed overhead capacity and efficiency variances**

The fixed overhead absorption rate for our hotel is based on the budgeted overhead expenditure for the period, divided by the budgeted number of guests.

$$\text{Fixed overhead absorption rate} = \frac{\text{budgeted fixed overhead}}{\text{budgeted number of guests}}$$

If the actual overhead, or the actual number of guests, or both, are different from budget then over or under absorption of overhead may occur, so that there may be a fixed overhead variance.

A **volume variance** arises when the activity level is different from that budgeted, in our case if the actual number of guests is different from the budgeted number. In some organisations it may be possible to sub-divide the volume variance into two parts: the capacity variance and the efficiency variance.

The **capacity variance** arises when the utilisation of the available capacity is higher or lower than budgeted. It is usually calculated as the difference between budgeted and

standard costing – further aspects: answers

actual hours worked, multiplied by the fixed overhead absorption rate. Under or over utilisation of capacity can potentially lead to under– or over-absorbed overhead.

The **efficiency variance** arises when employees are working at a more or less efficient rate than standard to produce a given output. Producing output at a faster or slower rate could also potentially lead to under– or over-absorbed overhead.

iii) **Calculating the fixed overhead capacity and efficiency variances for the Bare Foot Hotel complex**

The above descriptions of the fixed overhead capacity and efficiency variances highlight the need to be able to measure hours of work so that the volume variance can be subdivided.

It is not feasible to do this for the Bare Foot Hotel complex. We do have a measure of hours worked within the catering activity, but a large proportion of overheads are incurred on entertainment, for which we have no record of hours worked.

The absence of an activity measure based on hours worked therefore makes it difficult and meaningless to subdivide the fixed overhead volume variance into its capacity and efficiency elements.

15 a) i) Actual cost of a telephone unit = total actual cost ÷ total actual units = £79,200 ÷ 1,200,000 = £0.066

ii) Actual hourly wage rate of operators = actual total cost of operators' wages ÷ actual hours worked = £877,800 ÷ 114,000 hours = £7.70

iii) Standard number of operator hours per call = 6 mins = 0.1 hr

Standard number of operator hours for 1,000,000 calls = 0.1 hr × 1,000,000 = 100,000 hours

iv) Fixed overheads are based on budgeted operator hours.

Budgeted number of calls = 900,000

Budgeted number of operator hours = 900,000 × 0.1 hour = 90,000

Fixed overhead absorption rate = £6.50 per hour

Budgeted cost of fixed overheads = 90,000 hours × £6.50 per hour
= £585,000

v) See (iv) above

vi) Standard cost of actual operations = actual number of calls × standard cost per call = 1,000,000 × £1.42 = £1,042,000

233

standard costing – further aspects: answers

b)

i) **Price variance for telephone calls**

	£
1,200,000 units should have cost (× £0.07)	84,000
but did cost	79,200
	4,800 (F)

ii) **Usage variance for telephone calls**

1,000,000 calls should have used (× 1 unit)	1,000,000 units
but did use	1,200,000 units
Variance in units	200,000 units (A)
× standard rate per unit	× £0.07
	£14,000 (A)

iii) **Labour rate variance for the telephone operators**

	£
114,000 hours should have cost (× £7.00)	798,000
but did cost	877,800
	79,800 (A)

iv) **Labour efficiency variance for the telephone operators**

1,000,000 calls should have taken (from a)iii))	100,000 hrs
but did take	114,000 hrs
Variance in hours	14,000 hrs (A)
× standard rate per hour	× £7.00
	£98,000 (A)

v) **Fixed overhead expenditure variance**

	£
Budgeted expenditure (from a)iv))	585,000
Actual expenditure	540,400
	44,600 (F)

vi) **Fixed overhead volume variance**

	£
Budgeted number of calls	900,000
Actual number of calls	1,000,000
Variance in calls	100,000 (F)
× standard fixed overhead per call	× £0.65
	65,000 (F)

vii) **Fixed overhead capacity variance**

Budgeted operator hours (from a)v))	90,000 hrs
Actual operator hours	114,000 hrs
Variance in units	24,000 hrs (F)
× standard absorption rate per hour	× £6.50
	£156,000 (F)

viii) **Fixed overhead capacity variance**

Labour efficiency variance (as overheads are absorbed on a labour hour basis)(from b)iv))	14,000 hrs (A)
× standard absorption rate per hour	× £6.50
	£91,000 (A)

c) **Reconciliation statement – 3 months ended 31 May 2006**

	£	£	£
Standard cost of actual operations (from a)vi))			1,420,000
	(F)	(A)	
Variances			
Price for telephone calls	4,800		
Usage for telephone calls		14,000	
Labour rate		79,800	
Labour efficiency		98,000	
Fixed overhead expenditure	44,600		
Fixed overhead capacity	156,000		
Fixed overhead efficiency		91,000	
	205,400	282,800	77,400 (A)
Actual cost of actual operations			1,497,400

16 a) i) **Actual litres of material used** = actual total cost of materials/actual cost per litre = £23,985/£58.50 = 410 litres

ii) **Standard litres of material required for 40 barrels of X14** = standard litres per barrel × 40 = 10 litres × 40 = 400 litres

iii) **Average actual labour rate per hour** = actual total cost of labour/actual number of hours = £2,788/328 hours = £8.50

iv) **Standard labour hours required for 40 barrels of X14** = standard labour hours per barrel × 40 = 8 hours × 40 = 320 hours

v) **Budgeted number of machine hours** = budgeted production × budgeted number of hours per barrel = 45 barrels × 16 = 720 hours

vi) **Budgeted fixed overheads** = standard fixed overhead per barrel × budgeted production = £320 × 45 = £14,400 (or = budgeted number of machine hours for processing department × standard rate per machine hour = 720 hours × £20 = £14,400 or = (budgeted machine hours for processing department/factory budgeted machine hours) × factory budgeted fixed overheads = (720 hours/1,152 hours) × £23,040 = £14,400)

standard costing – further aspects: answers

    vii) **Actual fixed overheads** (for the processing department) = (budgeted machine hours for processing department/factory budgeted machine hours) × factory actual fixed overheads = (720 hours/1,152 hours) × £26,000 = £16,250

    viii) **Standard machine hours produced** = actual production output × standard machine hours per barrel = 40 barrels × 16 machine hours = 640 standard machine hours

    ix) **Standard absorption cost of actual production** = standard absorption cost per barrel × actual production = £984 × 40 barrels = £39,360

    x) **Actual absorption cost of actual production** = actual cost of material + labour + fixed overheads = £(23,985 + 2,788 + 16,250) = £43,023

b)

    i) **Material price variance**

	£
410 litres (from a)i)) should have cost (× £60)	24,600
but did cost	23,985
	615 (F)

    (ii) **Material usage variance**

40 barrels should have used (× 10 litres) (from a)ii))	400	litres
but did use (from (a)(i))	410	litres
Variance in litres	10	litres (A)
× standard cost per litre	× £60	
	£600	(A)

    iii) **Labour rate variance**

	£
328 hours should have cost (× £8)	2,624
but did cost	2,788
	164 (A)

    iv) **Labour efficiency variance**

40 barrels should have taken (× 8 hours) (from a)iv))	320	hours
but did take	328	hours
Variance in hours	8	hours (A)
× standard cost per hour	× £8	
	£64	(A)

    v) **Fixed overhead expenditure variance**

	£
Budgeted fixed overhead expenditure (from a)vi))	14,400
Actual fixed overhead expenditure (from a)vii))	16,250
	1,850 (A)

standard costing – further aspects: answers

Fixed overhead volume variance

	£	
Actual production at standard rate (40 barrels × £320)	12,800	
Budgeted production at standard rate (45 barrels × £320)	14,400	
	1,600	(A)

vii) **Fixed overhead efficiency variance**

40 barrels should take (× 16 hours) (from a)viii))	640	hours
but did take	656	hours
Variance in hours	16	hours (A)
× standard rate per hour	× £20	
	£320	(A)

viii) **Fixed overhead capacity variance**

Budgeted machine hours (from a)v))	720	
Actual machine hours	656	
Variance in hours	64	(A)
× standard absorption rate per hour	× £20	
	£1,280	(A)

c) **Reconciliation statement – five weeks ended 31 May 2006**

			£	
Standard absorption cost of actual production (from (a)(ix))			39,360	
	£	£		
	(F)	(A)		
Variances				
Material price	615			
Material usage		600		
Labour rate		164		
Labour efficiency		64		
Fixed overhead expenditure		1,850		
Fixed overhead efficiency		320		
Fixed overhead capacity		1,280		
	615	4,278	3,663	(A)
Actual absorption cost of actual production (from (a)(x))			43,023	

237

standard costing – further aspects: answers

d) **MEMO**

To: Judith Green, production manager
From: Accounting technician
Date: xx.xx.xx
Subject: **Croxton Ltd – analysis of variances for 5 weeks ended 31 May 2006**

Following our recent meeting, I set out below some issues to consider in relation to our discussions.

i) **Revised standard material price per litre** = £60 x 133/140 = £57

ii) **Subdivision of material price variance**

	£	£	
410 litres were expected to have cost (at the original standard of £60 per litre)	24,600		
but should then have been expected to have cost (at the revised standard of £57 per litre)	23,370		
Variance due to the change in the price index		1,230	(F)
410 litres should have cost, if the revised standard of £57 had been used	23,370		
but did cost	23,985		
Variance due to other reasons		615	(A)
Total material price variance		615	(F)

iii) **Reasons for the occurrence of the material price variance**

A favourable material price variance of £615 was reported for the five weeks ended 31 May 2006. The standard price used as the basis for this calculation was out of date, however, and was too high. If a more realistic standard had been used, the actual cost was in fact greater than the standard cost, not less than the standard cost. The purchasing department had therefore purchased material at a price greater than the realistic standard (although at a price lower than the out of date standard).

The purchasing department have therefore been inefficient, not efficient.

iv) **Implications of one scrapped barrel**

1) **Material usage variance**

The material usage variance shows that 10 litres more than standard were used. As the standard usage per barrel is 10 litres it is possible that the scrapped barrel is the reason for this adverse variance.

2) **Labour efficiency variance**

The labour efficiency variance shows that eight hours more than standard were worked. As a standard eight hours should be worked per barrel it is possible that the scrapped barrel is the reason for this adverse variance.

3) **Labour rate variance**

328 hours were actually worked during the five weeks. Overtime is paid on hours in excess of 320 hours, and hence an overtime premium of eight hours x £8 = £64 was paid in the period. Suppose the eight hours of overtime were worked because one barrel was scrapped (see (2) above). The total labour rate variance is £164 and so there is still £164 - £64 = £100 of the variance not explained by the scrapping of the barrel. This £100 would be due to other, unexplained reasons.

v) **Why the fixed overheads might not be controllable by the processing department**

1) The apportionment of both budgeted and fixed overheads to the department is done on the arbitrary basis of budgeted machine hours. Budgeted machine hours are determined by budgeted production volume, which is outside the control of the processing department.

2) The actual overheads apportioned to the processing department are a share of total fixed overheads. The processing department is unable to control the fixed overheads incurred in other parts of Croxton Ltd, however.

answers to chapter 6:
PERFORMANCE INDICATORS

1

	November	December	January	February
i)	$\dfrac{98{,}200}{64{,}300}$	$\dfrac{107{,}300}{68{,}900}$	$\dfrac{90{,}200}{62{,}100}$	$\dfrac{92{,}000}{60{,}200}$
	1.53 hours per unit	1.56 hours per unit	1.45 hours per unit	1.53 hours per unit
ii)	$\dfrac{64{,}300 \times 1.5}{98{,}200}$	$\dfrac{68{,}900 \times 1.5}{107{,}300}$	$\dfrac{62{,}100 \times 1.5}{90{,}200}$	$\dfrac{60{,}200 \times 1.5}{92{,}000}$
	98.2%	96.3%	103.3%	98.2%
iii)	$\dfrac{98{,}200}{65{,}000 \times 1.5}$	$\dfrac{107{,}300}{65{,}000 \times 1.5}$	$\dfrac{90{,}200}{60{,}000 \times 1.5}$	$\dfrac{92{,}000}{62{,}000 \times 1.5}$
	100.7%	110.1%	100.2%	98.9%
iv)	$\dfrac{64{,}300}{65{,}000}$	$\dfrac{68{,}900}{65{,}000}$	$\dfrac{62{,}100}{60{,}000}$	$\dfrac{60{,}200}{62{,}000}$
	98.9%	106.0%	103.5%	97.1%

2 Productivity is the quantity of output, either goods or services, in relation to the resources used to produce the output. Productivity measures how efficiently the resources of the organisation are being used.

An increase in productivity does not necessarily lead to an increase in profitability although in many cases it does. For example in a manufacturing business if the number of units produced per hour increases this is an increase in productivity. We now have more units of product to sell and if these can be sold at the same price as the current number of products then profit should increase. However if the additional units have to be sold at a lower price as there is not enough demand for these units then profitability may fall.

A further example would be an increase in units produced per hour with associated higher levels of materials wastage. This is an increase in productivity which will not necessarily lead to an increase in profit due to the additional costs of the materials wastage.

performance indicators: answers

3 i) a taxi firm — number of fares per shift
– number of miles per shift

ii) a hospital — out-patients seen per day

iii) a motorbike courier service — miles per week
– number of packages per day

iv) a firm of accountants — chargeable hours as a percentage of total hours

v) a retail store — sales per employee
– sales per square metre of shop floor

vi) a maker of hand-made pottery — number of pots thrown per day
– number of pots painted per day

4

	£
Sales	1,447,600
Less: cost of materials	(736,500)
cost of services	(316,900)
Total value added	394,200
Value added per employee	£394,200/15
	£26,280

5 a)

		January	February	March
i)	Productivity per labour hour	$\dfrac{8,540}{8,635}$	$\dfrac{8,670}{7,820}$	$\dfrac{9,320}{9,280}$
		0.99 units per hour	1.11 units per hour	1.00 unit per hour
ii)	Efficiency ratio	$\dfrac{8,540 \times 1.1}{8,635}$	$\dfrac{8,670 \times 1.1}{7,820}$	$\dfrac{9,320 \times 1.1}{9,280}$
		108.8%	122.0%	110.5%
iii)	Capacity ratio	$\dfrac{8,635}{8,500 \times 1.1}$	$\dfrac{7,820}{8,200 \times 1.1}$	$\dfrac{9,280}{9,500 \times 1.1}$
		92.4%	86.7%	88.8%
iv)	Activity ratio	$\dfrac{8,540}{8,500}$	$\dfrac{8,670}{8,200}$	$\dfrac{9,320}{9,500}$
		100.5%	105.7%	98.1%

performance indicators: answers

v)	Cost per unit	$\dfrac{£657,100}{8,540}$	$\dfrac{£666,800}{8,670}$	$\dfrac{£740,300}{9,320}$
		£76.94 per unit	£76.91 per unit	£79.43 per unit
vi)	Value added per employee	£	£	£
	Sales	916,000	923,000	965,000
	Production costs	(552,300)	(568,500)	(629,500)
	Value added	363,700	354,500	335,500
	Value added per employee	£6,613	£6,445	£5,784

b) Both the productivity per hour and efficiency indicators show that in all three months the time taken to produce units is less than the standard time of 1.1 hours. Although the activity ratio shows that in all three months the actual activity level was fairly close to the budgeted level the capacity ratio indicates that the available hours of work were never exceeded. Production significantly increased in March but this appears to have caused a higher cost per unit and lower value added per employee.

6   a)   i)   Efficiency ratio $= \dfrac{\text{Standard hours for actual production}}{\text{Actual hours worked}} \times 100$

$= \dfrac{14{,}200 \times 3}{46{,}000} \times 100$

$= 92.61\%$

As the efficiency ratio is less than 100% this indicates that the workforce have not worked as efficiently as was anticipated. The actual hours worked are more than the standard hours for that level of production.

ii)   Capacity ratio $= \dfrac{\text{Actual hours worked}}{\text{Budgeted hours}} \times 100$

$= \dfrac{46{,}000}{15{,}000 \times 3} \times 100$

$= 102.22\%$

The capacity ratio indicates whether as many hours have been worked as were budgeted for. In this instance the capacity ratio is greater than 100% meaning that the number of hours worked was more than those budgeted for.

performance indicators: answers

iii) Production volume ratio = $\dfrac{\text{Actual output}}{\text{Budgeted output}} \times 100$

$= \dfrac{14{,}200}{15{,}000} \times 100$

$= 94.67\%$

The production volume ratio is an indicator of how the volume of actual production compares to the budgeted level of output. In this instance as the production volume ratio is below 100% this indicates that the actual level of output was below the budgeted level.

b) Production volume ratio = Efficiency ratio x Capacity ratio

$= 92.61\% \times 102.22\%$

$= 94.67\%$

c) Hours worked @ 95% efficiency $= \dfrac{14{,}200 \times 3}{0.95}$

$= 44{,}842$

Hours saved (46,000 − 44,842) = 1,158 hours

7 i) Cost per unit = £3,204,430/467,800 units

= £6.85 per unit

ii) Efficiency ratio = $\dfrac{\text{Standard hours for actual production}}{\text{Actual hours worked}} \times 100$

$= \dfrac{467{,}800 \times 1.5}{748{,}500} \times 100$

$= 93.7\%$

iii) Capacity ratio = $\dfrac{\text{Actual hours worked}}{\text{Budgeted hours}} \times 100$

$= \dfrac{748{,}500}{428{,}000 \times 1.5} \times 100$

$= 116.6\%$

iv) Activity ratio = $\dfrac{\text{Standard hours for actual production}}{\text{Budgeted hours}} \times 100$

= $\dfrac{467,800 \times 1.5}{428,000 \times 1.5} \times 100$

= 109.3%

8 a) i) Gross profit margin = $\dfrac{\text{Gross profit}}{\text{Turnover}} \times 100$

= $\dfrac{1,007,200}{2,650,400} \times 100$

= 38%

ii) Net profit margin = $\dfrac{\text{Operating profit}}{\text{Turnover}} \times 100$

= $\dfrac{336,600}{2,650,400} \times 100$

= 12.7%

iii) Return on capital employed = $\dfrac{\text{Operating profit}}{\text{Capital employed}} \times 100$

= $\dfrac{336,600}{2,337,500} \times 100$

= 14.4%

iv) Asset turnover = $\dfrac{\text{Turnover}}{\text{Capital employed}}$

= $\dfrac{2,650,400}{2,337,500}$

= 1.13

v) Fixed asset turnover = $\dfrac{\text{Turnover}}{\text{Fixed assets}}$

= $\dfrac{2,650,400}{1,920,400}$

= 1.38

performance indicators: answers

vi) Current ratio $= \dfrac{\text{Current assets}}{\text{Current liabilities}}$

$= \dfrac{607,400}{190,300}$

$= 3.19 : 1$

vii) Quick ratio $= \dfrac{\text{Current assets} - \text{stock}}{\text{Current liabilities}}$

$= \dfrac{607,400 - 191,200}{190,300}$

$= 2.19 : 1$

viii) Debtors collection period $= \dfrac{\text{Debtors}}{\text{Turnover}} \times 365$

$= \dfrac{399,400}{2,650,400} \times 365$

$= 55 \text{ days}$

ix) Stock turnover $= \dfrac{\text{Average stock}}{\text{Cost of sales}} \times 365$

$= \dfrac{(180,000 + 191,200)/2}{1,643,200} \times 365$

$= 41 \text{ days}$

x) Creditors payment period $= \dfrac{\text{Creditors}}{\text{Purchases}} \times 365$

$= \dfrac{190,300}{1,654,400} \times 365$

$= 42 \text{ days}$

b) Increase in cash balance $= \dfrac{£1,654,400}{365} \times (60 - 42)$

$= £81,587$

performance indicators: answers

9 a)

		July	Aug	Sept	Oct	Nov	Dec
i)	Gross profit margin	34%	34%	34%	32%	31%	31%
ii)	Net profit margin	12%	12%	12%	11%	10%	9%
iii)	Expenses to sales %	22%	22%	22%	21%	21%	22%
iv)	Return on capital employed (W1)	15.2%	14.6%	13.1%	11.6%	10.9%	10.0%
v)	Asset turnover	1.27	1.21	1.09	1.06	1.09	1.11

b) Sales revenue decreased from July to September and then increased significantly until the end of the year. However the increase in sales has been at the cost of the gross profit margin which has decreased from 34% to 31%. Although the expenses to sales percentage has remained reasonably constant over the period the net profit margin has fallen due to the decrease in gross profit margin.

Return on capital employed fell dramatically in the first four months of the period although this was due to a significant decrease in asset turnover in that period more than a decline in profitability. The fall in return on capital employed continues in the last three months of the year due to the fall in net profit margin; however the drop in return is not as bad as it might have been as the asset turnover is again improving.

Workings

1 Here, return on capital employed is calculated as

$$\text{ROCE} = \frac{\text{Profit before interest}}{\text{Capital employed (shareholders funds + loans)}} = \frac{(550 - 374 - 116)}{468 + 50} = 11.6\% \text{ for October, etc}$$

Alternatively, it may be computed as a return on equity:

$$\text{ROCE (RoE)} = \frac{\text{Profit after interest}}{\text{Shareholders' funds}} = \frac{(550 - 374 - 116 - 3)}{468} = 12.2\% \text{ for October, etc}$$

2 To be consistent with the ROCE definition used, asset turnover has been calculated as

$$\text{Asset turnover} = \frac{\text{Turnover}}{\text{Total capital employed (assets - current liabilities)}} = \frac{550}{468 + 50} = 1.06 \text{ for October, etc}$$

247

performance indicators: answers

10

		2004	2005	2006
i)	Gross profit margin	40.1%	39.1%	37.9%
ii)	Net profit margin	14.1%	13.0%	11.0%
iii)	Return on capital employed (Note: total CE used)	13.3%	11.9%	10.6%
iv)	Asset turnover	0.95	0.92	0.97
v)	Fixed asset turnover	1.29	1.20	1.16
vi)	Current ratio	3.9 : 1	3.5 : 1	2.55 : 1
vii)	Quick ratio	3.1 : 1	2.6 : 1	1.6 : 1
viii)	Debtors' collection period	40 days	46 days	48 days
ix)	Stock turnover	45 days	54 days	64 days
x)	Creditors' payment period	60 days	62 days	65 days

Profitability has fallen significantly over the three year period. Return on capital employed has fallen by almost 3% and this is due solely to decreases in gross and net profit margins as asset turnover has remained fairly constant with a minor increase in 2006. Although both gross profit margin and net profit margin have fallen, the net profit margin has fallen proportionally a great deal more. This means that as well as the gross profit margin falling the expenses of the business are increasing.

There also seems to have been some loss of control regarding the working capital of the business. The stock turnover period has increased dramatically, meaning that large amounts of funds are being tied up in stock holding. Debtors' days have also increased by 8 days whereas the creditors' payment period has only increased by 5 days over the three year period.

The overall working capital of the business does appear to be high, particularly the high cash balances at the end of 2004 and 2005. This has improved by 2006 but this may be as a result of the stock turnover increase rather than a conscious policy.

Workings

	2004 £'000	2005 £'000	2006 £'000
Profit and loss summary			
Sales	1,420	1,560	1,740
Cost of sales	(850)	(950)	(1,080)
Gross profit	570	610	660
Expenses	(370)	(407)	(469)
Profit before interest	200	203	191
Interest	–	(7)	(6)
Profit after interest	200	196	185
Balance sheet summary			
Fixed assets	1,100	1,300	1,500
Stock	105	140	190
Debtors	155	198	230
Cash	280	224	73
Creditors	(140)	(162)	(193)
	1,500	1,700	1,800
Long term loan	–	(100)	(100)
Capital and reserves	1,500	1,600	1,700

11 a)

		North	South	Central
i)	Gross profit margin	32.0%	30.0%	35.0%
ii)	Net profit margin	18.0%	11.1%	13.4%
iii)	Return on capital employed	16.0%	9.0%	14.0%
iv)	Asset turnover	0.89	0.81	1.04
v)	Stock turnover	0.6 months	1.1 months	1.0 months
vi)	Debtors' collection period	1.4 months	2.3 months	1.6 months
vii)	Creditors' payment period	2.1 months	1.3 months	1.9 months
viii)	Units per square metre	34.0 units	25.5 units	29.3 units
ix)	Units per employee	944 units	850 units	820 units
x)	Units per hour	2 units	1.8 units	1.8 units

b) In terms of profitability North is clearly the most profitable with the highest net profit margin and return on capital employed. However Central has a higher gross profit margin which may be due to production of a different product to North or due to higher local selling prices or lower purchasing prices for Central. Although Central's net profit margin is significantly lower than North's its return on capital employed is not so different due to a higher asset turnover in Central. South seems to have profitability problems with gross and net profit margins, asset turnover and return on capital employed significantly lower than those of the other two divisions.

performance indicators: answers

North again appears to have the best working capital control with the lowest stock turnover and debtors collection period and the longest creditors payment period. Central's working capital control appears to be adequate but again there are questions to be asked at South with a relatively long debtors collection period and a month shorter creditors payment period.

Finally, whichever way productivity is measured, the productivity at North is significantly greater than at either of the other two divisions. Central makes the same number of units per hour as South but less per employee indicating that there could be room for improvement in employee productivity at Central.

Workings		North £	South £	Central £
Profit and loss				
Sales		870,000	560,000	640,000
COS:	o/stock	34,000	41,000	34,000
	purchases	590,000	380,000	420,000
	c/stock	(32,000)	(29,000)	(38,000)
		592,000	392,000	416,000
Gross profit		278,000	168,000	224,000
Expenses		(121,000)	(106,000)	(138,000)
Net profit		157,000	62,000	86,000
Balance sheet				
Debtors		100,100	107,300	87,600
Creditors		(103,400)	(42,600)	(66,700)
Other net assets		983,300	625,300	594,100
Capital		980,000	690,000	615,000

12 i) Gross profit   = 380,000 x 0.48
                          = £182,400

    ii) Sales   = £425,000/0.34
                          = £1,250,000

    iii) Gross profit   = £85,000 x 0.40
                          = £34,000

         Net profit   = £85,000 x 0.115
                          = £9,775

         Expenses   = £34,000 – £9,775
                          = £24,225

    iv) Capital employed = £100,000/0.116
                          = £862,069

    v) Asset turnover   = 0.10/0.08
                          = 1.25

vi) Average stock = (£158,000 + £182,000)/2
                  = £170,000

    Cost of sales = £158,000 + £560,000 – £182,000
                  = £536,000

    Stock turnover = £536,000/170,000
                   = 3.2 times

vii) Sales = £96,000/48 x 365
          = £730,000

13 The decrease in gross profit margin could have been due to a number of factors:

- decrease in selling price
- increase in suppliers' prices
- loss of trade discount on purchases
- significant decrease in stock levels
- significant stock write-offs
- any combination of the above

14 a)

		Y/e 31 Dec 2006	Y/e 31 Dec 2005
i)	Gross profit margin	45.3%	42.4%
ii)	Net profit margin (Profit before tax/turnover)	16.6%	15.2%
iii)	Return on capital employed (Profit before tax/ capital + reserves + loan)	13.3%	12.5%
iv)	Asset turnover	0.80	0.82
v)	Fixed asset turnover	0.85	0.89
vi)	Current ratio	1.75 : 1	2.3 : 1
vii)	Quick ratio	1.2 : 1	1.6 : 1
viii)	Debtors' collection period	40 days	44 days
ix)	Stock turnover	31 days	36 days
x)	Creditors' payment period	61 days	51 days

b) Return on capital employed has increased over the two year period and this is solely due to increased profitability as both the asset turnover and fixed asset turnover have decreased over the period. There has been a significant increase in gross profit margin in 2006 and, although net profit margin has also increased, it has not done so at the rate of the gross profit margin, indicating that expenses are in fact increasing at a faster rate than sales. This may be due to a large advertising campaign which has increased costs but allowed the gross profit margin to increase or some similar reason.

As well as an increase in sales and profitability there also appears to be general improvement in the working capital management. Both the current and quick ratios have fallen but are still at acceptable levels. The debtors collection period and stock turnover period have both been reduced by a few days and in combination with the increase in the creditors payment period by 10 days this will have a significant positive effect on the cash flows of the business.

15 Ratio analysis can be a useful tool for providing information to management about the performance of a business or part of a business. However care must be taken with the analysis as there are a number of limitations that must be borne in mind:

Comparison of like with like – if ratios are to be compared then they must have been calculated in the same way and using comparable figures. When comparing ratios over time in an organisation, any change in accounting policies over the period may impact upon the ratios. If comparing the accounts of two different organisations, it is likely that they will have different accounting policies and ideally adjustments should be made to bring the accounting policies in line before calculating the ratios.

Inflation – if ratios are being compared over time on the basis of historical cost accounting figures then adjustment must be made using an appropriate index in order to restate all the figures in terms of a common price basis.

Representative figures – in many cases we are using year end balance sheet amounts to calculate ratios and these may not necessarily be representative of the value throughout the year, for example when calculating stock turnover or the debtors collection period.

Year-end transactions – as year end figures are used for the ratios just one significant accounting adjustment or transaction before the year end can alter the position shown by the balance sheet and the resulting ratios. For example if a large cash payment were made to creditors just before the year end this would significantly improve the current ratio and reduce the creditors collection period calculated.

Age of fixed assets – if comparing one company with another using ratio analysis the figures may not be entirely comparable unless the fixed assets are of similar age. Older fixed assets will have a lower balance sheet value as they have been depreciated for longer and this can serve to improve figures such as asset turnover and return on capital employed.

16 a) **Performance indicators for Melosoven Ltd for quarter 4**

	i)	Quarterly return on capital employed	(352/8,111) × 100%	4.3%
	ii)	Operating profit margin	(352/4,759) × 100%	7.4%
	iii)	Quarterly asset turnover	4,759/8,111	0.59 times
	iv)	Average age of period-end debtors in days	(2,040/4,759) × 91	39 days
	v)	Average age of period-end trade creditors in days	[2,362/(1,583 + 43)] × 91	132 days
	vi)	Average age of period end materials stocks in days	(305/1,583) × 91	18 days

vii) Average age of period-end finished
goods stocks in days   (1,326/3,980) × 91   30 days

b) i) **Performance indicators for Melosoven Ltd for Quarters 1 to 4**

	Q1	Q2	Q3	Q4
Return on capital employed	4.3%	1.2%	2.8%	4.3%
Operating profit margin	9.0%	2.6%	5.3%	7.4%
Quarterly asset turnover	0.54	0.55	0.52	0.59
Age of debtors in days	39	38	44	39
Age of trade creditors in days	192	167	158	132
Age of materials stocks in days	29	24	18	18
Age of finished goods stocks in days	51	41	28	30

ii) **Briefing note**

To: Louise Simpson
From: Financial analyst
Date: xx/xx/xx
Subject: **Performance of Melosoven Ltd in Quarters 1 to 4**

The above financial performance ratios expose a sharp drop in performance between quarter 1 and quarter 2. Quarters 3 and 4 showed an improvement and the key ratios (return on capital employed, operating profit margin and asset turnover) are returning to the levels achieved in Quarter 1.

1) **Return on capital employed**. This ratio dropped from 4.3% to 1.2%. Between quarters 1 and 2, but has now returned to its earliest level.

2) **Operating profit margin**. This fell in quarter 2 and, although it improved in quarters 3 and 4, is not yet back to the level of quarter 1. The drop in profit margin in quarter 4 was the reason for the fall in ROCE.

3) **Quarterly asset turnover**. This was higher in quarter 4 than in any of the earlier quarters and is the reason that the return on capital employed is back to 4.3% in quarter 4 despite the profit margin being lower than in quarter 1.

4) **Age of debtors in days**. This ratio has remained comparatively stable during the year, and at 39 days is not excessively high.

5) **Age of trade creditors in days**. At the end of quarter 1 Melosoven was taking an average of 192 days (more than six months) to pay its trade creditors, which seems excessive. This figure has been progressively reduced during the year to 132 days (still more than 4 months, however) by the end of quarter 4.

6) **Age of materials stocks in days**. Material stocks have fallen from 29 days at the end of quarter 1 to stabilise at 18 days in quarters 3 and 4.

7) **Age of finished goods stocks in days**. Finished goods stocks have dropped from 51 days sales at the end of quarter 1 to 30 days at the end of the year. This is a significant improvement.

performance indicators: answers

17 a) To: Angela Wade
From: A Technician
Date: xx.xx.xx
Subject: **West Ltd and East Ltd – Performance Report**

i) **Return on capital employed (ROCE)**

The ROCE is a key financial ratio which shows the amount of profit which has been made in relation to the amount of resources invested. It also gives some idea of how efficiently the company has been operating.

$$ROCE = \frac{Operating\ profit}{Net\ assets}$$

$$ROCE\ (West\ Ltd) = \frac{3,068}{15,340} = 0.2 \times 100\% = 20\%$$

$$ROCE\ (East\ Ltd) = \frac{2,795}{6,500} = 0.43 \times 100\% = 43\%$$

ii) **Asset turnover**

The asset turnover is one of the main balance sheet ratios, and is a measure of how well the assets of a business are being used to generate sales.

$$Asset\ turnover = \frac{Net\ turnover}{Net\ assets}$$

$$Asset\ turnover\ (West\ Ltd) = \frac{17,910}{15,340} = 1.17\ times$$

$$Asset\ turnover\ (East\ Ltd) = \frac{17,424}{6,500} = 2.68\ times$$

iii) **Sales margin**

The sales margin ratio is a measure of overall profitability and it provides a measure of performance for management. Unsatisfactory sales margins are investigated by management, and are generally followed by control action. Increasing selling prices and reducing costs will have a direct effect on this ratio.

$$Sales\ margin = \frac{Operating\ profit}{Net\ turnover}$$

$$Sales\ margin\ (West\ Ltd) = \frac{3,068}{17,910} = 0.171 \times 100\% = 17.1\%$$

$$Sales\ margin\ (East\ Ltd) = \frac{2,795}{17,424} = 0.16 \times 100\% = 16\%$$

b) **Measure of customer service : faulty sales**

The percentage of faulty sales as a measure of the level of customer service is calculated as :

$$\frac{\text{Returns}}{\text{Gross sales}}$$

West Ltd = $\frac{100}{20,000}$ = 0.005% x 100% = 0.5%

East Ltd = $\frac{220}{22,000}$ = 0.01% x 100% = 1%

c) **Further measure of customer service**

Another possible measure of the level of customer service which could be derived from the accounting data is the number of days between order and delivery of goods.

This can be calculated as follows.

$$\text{Time between order and delivery} = \frac{\text{Orders received in year - net sales ('000 litres)}}{\text{Net sales ('000 litres)}} \times 365 \text{ day}$$

West Ltd = $\frac{20,173 - 19,000}{19,900}$ x 365 days = 5 days

East Ltd = $\frac{22,854 - 21,780}{21,780}$ x 365 days = 18 days

The amount of money which the subsidiaries invest in research and development, and training could also provide a measure of customer service.

d) **Limitations of financial ratios**

Financial ratios as a measure of performance are only concerned with the data recorded in the accounts. For example, East Ltd appears to be a much more efficient company than West Ltd based on its ROCE and asset turnover ratios. However, when calculations are made to measure customer service, West Ltd has far fewer days between order and delivery of goods, and half as many faulty sales (as a percentage of gross sales).

The financial ratios also treat research and development, and training costs as expenses which are written off to the profit and loss account. These expenses are likely to have an impact on the future profitability of the company, and are more of an investment than expense.

Both West Ltd and East Ltd use plant of similar size and technology. There is however, a large difference in the net book values of the plant, and hence a large difference in the net assets of each company.

East Ltd purchased its plant before West Ltd, and has a lower cost, and a higher depreciation to date than West Ltd. These differences arise mainly due to the fact that the accounts are prepared using historical cost accounting. The fact that East Ltd's net assets are so much lower than those of West Ltd, means that the ROCE of East Ltd will be much higher than that of West Ltd.

performance indicators: answers

18 a) i) **Return on capital employed** = (operating profit ÷ net assets) x 100%
= (£975,000/£4,875,000) x 100% = 20%

ii) **Asset turnover** = turnover/net assets = £3,900,000/£4,875,000 = 0.8

iii) **Sales (operating profit) margin** = (operating profit/turnover) x 100%
= (£975,000/£3,900,000) x 100%
= 25%

iv) **Average age of debtors (in months)** = (debtors/turnover) x 12
= (£325,000/£3,900,000) x 12
= 1 month

v) **Average age of finished stock (in months)** = (finished goods stock/cost of sales) x 12
= (£140,000/£840,000) x 12 = 2 months

b) **Briefing notes on the usefulness of performance indicators**

Prepared for Angela Frear

Prepared by Financial Analyst

Dated: xx.xx.xx

i) **Return on capital employed**

The return on capital employed can be misleading.

1) Profits should be related to average capital employed but we compute the ratio using year-end assets. Using year-end figures can distort trends and comparisons. If a new investment is undertaken near to a year end and financed, for example, by an issue of shares, the capital employed will rise by the finance raised but profits will only have a month or two of the new investment's contribution.

2) The ROCE would be higher if costs such as marketing, research and development and training were not treated as revenue expenditure but were viewed as investment for the future and were capitalised.

ii) **Sales (operating profit) margin**

The sales (or operating profit) margin can be manipulated in a number of ways. The following activities would result in short-term improvements in the margin, but probably at the expense of the organisation's long-term viability.

1) Reducing expenditure on discretionary cost items such as research and development

2) Depreciating assets over a longer period of time, so that the depreciation charge is less

3) Choosing an alternative stock valuation method to increase the value of closing stock

iii) **Average delay in fulfilling orders**

	£
Orders during the year	4,550,000
Turnover during the year	3,900,000
Unfulfilled orders	650,000

Average delay = (£650,000/£3,900,000) × 12 months = 2 months

iv) **Measures of customer satisfaction**

As well as the delay in fulfilling orders, other measures of customer satisfaction include the following.

- Repeat business ((£3,120,000/£3,900,000) × 100% = 80%)
- Cost of customer support per £ of turnover (£400,000/£3,900,000 = 10p)
- Cost of customer support per customer (information not available)

v) **Measuring performance from an internal perspective**

A number of indicators may help to measure performance from an internal perspective.

- Training costs as a percentage of production costs ((£140,000/£930,000) × 100% = 15.05%)

- Reworked faulty production as a percentage of total production ((£37,200/£930,000) × 100% = 4%)

- Returns as a percentage of sales ((£100,000/£4m) × 100% = 2.5%)

The first indicator should be relatively high, the second and third as low as possible.

vi) **Measuring the innovation and learning perspective**

The innovation and learning perspective could be measured with one of the following indicators.

- Turnover from new products as a percentage of total turnover ((£1.56m/£3.9m) × 100% = 40%)

- Research and development expenditure as a percentage of cost of production ((£750,000/£930,000) × 100% = 81%)

- Research and development expenditure as a percentage of turnover ((£750,000/£3.9m) × 100% = 19.2%)

performance indicators: answers

19 a)

i) Gross profit margin $= \dfrac{£221,760}{£633,600} \times 100\% = 35\%$

ii) Net profit margin $= \dfrac{£76,032}{£633,600} \times 100\% = 12\%$

iii) Return on capital employed $= \dfrac{£76,032}{£95,040} \times 100\% = 80\%$

iv) Asset turnover $= \dfrac{£633,600}{£95,040} = 6.7 \text{ times}$

v) No. of passengers in the year $= \dfrac{\text{turnover}}{\text{fare per passenger}} = \dfrac{£633,600}{£1}$

$= 633,600 \text{ passengers}$

vi) Total cost per mile $= \dfrac{£633,600 - £76,032}{356,400} = £1.56$

vii) No. of journeys in the year $= \dfrac{356,400 \text{ miles}}{18 \text{ miles per journey}} = 19,800 \text{ journeys}$

No. of journeys per day $= \dfrac{19,800}{360} = 55 \text{ journeys}$

viii) Maintenance cost per mile $= \dfrac{£28,512}{356,400} = £0.08$

ix) Passengers per day $= \dfrac{633,600 \text{ (from v))}}{360} = 1,760 \text{ passengers}$

x) Passengers per journey $= \dfrac{1,760 \text{ (from(ix))}}{55 \text{ (from(vii))}} = 32 \text{ passengers}$

xi) Number of drivers $= \dfrac{\text{wages paid}}{\text{wages per driver}} = \dfrac{£142,000}{£14,200}$

b) **MEMO**

To: Chief executive
From: Management accountant
Date: xx.xx.xx
Subject: **Performance of Travel Bus Ltd for the year to 30 November 2006**

This memo addresses a number of issues concerning the productivity and profitability of Travel Bus Ltd.

i) **Productivity and profitability**

Productivity is the quantity of service produced (output) in relation to the resources put in (input). It measures how efficiently resources are being used.

An increase in productivity does not always lead to increased profitability. For example the number of passengers carried per driver, a measure of productivity, could increase. The extra passengers may have been attracted by offering substantial fare reductions, however, and this could lead to reduced profitability.

Another example might be an increase in productivity in terms of the number of journeys per bus. This increase in 'output' arising from the increase in productivity may not be saleable: the buses may be running empty. The revenue gained might be less than the additional costs incurred, leading to reduced profitability.

ii) **Driver productivity**

A possible measure of driver productivity is the number of miles per driver.

	2005	2006
Miles per driver	$\dfrac{324{,}000}{8} = 40{,}500$	$\dfrac{356{,}400}{10} = 35{,}640$

The number of miles per driver has decreased between 2005 and 2006 and so, in terms of this measure of productivity, the drivers' claim that their productivity has increased is incorrect.

Even if the productivity had increased the drivers might still be unable to claim that this had resulted in improved profitability. As discussed above, the extra miles might have been travelled with too few fare-paying passengers, so profitability would not necessarily have improved.

iii) **Reason for improved profitability**

A major reason for the improved profitability was the Council's decision not to charge for parking. This reduced the overall cost of using the service for passengers, and demand therefore increased considerably. Since many of the costs incurred by Travel Bus Ltd are fixed, costs did not increase at the same rate as turnover, and profitability improved.

iv) **Performance indicators to measure the satisfaction of passenger needs**

1) The satisfaction of passenger needs could be monitored by the number of passengers per journey.

	2005	2006
Number of passengers per journey	30	32

Depending on the size of the buses, passenger needs may have been less satisfied during 2006 because of more crowding or the need to stand because no seats were available.

Another measure of the satisfaction of passenger needs is the number of journeys per day.

	2005	2006
Number of journeys per day	50	55

This increase probably led to reduced waiting times and so passenger needs may have been better satisfied in 2006.

performance indicators: answers

2) A measure of the satisfaction of customer needs that cannot be derived from the existing data is cleanliness of the buses.

Monitoring the cleaning cost per day or per bus might give some indication of the effort put into keeping the buses clean.

Another measure of the satisfaction of customer needs **is punctuality** of the buses and their **adherence to published** timetables.

Monitoring the percentage of buses arriving and departing within five minutes of their published time would give an indication of performance in this area.

v) **Monitoring the safety aspect of Travel Bus's operations**

1) The safety aspect of Travel Bus's operations could be monitored by the maintenance cost per mile.

	2005	2006
Maintenance cost per mile	£0.10	£0.08

This has reduced, which may indicate a reduction in attention to safety, especially as maintenance costs are likely to increase as buses become older. No new buses have been added to the fleet (cost value of buses has remained at £240,000); the buses are older and likely to require more maintenance.

On the other hand, some of this reduction in the cost per mile may have been caused by the spreading of the fixed element of maintenance costs over a higher number of miles in the year 2006.

Another indicator of attention to the safety aspect might be the average age of the buses. The depreciation charge for the year 20X0 was £12,000 (£180,000 – £168,000). On a cost value of £240,000, assuming straight line depreciation and no residual value, this suggests a useful life of 20 years. Accumulated depreciation of £180,000 means that the buses were on average 15 years old by the end of 2006, and thus nearing the end of their useful lives.

2) A measure of the safety aspect that cannot be derived from the existing data is the number of accidents per year.

Another measure could be the percentage of maintenance cost that is incurred to prevent faults compared with the percentage incurred to correct faults. This would indicate whether faults were being prevented before they occurred, or whether maintenance was being carried out 'after the event', which could compromise safety.

20 a) i) **Sales (or net profit) margin** = (operating profit/turnover) x 100%
= (138/480) x 100% = 28.75%

ii) **Gross profit margin** = (gross profit/turnover) x 100%
= (270/480) x 100% = 56.25%

iii) **Asset turnover** = (turnover/net assets)
= (480/240) = 2 times

iv) **Return on capital employed** = (operating profit/net assets) x 100%
= (138/240) x 100% = 57.5%

v) **Average age of stocks** = (closing stock/cost of sales) x 12 months
= (140/210) x 12 months = 8 months

vi) **Average age of debtors** = (debtors/sales) x 12 months
= (40/480) x 12 months = 1 month

vii) **Added value per employee** = (turnover − cost of sales (as no bought-in services))/number of employees

= £(480 − 210)m/4,000 = £67,500

viii) **Average sales value per transaction** = turnover/number of transactions
= £480m/60 million = £8

ix) **Sales per employee** = turnover/number of employees
= £480m/4,000 = £120,000

x) **Transactions per employee** = number of transactions/number of employees

= 60 million/4,000 = 15,000

xi) **Sales per square metre** = turnover/square metres of floor space
= £480m/200,000 = £2,400

b) i) **Meaning of productivity and efficiency**

1) **Productivity**

Productivity is a measure of output relative to some sort of input.

- The output might be socks, cars, meals served in a restaurant, calls answered in a customer service department and so on.
- The input might be the workforce, machines or raw materials.

Productivity measures compare the output achieved from a certain amount of input. Here are some examples.

- Number of customers served per employee per day
- Number of components produced per machine per month
- Number of hotel rooms occupied as a percentage of rooms available.

Input or output or both can also be expressed in financial terms. So other measures of productivity include:

- Number of litres of chemical X produced per £ of labour
- Revenue per employee
- Revenue per £ of labour

Asset turnover (turnover/assets) is a commonly-used measure of productivity, with both input and output expressed in financial terms. It gives an indication of how well the assets of the business (the input) are being used to generate sales (the output).

2) **Efficiency**

Efficiency also looks at output relative to input, but it is not the same as productivity because the output is considered in terms of financial gain or value to the organisation. If the value of the output is greater than the value of the input, the operation is efficient. The greater the difference between the values of the input and output, the greater the efficiency.

In most organisations, the value generated is normally some sort of profit.

Return on capital employed is one of the major measures of efficiency in organisations with an objective to earn profit. It measures the efficiency with which managers have used resources under their control (capital employed) to generate profit.

ii) **Reasons for a difference in the net book value of the fixed assets of the two companies**

1) With rising prices, the older an asset, the lower its initial cost. Even with the same depreciation policies and rates, the older asset will have a lower net book value.

    Both companies depreciate their leasehold buildings over fifty years (£500m/£10m for Alderton Ltd, £200m/£4m for Brandon Ltd). The average age of Alderton Ltd's buildings is 10 years (given that annual depreciation is £10m and total depreciation to date is £100m). The average age of Brandon Ltd's buildings is 46 years, however (given that annual depreciation is £4m and total depreciation to date is £184m).

2) If two assets have the same initial cost and the same depreciation policy and rate is applied to each, but one is older than the other, the older asset will have been depreciated more and so will have a lower net book value. The net book value of Brandon Ltd's leasehold buildings is only 8% of the initial cost, whereas that of Alderton is 80% of initial cost.

3) The use of different depreciation rates will affect net book values. Brandon Ltd depreciates its fixtures and fittings over ten years (£80m/£8m), whereas Alderton Ltd depreciates over five years (£200m/£40m).

iii) **How the difference in net book value of Alderton's fixed assets affects return on capital employed**

1) Alderton Ltd has newer assets and hence their net book value is likely to be higher than for companies such a Brandon Ltd with older assets. This will increase net assets and hence reduce return on capital employed.

- 2) Even with the same depreciation policies, the depreciation charge on newer assets is likely to be higher than that on older assets because of the higher initial cost. A higher annual depreciation charge will reduce Alderton Ltd's profit and hence reduce return on capital employed.

- 3) Different depreciation rates will affect the depreciation charge against profit. Alderton Ltd depreciates its fixtures and fittings over a shorter period of time than Brandon Ltd, and so its annual depreciation charge will be higher, thereby reducing profit and return on capital employed.

iv) Likely effect of first in, first out (FIFO) and last in, first out (LIFO) stock valuation policies on operating profits

During the twelve months to 31 May 2006, the cost of purchases has been falling. Using a FIFO valuation basis, cost of sales will reflect the earlier, more expensive purchases while closing stock will reflect the more recent, cheaper purchases. The reverse is true if LIFO is used.

Alderton Ltd's operating profit is therefore lower than it would have been if it had used LIFO, and its closing stock valuation (and hence its net assets) is lower than it would have been.

The reverse situation applies to Brandon Ltd, which would have reported lower operating profit and lower net assets if it had used FIFO instead of LIFO.

v) Limitations of using added value per employee as a measure of employee productivity

Measures of employee productivity compare the output received from a certain amount of input from employees. In this instance the output is value added, which is sales value minus cost of purchased materials and bought-in services.

- 1) Improvements (or deteriorations) in value added may not be due to employees' efforts. Improvements to shop layouts or facilities may encourage more customers into the stores.

- 2) Some accounting policies influence the measure. For example, the stock valuation policy will affect cost of sales and hence value added.

vi) Alternative measures of employee productivity

The number of transactions per employee per day could be used to measure employee productivity as the number of transactions is a valid reflection of the level of employees' work effort. Sales revenue per employee per day could also be used.

answers to chapter 7: QUALITY

1 Quality could be described as the 'degree of excellence of the product or service' or 'how well the product or service serves its purpose'.

Quality is therefore judged by the customer. The product or service will only be perceived as having quality if it satisfies the customers' requirements. Therefore the product or service must have two main elements if it is to satisfy the customer and have quality:

- It must be fit for the purpose for which it has been acquired
- It must represent value for money to the customer

This does not mean that products or services need to be made more expensive by using better materials or more highly skilled staff. Provided that the product or service does what it is meant to do and is viewed as value for money to the customer then this product or service will have quality.

2 Prevention costs are the costs incurred with the aim of reducing substandard output to a minimum. They are the costs of actions taken to investigate, prevent or reduce defects in products or mistakes in services.

Examples of prevention costs are:

- improvements in product design or specification to reduce defective products
- improvements in systems designed to reduce mistakes in the provision of services
- design, development and maintenance of quality control or inspection equipment

Appraisal costs are the costs incurred in initially ascertaining how the product or service conforms to quality requirements. They are all of the costs associated with assessing the level of quality achieved.

Examples of appraisal costs are:

- inspection of goods and raw materials received
- inspection of production processes and work in progress
- inspection or performance testing of finished goods

Internal failure costs are the costs arising from inadequate quality identified before the goods or services are sold to the customer. Therefore they are costs arising within the organisation due to the failure to achieve the required level of quality.

Examples of internal failure costs are:

- investigation and analysis of failed units

- lost contribution on defective units scrapped or sold at a lower price than normal
- losses due to faults in raw materials purchased

External failure costs are costs arising from inadequate quality discovered after the goods or services have been sold to the customer.

Examples of external failure costs are:

- costs of running a customer service department
- product liability costs
- costs of replacing or repairing goods returned from customers

3

			Type of cost
	i)	Lost contribution on defective products sold as seconds	Internal failure
	ii)	Cost of replacing faulty products	External failure
	iii)	Claims from customers relating to defective products	External failure
	iv)	Products scrapped due to faulty raw materials	Internal failure
	v)	Training for quality control staff	Prevention
	vi)	Maintenance of quality control equipment	Prevention
	vii)	Performance testing of finished goods	Appraisal
	viii)	Costs of customer after sales service department	External failure
	ix)	Costs of inspection of raw materials	Appraisal
	x)	Costs of production delays due to re-working defective products discovered in quality inspection	Internal failure

4 i) New zipper design

Prevention costs – will have increased due to the costs of the design

Appraisal costs – no effect

Internal failure costs – these should be reduced as the product is more reliable

External failure costs – these should be reduced as the new zipper has a longer lifespan and will reduce returns of products

ii) Faulty jumpers

Prevention costs – no obvious effect

Appraisal costs – these will probably increase as machines should be checked regularly to ensure that this problem is not repeated

Internal failure costs – these will increase due to investigation of the failure, repairs to the machines which may cause disruption to the production process and re-inspection costs

External failure costs – any damages claims received from customers and the loss of these customers for future sales

iii) Flawed fabric

Prevention costs – finding a new supplier for the fabric

Appraisal costs – these will increase with the costs of inspection procedures

Internal failure costs
- the lost contribution from having to sell the suits at a lower price
- reduction of costs as the benefits of the inspection controls are felt

External failure costs – these should reduce as fewer defective products will be sold to customers

5 Explicit costs of quality are the costs of quality that can be identified and valued from the cost accounting records. Implicit costs are other types of cost which are not recorded in the accounting records and which can often only be estimated.

Examples of explicit costs are:

- costs of repairing defective products
- costs of quality control inspections
- costs of repair of returned goods from customers

Examples of implicit costs are:

- the opportunity cost of lost sales to customers who are dissatisfied due to faulty goods and will not purchase from the organisation again

- loss of goodwill or reputation due to factors such as the widespread recall of one of an organisation's products

- costs of production disruption due to reworking of faulty products – these costs will be included in the production costs but cannot be separately identified

6 Number of estimated defective goods 10 million/1,000 × 3 = 30,000 units

	£
Appraisal costs – quality inspections	35,000
Internal failure costs – lost contribution on sales of seconds 4,000 × (£15 – £11)	16,000
External failure costs – replacement cost 30,000 × £10 × 70%	210,000
	261,000

There are also implicit costs of the lost sales to customers who have purchased faulty products.

quality: answers

7

	£
Appraisal costs	60,000
Internal failure costs – lost contribution	
7,500 units x (£33 – £20)	97,500
Total quality cost	157,500

8

Cost of repair of returned goods	
8,000,000/6,000 x 75% x £10	£10,000 – external failure cost
Advertising cost	£5,000 – external failure cost
Lost customers	
8,000,000/6,000 x 25% = 333 units	Implicit cost, cannot be estimated – external failure cost

9

Quality inspection costs	£340,000	– appraisal cost – explicit
Lost contribution		
5,200 units x (£200 – 108)	£478,400	– internal failure cost – implicit
Replacement of defective units		
1,000,000/2,000 x 60% x £120	£36,000	– external failure cost – explicit
	£12,000	
Lost customers	–	– external failure cost – implicit

10

Under traditional costing methods the costs of a product are only recorded and analysed once production of the product has begun. However, it is recognised that a large proportion of the costs of a product are incurred before production has started in the early stages of the product life cycle. Life cycle costing recognises all of these pre-production costs of the product such as:

- design costs
- prototyping
- programming
- process design
- equipment acquisition

The aim of life cycle costing is to ensure that all the costs of the product are accumulated over the whole of its life cycle in order to ensure that all costs are covered by revenue from the product.

quality: answers

11 a) The four general headings making up the cost of quality are as follows.

   i) Prevention costs
   ii) Appraisal costs
   iii) Internal failure costs
   iv) External failure costs

b) Examples of types of cost likely to be found in each category are as follows.

   i) Prevention costs. Maintenance of quality control and inspection equipment, training in quality control

   ii) Appraisal costs. Inspection of goods inwards, inspection costs of in-house processing

   iii) Internal failure costs. Losses from failure of purchased items, losses due to lower selling prices for sub-quality goods

   iv) External failure costs. Costs of customer complaints section, cost of repairing products returned from customers

c) Implications for the existing costing system

   i) If there are fixed price contracts with guaranteed levels of quality there are likely to be few, if any, material price variances or material usage variances due to poor quality.

   ii) The cost of labour will effectively become a fixed cost, the actual unit cost of labour simply depending on the volume produced. Labour efficiency variances could therefore be calculated but they will not reflect costs saved or excess wages paid. Labour rate variances are likely to be minimal if there is a guaranteed weekly wage.

   iii) Predetermined standards conflict with the TQM philosophy of continual improvement.

   iv) Continual improvements should alter prices, quantities of inputs and so on, whereas standard costing systems are best used in stable, standardised, repetitive environments.

   v) Standard costing systems often incorporate a planned level of scrap in material standards. This is at odds with the TQM aim of 'zero defects'.

   Results of these implications

   i) There is less need for a standard costing system: variances are likely to be small or non-existent and, if incurred, non-controllable; the use of standards is inappropriate in a TQM environment.

   ii) With the flexible work practices, capture of actual labour costs by individual jobs would be very difficult. Only material costs could be collected in the normal way. It is therefore unlikely that the full marginal cost of individual jobs could be collected.

d) A cost saving not recorded in the existing costing system

With the introduction of a system of just-in-time, the cost of having money tied up in high levels of stocks will be saved. This cost would not normally be captured by Barnet Ltd's existing costing system.

quality: answers

12 a) Background paper for meeting on 7 July 20X8

To: Jane Greenwood, Management Accountant
From: Assistant Management Accountant
Subject: Total quality management and the cost of quality
Date: 30 June 20X8

i) **The meaning of Total Quality Management**

Total Quality Management (TQM) is a philosophy that guides every activity within a business. It is concerned with developing and sustaining a culture of continuous improvement which focuses on meeting customers' expectations.

One of the basic principles of TQM is therefore a dissatisfaction with the status quo: the belief that it is always possible to improve and so the aim should be to 'get it more right next time'. This involves the development of a commitment to quality by all staff and a programme of continuous learning throughout the entire organisation, possibly by empowering employees and making them responsible for the quality of production or by introducing quality circles.

The customer-centred approach of TQM hinges upon identifying the 'customers', focusing attention on them and then meeting their needs in terms of price, quality and timing. Organisations must therefore be customer orientated rather than, as is traditionally the case, production orientated.

One of the goals of TQM is to get it right first time. By continuously improving towards zero defects, the quality of the product delivered to the customer is improved. The quality of output depends on the quality of materials input, however, and so either extensive quality control procedures are needed at the point where goods are accepted and inspected or quality assurance schemes, whereby the supplier guarantees the quality of the goods supplied, must be in place.

A small proportion of mistakes are inevitable in any organisation but more often than not those mistakes have been 'designed' into the production process. Because TQM aims to get it right first time, however, quality and not faults must be designed into an organisation's products and operations from the outset. Quality control must therefore happen at the production design and production engineering stages of a product's life, as well as actually during production.

In summary, TQM involves getting it right first time and improving continuously.

ii) **Failure of the current accounting system to highlight the cost of quality**

Traditionally, the costs of scrapped units, wasted materials and reworking have been subsumed within the costs of production by assigning the costs of an expected level of loss (a normal loss) to the costs of good production, while accounting for other costs of poor quality within production or marketing overheads. Such costs are therefore not only considered as inevitable but are not highlighted for management attention. Moreover, traditional accounting reports tend to ignore the hidden but real costs of excessive stock levels (held to enable faulty material to be replaced without hindering production) and the facilities necessary for storing that stock.

iii)/iv) **Explicit costs of quality**

There are four recognised categories of cost identifiable within an accounting system which make up the cost of quality.

1) Prevention costs are the costs of any action taken to investigate, prevent or reduce the production of faulty output. Included within this category are the costs of training in quality control and the cost of the design/development and maintenance of quality control and inspection equipment.

2) Appraisal costs are the costs of assessing the actual quality achieved. Examples include the cost of the inspection of goods delivered and the cost of inspecting production during the manufacturing process.

3) Internal failure costs are the costs incurred by the organisation when production fails to meet the level of quality required. Such costs include losses due to lower selling prices for sub-quality goods, the costs of reviewing product specifications after failures and losses arising from the failure of purchased items.

4) External failure costs are the costs which arise outside the organisation (after the customer has received the product) due to failure to achieve the required level of quality. Included within this category are the costs of repairing products returned from customers, the cost of providing replacement items due to sub-standard products or marketing errors and the costs of a customer service department.

v) **Quality costs not identified by the accounting system**

Quality costs which are not identified by the accounting system tend to be of two forms.

1) Opportunity costs such as the loss of future sales to a customer dissatisfied with faulty goods.

2) Costs which tend to be subsumed within other account headings such as those costs which result from the disruption caused by stockouts due to faulty purchases.

b) i) **Explicit cost of quality**

	£
Reworking (labour cost)	13,500
Customer support (contractors)	24,300
Store inspection costs	10,000
Cost of returns	4,500
	52,300

ii) **Cost of quality not reported in the accounting records**

Opportunity cost (lost contribution from 100 X4s due to faulty circuit board) = £795 (W1) x 100 = £79,500.

quality: answers

Workings

			£
1	Labour (W2)		200
	Printed circuit board (£120,000 ÷ 1,000)		120
	Other material (£121,500 ÷ 900)		135
	Marginal cost		455
	Selling price		(1,250)
	Contribution		795

		£
2	Total labour cost	193,500
	Less: cost of reworking	(13,500)
		180,000

Unit cost per good unit = £180,000 ÷ 900 = £200

answers to chapter 8:
BUDGETARY CONTROL SYSTEMS

1 a) A budget is a formalised, numerical plan of action for all areas of a business for the forthcoming period, normally set for the next twelve month period.

b) A budgetary control system can help management to perform their duties and carry out their responsibilities in two main areas.

One of the roles of management is in terms of planning for the business – both long term strategic plans and shorter term operational plans. Budgets are formal, numerical plans which can help to ensure that all areas of the business are aiming at the same goals. For example, if the sales demand for the product is the key budget factor, by setting manufacturing budgets management can ensure that these are in line with the sales budget. It would be bad management to produce 100,000 units of a product if only 60,000 units of the product are likely to be sold in the forthcoming period.

A further example would be that, once the sales and manufacturing budgets are set, management can then ensure that the budgets for other areas of the business such as the canteen and the sales department are in line with these budgets. So, for example, if it is budgeted that there will be 200 factory workers each day then the canteen should not be budgeting to buy food for 400. Or if sales are expected to be 60,000 units in the period it is important that the sales department budgets in order to be able to deal with this level.

A further important role of management is that of control of operations and of costs in particular. A budgetary system can assist in this area as the eventual actual results can be compared to the budgeted figures and any variances can be calculated and investigated. Where necessary management can then take corrective action to deal with these variances from planned costs.

2 a) The strategic plans of a business are the long-term plans of the business. These plans will be based upon the strategic objectives of the management of the business which may concern maximisation of profitability, increase of market share, growth by acquisition of other businesses or expansion of the product range. Once the strategic objectives have been determined then the strategic plans are the long term plans of how the business is to meet these objectives.

Once the strategic plan is in place then the management can look at shorter term plans necessary in order to meet the strategic objectives of the business. These are the operational plans and will take a variety of forms such as plans for the purchase of fixed assets, plans for the amount of production and plans for the financing of the business. All of these plans take the form of budgets.

b) When a business is started then the management must determine a long-term plan of how the business is to be operated and where its future lies. This will mean that the senior management of the business must determine the strategic objectives of the business. The strategic plan will remain in place for the life of the business but may be altered from time to time as circumstances change or opportunities become available.

The strategic plan shows where the business is going but the next stage of the planning process is to determine how the business is going to get there. This will involve a detailed review of the business both from an internal and external perspective in order to decide what possible strategies there are in order to move the business closer to the strategic objective.

Information will need to be gathered about all of the resources of the business, the state of its products or services and the amount of finance that is available. External information about the market, competitors and the general economic environment will also be required. This detailed review of the position of the business is often called a SWOT analysis, a review of the strengths, weaknesses, opportunities and threats to the business.

Once this analysis has been carried out, management will be in a position to identify the various strategies that are available to the organisation, such as marketing a new product or concentrating on the production of its current products.

Once the various available strategies have been identified then the management will be in a position to choose which strategy is the most suitable and has the greatest potential for achieving the overall strategic objective. When the strategies for the future have been chosen then they can be co-ordinated into the strategic plan for the business.

Once the strategic plan is in place then the management can look at shorter term plans necessary in order to meet the strategies chosen for the business, the operational plans.

3   A capital budget details the timing and value of the purchases of fixed assets. This is important for a number of reasons.

- The purchase of fixed assets will normally be the most significant outgoing of a business and therefore it is important that such major purchases are properly planned.

- The purchase of fixed assets will normally be costly and it is therefore important that appropriate finance is available at the precise time that it is required.

- Fixed assets are frequently fundamental to the production and processes of an organisation therefore it is vital that fixed assets are fully functioning and are replaced or updated at the appropriate time.

4 Resource budgets are those that deal with all aspects of the short term operations of the business. The resource budgets will include:

Production budget – this is a budget for the number of units that it is planned to produce during the forthcoming period – this will be based upon the key budget factor which is frequently the sales demand which will be forecast in the sales budget.

Materials usage budget – this is based upon the production budget and is a budget for the estimated quantity of materials that is to be used in the forthcoming period.

Materials purchases budget – this is the amount of raw materials that must be purchased each period to satisfy the production and stock demands and will be expressed in both units and monetary amounts. These figures will be based upon the materials usage budget.

Labour usage budget – this is based upon the production budget and is an estimate of the labour hours required during the period to meet the production figures. The production budget will be the starting point for determining the labour usage budget.

Labour cost budget – this is based upon the labour usage budget and is the monetary cost of the labour hours required for the period including any overtime.

Machine hours budget – this is based upon the production plans and shows the number of hours that the machinery must be working in order to produce the required level of production. The figures can be calculated using the quantity of production from the production budget.

Variable overheads budget – this will be based upon the production budget as the variable overheads will vary with the amount of production. Therefore the production budget will provide the quantities of production which can then be used to determine the variable overheads expected to be incurred.

Fixed overheads budget – this is independent of the level of production as this should not affect the amount of fixed overheads. Therefore the budget for fixed overheads will be based upon estimates of fixed overhead costs and previous experience.

There may also be sundry other resource budgets such as the selling and distribution costs budget, advertising budget and the administration budget which will again all be set within the context of the sales budget.

5 a) The key budget factor is the element or resource of the business that is likely to be the one that places limitations on the activities of the business. It is unlikely in a business that it will be able to produce and sell an unlimited number of its products. There will normally be one factor at least that will limit the quantity of sales and/or production. The importance of the key budget factor is that as it places a limit on all of the other operations of the business then the forecast for the key factor must be made first and all other budgets will be based upon this one.

The most common key budget factor is that of sales demand. Therefore the sales forecast must be made first and the production budget will then be based upon the forecast sales levels.

budgetary control systems: answers

b) Any three of the following:
- limitations on the amount of raw materials that can be purchased
- manpower limitations – a limit to the number of hours that can be worked in the period by the labour force
- capacity limitations – a limit to the number of machine hours available
- a limit to the quantity that can be produced by a production line in the period

6   i)   There would appear to be no limits regarding demand for beds or the labour force. The key budget factor would seem to be the number of beds available.

    ii) In a busy shopping centre demand for the ice cream is probably not the key factor therefore it is likely to be the quantity of ice cream that can be stored each day.

    iii) Sales demand is not a limiting factor however as this is highly skilled work the available hours of the three partners will be the key budget factor.

    iv) As the products are similar to those of other manufacturers and therefore can be replaced by similar products by the retail stores then it is highly likely that the demand from the retail stores will be the key budget factor.

7   i)   The budget manual is a set of detailed instructions as to how the budget is to be prepared. The budget manual might typically include the following:
    - the names of the budget holders – those responsible for producing each budget
    - to whom each budget holder reports
    - an organisation chart
    - the timescale for the production of each budget
    - the procedures for preparing each budget
    - the format of the budgets
    - how and when actual performance is compared to budget

    ii) The budget committee is responsible for co-ordinating and administering all of the individual budgets and will review and authorise each individual budget. The budget committee will normally be made up of senior executives and each function of the business should be represented on the budget committee in order to ensure that there is full communication between all areas of the business. The budget committee will normally be assisted by an accountant known as the budget officer.

    iii) Budget holders are the managers within a business that are responsible for preparing each resource budget. In most cases the budget holder should be the manager who will also be responsible for ensuring that the activities meet the budget.

    iv) The master budget is the final overall budget for all areas of the business. It is normally set out in the form of a budgeted profit and loss account, budgeted balance sheet and cash flow budget.

8 The budgeting process starts with the setting of the budget (forecast) for the key budget factor. This will frequently be the sales budget although if manufacturing resources are the key budget factor this may be the labour budget or machine hours budget. Once the key budget factor budget has been set then the production budget will be set by the production manager and the various other resource budgets set by the relevant budget holders.

Once the budget holder has drafted his budget then he will submit this to the budget committee. The budget officer will ensure that the budget is consistent with the other resource budgets checking, for example, that it has been prepared in line with the production budget.

There will then frequently be negotiations between the budget committee and the budget holder regarding the detailed content of the budget. The manager might for example have built in an increase in costs over previous years which the budget committee does not agree with. The budget holder may well have to change his draft budget and re-submit it to the budget committee a number of times before the budget committee is satisfied with it.

Once the budget committee have agreed all of the resource budgets with the budget holders then they will be formed into the master budget.

9 A rolling budget is one which is constantly being updated and added to. It will be set in detail for the next short accounting period and in outline for the remainder of the 12 month period. As each accounting period passes the details of the next period's budget are produced and the budget extended to maintain a 12 month coverage.

For example if budgets are set for each of 13 four week periods in a year initially the detailed budget will be set for period 1 and the remaining 12 periods' budgets will be in outline. Towards the end of period 1 the detail for period 2's budget will be set and the outline budget for period 1 of the following year added.

The benefits of a rolling budget are that the detailed budgeting only has to be performed for the next accounting period rather than for periods a long time in advance therefore the budget is potentially more accurate. It also means that when setting the detail of each period's budget the budget holder can react to changes in circumstances that are revealed by comparison of the actual figures for each period to the budgeted figures.

10 i) Incremental budgeting is one of the most common methods in practice of setting budgets. Under this method the budget for the forthcoming period is set by taking the previous period's budget and adding a percentage to reflect any increases in prices since the last budget was set or any increase in activity level.

ii) Zero based budgeting is a method of budgeting that looks at the costs of each cost centre from scratch for each period. Each cost is then considered in the context of the production budget and the amount of each cost must then be specifically justified and not just included in the budget because if was in last year's budget.

budgetary control systems: answers

For each item of activity which causes a cost the following types of questions must be asked:

- is the activity necessary?
- are there alternatives to this activity?
- what are the costs of the alternative?
- what would happen if the activity were not carried out?
- is the expense of the activity worth the benefit?

By asking such questions the activity and its related costs can either be justified for inclusion in the budget or a cheaper alternative found.

iii) Activity based budgeting is a system of setting budgets based upon Activity Based Costing principles. Under this method of budgeting the costs that are incurred by each activity are budgeted for rather than the costs of individual cost centres. For example, a budget might be set for the production set-up process or the quality control procedures rather than the factory cost centre as a whole.

11 Spreadsheet design to produce the labour requirements budget for August 2006

The labour requirements budget for August would be determined by the production budget, which is in turn dependent on the requirement for sales and stock. Consequently, there would be a 'cascade' approach.

Once the production requirement has been determined there would need to be an adjustment for the 10% defect rate. This would provide a figure for actual production required. This adjustment is complicated by the fact that whole units are required, and so a correction to bring the output up to the next complete unit may be necessary. This correction could be dispensed with in the interests of simplicity, however.

The next step would be to convert the actual production into labour hours by multiplying output by hours per unit. The hours per unit may well be contained in a data table to permit easy adjustment of the budget if production levels change.

The final step would be to convert the labour hours into money by reference to an hourly rate of pay. The hourly rate also could be located in the data table to permit easy amendment of the budget.

budgetary control systems: answers

A cell layout diagram is set out below.

	A	B	C	D	E	F	G	H
1	**Labour budget**							
2	**Data table**							
3	Closing stock as a proportion of following month's sales						0.5	
4	Defect rate						0.1	
5	Labour hours per unit						10	
6	Labour wage rate per hour						£8	
7								
8	Month					*August*	*September*	
9	Budgeted sales units					300	600	
10	Opening stock					= F9 * G3		
11	Closing stock					= G9 * G3		
12	Good production required					= F9 – F10 + F11		
13	Actual production in units after adjustment for defect rate					= F12 /(1–G4)		
14	Labour hours budget					= F13 * G5		
15	Wages budget					= F14 * G6		

279

answers to chapter 9:
FORECASTING INCOME

1   The general limitations of forecasting are:

    - the less historical data that is used the more unreliable the results of the forecast will be
    - the further into the future that the forecast considers the more unreliable it will become
    - forecast figures will often be based upon the assumption that current conditions will continue in the future. A trend of results may be based upon historical data, but you cannot always assume that the trend will continue in the future
    - if the forecast is based upon a trend there are always random elements or variations which cause the trend to change
    - the forecast produced from the historical data may be quite accurate but the actual future results may be very different from the forecast figures due to changes in the political, economic or technological environment within which the business operates

2

	Trend	Seasonal variation		Forecast
Quarter 2 ((122,000 – 6,000) x 1.035)	120,060	–8,000	=	112,060
Quarter 3 (120,060 x 1.035)	124,262	+12,000	=	136,262
Quarter 4 (124,262 x 1.035)	128,611	–10,000	=	118,611

3

	Trend		Seasonal variation		Forecast
Quarter 1	340,000	x	0.82	=	278,800
Quarter 2	345,000	x	1.21	=	417,450
Quarter 3	350,000	x	1.07	=	374,500
Quarter 4	355,000	x	0.90	=	319,500

forecasting income: answers

4

	Trend		Seasonal variation		Forecast
Quarter 1 (90,000/1.11) x 1.02)	82,703	x	0.69	=	57,065
Quarter 2 (82,703 x 1.02)	84,357	x	0.97	=	81,826
Quarter 3 (84,357 x 1.02)	86,044	x	1.23	=	105,834
Quarter 4 (86,044 x 1.02)	87,765	x	1.11	=	97,419

5

	Trend		Seasonal variation		Forecast
Quarter 1 (+ 4,500)	178,000	x	1.07	=	190,460
Quarter 2 (+ 4,500)	182,500	x	1.09	=	198,925
Quarter 3 (+4,500)	187,000	x	0.97	=	181,390
Quarter 4 (+ 4,500)	191,500	x	0.87	=	166,605

6 i)

	Actual	Four quarter moving average	Centred four quarter moving average	Seasonal variation TREND
2003				
Quarter 3	1,900			
Quarter 4	2,300			
2004		2,500		
Quarter 1	2,800		2,563	+237
		2,625		
Quarter 2	3,000		2,650	+350
		2,675		
Quarter 3	2,400		2,725	−325
		2,775		
Quarter 4	2,500		2,825	−325
2005		2,875		
Quarter 1	3,200		2,888	+312
		2,900		
Quarter 2	3,400		2,925	+475
		2,950		
Quarter 3	2,500		2,988	−488
		3,025		
Quarter 4	2,700		3,063	−363
		3,100		
2006				
Quarter 1	3,500			
Quarter 2	3,700			

ii)	Seasonal variation	Quarter 1	Quarter 2	Quarter 3	Quarter 4
	2004	+237	+350	−325	−325
	2005	+312	+475	−488	−363
		+549	+825	−813	−688
	Average	+275	+412	−406	−344
	Adjustment (63/4)	+15	+16	+16	+16
		+290	+428	−390	−328

iii) We can forecast the quarter 3 sales for 2006 by estimating the trend figure for that quarter and then applying the seasonal adjustment. The trend is increasing, however the rate of increase seems to have slowed in recent quarters. As an estimate therefore assume trend increase of say 65 units each quarter.

Trend 3,063 + 65 + 65 +65	3,258
Seasonal variation for quarter 3	−390
Forecast sales	2,868

iv) The forecast results may be different from the actual results if the trend changes in quarter 1 or 2 of 2006 and if the seasonal variation for quarter 3 is different from that predicted. The actual results could also be different to the forecast results due to any random factors that affect the sales for the quarter.

7   The main limitations of using time series analysis for forecasting are:

- unless the data used covers many years it is impossible to isolate the cyclical changes due to general changes in the economy

- the seasonal variations are an average of the seasonal variation for each period and again unless this is based on a large amount of historical data the figure could be misleading

- any random variations are ignored

- the trend and the seasonal variations are assumed to continue in the future in the same manner as in the past

- if the time series analysis is based upon historic value the figures will include past inflation which may not be an indication of the future amounts

forecasting income: answers

8 a) The product life cycle is generally thought to split naturally into five separate stages:

- development
- launch
- growth
- maturity
- decline

During the development and launch stage of the product's life there are large outgoings in terms of development expenditure, fixed assets necessary for production, the building up of stock levels and advertising and promotion expenses. It is likely that even after the launch sales will be quite low and the product will be making a loss at this stage.

If the launch of the product is successful then during the growth stage there will be fairly rapid increases in sales and a move to profitability as the costs of the earlier stages are covered. However, these sales increases are not likely to continue indefinitely.

In the maturity stage of the product demand for the product will probably start to slow down and become more constant. In many cases this is the stage where the product is modified or improved in order to sustain demand and this may then see a small surge in sales.

At some point in a product's life, unless it is a consumable item such as chocolate bars, the product will reach the end of its sale life, this is known as the decline stage. The market will have bought enough of the product and sales will decline. This is the point where the business should consider no longer producing the product.

b) If the future demand for a product is to be forecast using time series analysis it is obviously important that the stage in the product life cycle that has been reached is taken into account. For example, if the trend is based upon the growth stage whereas in fact the product is moving into the maturity stage then the trend would show an overly optimistic forecast for sales.

9 Maturity stage.

forecasting income: answers

10 i)

	A	B	C	D	E
1	Unit sales price - £	150			
2	Annual sales volume - units	180,000			
3	Seasonal variation	-14%	-28%	+20%	+22%
4		Quarter 1	Quarter 2	Quarter 3	Quarter 4
5	Seasonal variation - units	=(B2/4)*B3/100	=(B2/4)*C3/100	=(B2/4)*D3/100	=(B2/4)*E3/100
6	Quarterly volume - units	=(B2/4)+B5	=(B2/4)+C5	=(B2/4)+D5	=(B2/4)+E5
7	Quarterly sales - £	=B6*B1	=C6*B1	=D6*B1	=E6*B1

ii)

	A	B	C	D	E
1	Unit sales price - £	150			
2	Annual sales volume - units	180,000			
3	Seasonal variation - %	-14	-28	+20	+22
4		Quarter 1	Quarter 2	Quarter 3	Quarter 4
5	Seasonal variation - units	-6,300	-12,600	+9,000	+9,900
6	Quarterly volume - units	38,700	32,400	54,000	54,900
7	Quarterly sales - £	5,805,000	4,860,000	8,100,000	8,235,000

11 a) **Calculation of trend sales values from the regression line**

Quarter				
17		£(2,000,000 + (40,000 × 17))	=	£2,680,000
18		£(2,000,000 + (40,000 × 18))	=	£2,720,000
	or	£(2,680,000 + 40,000)	=	£2,720,000
19		£(2,720,000 + 40,000)	=	£2,760,000
20		£(2,760,000 + 40,000)	=	£2,800,000

Calculation of seasonally-adjusted sales

Quarter	Trend value £	Seasonal variation	Absolute variation £	(i) Forecast £	Percentage variation %	(ii) Forecast £
17	2,680,000	A	+350,000	3,030,000	+15	3,082,000*
18	2,720,000	B	+250,000	2,970,000	+10	2,992,000
19	2,760,000	C	-400,000	2,360,000	-15	2,346,000**
20	2,800,000	D	-200,000	2,600,000	-10	2,520,000

*   £2,680,000 x 115%
** £2,760,000 x 85%

285

forecasting income: answers

b) i)

Quarter	Actual £	Absolute forecast £	Residual error £	Percentage forecast £	Residual error £
17					
18	3,079,500	3,030,000	+49,500	3,082,000	−2,500
19	3,002,400	2,970,000	+32,400	2,992,000	+10,400
20	2,346,500	2,360,000	−13,500	2,346,000	+500
20	2,490,200	2,600,000	−109,800	2,520,000	−29,800

In each of the four quarters, the residual error associated with percentage seasonal variations is lower than that associated with absolute seasonal variations. On the basis of the sample of four quarters, the **percentage seasonal variations method appears to be the more accurate forecasting method**.

ii)

Quarter	Season	Trend £	Seasonal variation %	Forecast £
21	A	2,840,000*	+15	3,266,000
22	B	2,880,000	+10	3,168,000
23	C	2,920,000	−15	2,482,000
24	D	2,960,000	−10	2,664,000

*Trend for Q20 + £40,000

c) **Memorandum**

To: Managing Director
From: Assistant Management Accountant
Date: xx.xx.xx
Subject: **Forecasting, seasonal variations and seasonally-adjusted data**

I have recently tested a statistical software package which can be used for estimating demand for fuel oil. I set out below some information which you may find useful.

i) **Seasonal variations** are regular, predictable and consistent changes in recorded values due to different circumstances which affect results at different times of the year, on different days of the week, at different times of day or whatever. For oil distribution, it is likely that demand will be higher in winter than in summer and this is reflected in the seasonal variations for our organisation produced by the software package. The sales revenue in Quarter A, which includes the winter months, is 15% above the average quarterly sales revenue whereas the sales revenue in Quarter C, which includes the summer months, is 85% of the average quarterly sales revenue.

Seasonally-adjusted data is actual data from which seasonal variations (derived from historic data) have been removed, to leave a figure which might be taken to indicate the trend (if we assume that any random variations are negligible). For example, the estimated seasonal variations within the actual sales revenue for Quarter 17 = 15/115 x £3,079,500 = £401,674, say £402,000. Deducting this from the actual sales revenue leaves an underlying figure of £(3,079,500 − 402,000) = £2,677,500.

ii) The percentage seasonal variations method of seasonal adjustment might be more accurate than the absolute seasonal variations method because the trend in sales turnover is increasing over time. When a trend is increasing, it is likely that absolute seasonal variations are also increasing. The absolute seasonal variations method simply adds absolute and unchanging seasonal variations to the trend figures whereas the percentage seasonal variations method, by multiplying the increasing trend values by a constant factor, produces seasonal variations which increase in time with the trend in sales.

iii) There are a number of ways in which an understanding of seasonal variations and seasonally-adjusted data can help us to be more efficient. For example, it helps in stock control. If we are able to forecast demand we will not have to hold excessive stock. This helps cash flow in two ways.

1) It reduces cash tied up in stocks.
2) It minimises the interest charges on amounts owing to Star Fuels.

Accurate forecasts of demand will also enable us to forecast future profit levels more accurately.

iv) There are, however, a number of limitations to this forecasting technique

1) The use of the least squares regression equation assumes that there is a linear relationship between sales turnover and time.

2) The use of the equation also assumes that sales turnover is dependent only upon time. In reality it might depend on several other variables such as the actions of competitors or the state of the economy.

3) It assumes that what has happened in the past will provide a reliable guide for what will happen in the future. If, for example, a new competitor has entered the market, this will not be the case.

4) The data used was measured in monetary terms but part of any increase in sales turnover may be due to rising prices rather than increased demand. It might therefore be better to measure sales in litres rather than value.

5) The choice of a quarterly seasonal variation may be inappropriate. Forecasting on a weekly basis may be more suitable.

answers to chapter 10: FORECASTING EXPENDITURE

1 Total production $= \dfrac{129,000 \text{ kgs}}{5 \text{ kgs}}$

$= 25,800$ units

Monthly production $= \dfrac{25,800 \text{ kgs}}{12}$

$= 2,150$ units

2 a) Maximum shortage

	July	Aug	Sept	Oct	Nov	Dec
Requirement	4,800	4,300	4,100	4,900	4,200	5,000
Purchase	4,500	4,300	4,100	4,500	4,200	4,500
Shortfall	300	–	–	400	–	500

Total shortfall $= 300 + 400 + 500$

$= 1,200$ units

b) Purchasing plan

	July	Aug	Sept	Oct	Nov	Dec
Requirement	4,800	4,300	4,100	4,900	4,200	5,000
Purchase	4,500	4,500	4,500	4,500	4,500	4,500
Excess/(Shortfall)	(300)	200	400	(400)	300	(500)
Stock		200	600	200	500	–
Production	4,500	4,300	4,100	4,900	4,200	5,000

By purchasing the maximum available in August, September and November, even though it is not required, the shortages in October and December can be covered from materials held in stock. This leaves only the 300 kg shortage in July.

forecasting expenditure: answers

3 **a)** If the shortage is only temporary then there are a number of short-term solutions which could alleviate the problem.

- Using stocks of materials – the stocks of raw materials could be run down in order to maintain production and sales.

- Using stocks of finished goods – in order to maintain sales in the short-term finished goods stocks can be run down even though production levels are not as high as would be liked.

- Rescheduling purchases – if the amount of the raw material required is available in some periods but not in others then the raw materials purchases could be rescheduled to ensure that the maximum use is made of the available materials.

b) If the shortage is a long-term problem then the following are possible options for the business.

- Seeking an alternative supplier – this is an obvious solution but it may not always be possible to find another supplier who can supply the correct quality at an acceptable price.

- Finding an alternative material – in some instances a product can only be made from one particular material but it may be possible to adapt the design of the product and the manufacturing process in order to use a substitute material that is widely available.

- Manufacturing an alternative product – it may be possible to switch the production process to manufacture of an alternative product which uses a different material which is not in short supply.

- Buying in finished goods for resale – instead of producing the product it could be purchased in finished form from another producer who is not having the same problems with supply of the materials required. However this probably would lead to an under-utilisation of production resources and a major change in the organisation's strategy.

4 **a)**

	May	June	July	Aug	Sept	Oct
Material requirement	9,500	10,200	10,200	9,300	10,200	10,300
Potential shortage	–	200	200	–	200	300

Do not buy 10,000 kgs each month as this will lead to stocks that are not required. However buy enough in May and August to cover the potential shortages.

	May	June	July	Aug	Sept	Oct
Material requirement	9,500	10,200	10,200	9,300	10,200	10,300
Purchases	9,900	10,000	10,000	9,800	10,000	10,000
Stock	400	200	–	500	300	–
Production	9,500	10,200	10,200	9,300	10,200	10,300

b) No shortage

forecasting expenditure: answers

5 a) Total hours available (including overtime) = 12 x (38 + 8)
= 552 hours per week

Maximum production = 552/3
= 184 units

b) Possible solutions to this problem could be:

- increase the overtime worked – it may be possible to agree additional overtime with the employees in order to maintain production; however at 46 hours per week already this may not be an option here

- use sub-contractors – in some types of business it may be possible to use agency workers or to sub-contract the work in order to maintain production levels. This option is likely to be fairly costly

- use up finished goods stock – if production levels are lower than required to meet sales demand then for the short term sales can still be maintained by running down the finished goods stock. This is not, however, a long-term solution

- buying in finished goods stock – this could be an expensive option leaving factory capacity under-utilised and may have quality implications as well

- improving labour efficiency – this is not something that can be done quickly but with training over a period of time it may be possible to increase the number of employees with the skills required

6 Labour hours required = 1,860 units x 4 hours
= 7,440 hours

Labour hours available = 160 employees x 35 hours
= 5,600 hours

Overtime hours required = 7,440 – 5,600
= 1,840 hours

7 a) Hours of production line time = 2 shifts x 7 hours x 5 days x 2 production lines
= 140 hours

Maximum production = 140 hours x 30 units
= 4,200 units

b) If sales demand exceeds this maximum production level there are a number of options that could be considered.

- Introduce a third shift so that the production lines are in fact running for 21 hours a day.

- Lengthen the shift to, say, a 9 hour shift.

- Operate the factory for 6 or even 7 days a week.

- Speed up the production line so that more units are produced an hour.

forecasting expenditure: answers

8

	May £	June £	July £	Aug £	Sept £	Oct £
Production costs (production units x £10.50)	37,800	30,450	33,600	32,550	35,700	42,000
Selling costs (sales units x £3.80)	13,300	11,400	11,400	12,160	13,300	14,440

9

Quarter 1	£657,000 x 128.4/126.4	=	£667,396
Quarter 2	£692,500 x 131.9/126.4	=	£722,633

10 Variable production costs

		£
January	4,200 x £25 x 137.3/135.2	106,631
February	4,400 x £25 x 139.0/135.2	113,092
March	4,500 x £25 x 139.6/135.2	116,161
April	5,100 x £25 x 140.3/135.2	132,310
May	5,300 x £25 x 141.2/135.2	138,380
June	4,800 x £25 x 143.0/135.2	126,923

Variable selling costs

January	4,100 x £8 x 141.5/140.5	33,033
February	4,300 x £8 x 143.0/140.5	35,012
March	4,650 x £8 x 143.7/140.5	38,047
April	4,700 x £8 x 144.4/140.5	38,644
May	5,000 x £8 x 145.1/140.5	41,310
June	5,100 x £8 x 146.0/140.5	42,397

11

		£
Rent	£65,000 x 1.055	68,575
Insurance	£15,700 x 1.10	17,270
Power	£84,000 x 171.2/166.3	86,475
		172,320

forecasting expenditure: answers

12 i)

	Machine hours	Cost £
June (lowest)	14,200	285,000
August (highest)	15,200	300,000
Increase	1,000	15,000

Variable cost = £15,000/1,000 hours
= £15 per hour

ii)

	£
June	
Variable element £15 x 14,200 hours	213,000
Fixed element (bal fig)	72,000
Total cost	285,000

13 i)

	Activity level	Cost £
July (lowest)	63,000	608,000
September (highest)	76,000	699,000
Increase	13,000	91,000

Variable element = £91,000/13,000
= £7 per unit

	£
July	
Variable element £7 x 63,000 units	441,000
Fixed element (bal fig)	167,000
Total cost	608,000

ii) a) Production level of 74,000 units:

	£
Variable cost £7 x 74,000	518,000
Fixed cost	167,000
Total cost	685,000

b) Production level of 90,000 units:

	£
Variable cost £7 x 90,000	630,000
Fixed cost	167,000
Total cost	797,000

iii) The estimate for the 74,000 units of production is likely to be more accurate than the estimate for 90,000 units. Estimating the costs at 74,000 units is an example of interpolation, in that the estimate is being made for a production level that is within the range of production levels used to estimate the variable and fixed costs. 90,000 units of production is significantly higher than the levels of production used in estimating fixed and variable costs and therefore it is possible that the costs would behave differently at this level of production. This is an example of extrapolation.

forecasting expenditure: answers

14 a) y = a + bx

b) a is the point where the line intersects the vertical axis
b is the gradient of the line

c) a = the fixed element of the cost
b = the variable amount per unit/hour

15 Production costs = 138,000 + 6.4 x 105,000

= £810,000

16 Power costs:

		£
April	80,000 + 380,000 x 0.5	270,000
May	80,000 + 400,000 x 0.5	280,000
June	80,000 + 395,000 x 0.5	277,500
July	80,000 + 405,000 x 0.5	282,500
Aug	80,000 + 410,000 x 0.5	285,000
Sept	80,000 + 420,000 x 0.5	290,000

17 Month 1: sales trend = 3.1 + 0.9 x 25 (month 25)
= 25,600 units

Month 2: sales trend = 3.1 + 0.9 x 26
= 26,500 units

Month 3: sales trend = 3.1 + 0.9 x 27
= 27,400 units

18

	Trend		Seasonal variation		Estimate of actual
Quarter 1	400 + 105 x 13	=	1,765 – 175	=	1,590
Quarter 2	400 + 105 x 14	=	1,870 + 225	=	2,095
Quarter 3	400 + 105 x 15	=	1,975 + 150	=	2,125
Quarter 4	400 + 105 x 16	=	2,080 – 200	=	1,880

answers to chapter 11:
PREPARING BUDGETS

1

	Units
Sales	13,800
Less: opening stock (inventory)	(2,100)
Add: closing stock (inventory)	1,500
Production	13,200

2

	Units
Sales	200,000
Less: opening stock	(35,000)
Add: closing stock (70% x 35,000)	24,500
Production	189,500

3 Production required = 16,200 x 100/97
= 16,702 units

4 a) Production budgets

	Period 4 Units	Period 5 Units	Period 6 Units
Sales	10,800	11,500	11,000
Less: opening stock	(2,700)	(2,875)	(2,750)
Add: closing stock			
11,500 x 5/20	2,875		
11,000 x 5/20		2,750	
11,200 x 5/20			2,800
Good units required	10,975	11,375	11,050
Defective units			
10,975 x 4/96	457		
11,375 x 4/96		474	
11,050 x 4/96			460
Production	11,432	11,849	11,510

295

preparing budgets: answers

b)

	A	B	C	D	E
1		Period 4	Period 5	Period 6	Period 7
2	Sales - units	10,800	11,500	11,000	11,200
3	Opening stock	2,700	=B4	=C4	
4	Closing stock	=C2*0.25	=D2*0.25	=E2*0.25	
5	Good production	=B2-B3+B4	=C2-C3+C4	=D2-D3+D4	
6	Total production	=B5+ (B5*4/96)	=C5+ (C5*4/96)	=D5+ (D5*4/96)	

5   Materials usage:

	Kg
25,400 x 5kg	127,000
Add: wastage 127,000 x 10/90	14,112
Raw material required	141,112

6 a) Materials usage budget

    40,000 units x 5 kg = 200,000 kgs

  b) Materials purchases budget

	Kgs
Raw materials required	200,000
Less: opening stock	(30,000)
Add: closing stock (30,000 x 80%)	24,000
	194,000

7 a) Materials usage budget

	Period 1 Kg	Period 2 Kg	Period 3 Kg
Production x 8kg	256,000	280,000	320,000
Normal loss 256,000 x 20/80	64,000		
280,000 x 20/80		70,000	
320,000 x 20/80			80,000
Materials usage	320,000	350,000	400,000

preparing budgets: answers

Materials purchasing budget – units

	Period 1 Kg	Period 2 Kg	Period 3 Kg
Materials usage	320,000	350,000	400,000
Less: opening stock	(64,000)	(87,500)	(100,000)
Add: closing stock			
350,000 x 5/20	87,500		
400,000 x 5/20		100,000	
480,000 x 5/20			120,000
	343,500	362,500	420,000

Materials purchasing budget – value

	Period 1 Kg	Period 2 Kg	Period 3 Kg
343,500 kg x £2.50	858,750		
362,500 kg x £2.50		906,250	
420,000 kg x (£2.50 x 1.04)			1,092,000

b)

	A	B	C	D	E
1		Period 1	Period 2	Period 3	Period 4
2	Production - units	32,000	35,000	40,000	48,000
3	Usage before loss	=B2*8	=C2*8	=D2*8	=E2*8
4	Total usage	=B3*100/80	=C3*100/80	=D3*100/80	=E3*100/80
5	Opening stock	64,000	=B6	=C6	
6	Closing stock	=C4*5/20	=D4*5/20	=E4*5/20	
7	Purchases - units	=B4-B5+B6	=C4-C5+C6	=D4-D5+D6	
8	Purchases - £	=B7*2.5	=C7*2.5	=D7*2.5*1.04	

8   One unit requires   18 x 100/90   = 20 hours
    20 units require   20 x 20   = 400 hours

9   Standard hours 120,000 x 4   = 480,000 hours
    Actual hours 480,000 x 100/120   = 400,000 hours

preparing budgets: answers

10 Production budget

	Units
Sales	102,000
Less: opening stock	(17,000)
Add: closing stock (115,000 x 10/60)	19,167
Production	104,167

Labour usage budget

	Hours
Standard hours 104,167 x 5.5	572,919
Actual hours 572,919 x 100/95	603,073

11

	Period 1 £	Period 2 £	Period 3 £	Period 4 £
Sales budget	120,000	136,000	156,000	148,400

Production budget

	Units	Units	Units	Units
Sales	3,000	3,400	3,900	3,500
Less: opening stock	(600)	(680)	(780)	(700)
Add: closing stock				
3,400 x 4/20	680			
3,900 x 4/20		780		
3,500 x 4/20			700	
4,000 x 4/20				800
	3,080	3,500	3,820	3,600
Defective units				
3,080 x 3/97	96			
3,500 x 3/97		109		
3,820 x 3/97			119	
3,600 x 3/97				112
	3,176	3,609	3,939	3,712

Materials usage budget

	Kg	Kg	Kg	Kg
Production x 4kg	12,704	14,436	15,756	14,848
Normal loss (x 10/90)	1,412	1,604	1,751	1,650
Materials usage	14,116	16,040	17,507	16,498

preparing budgets: answers

Materials purchasing budget

	Kg	Kg	Kg	Kg
Materials usage	14,116	16,040	17,507	16,498
Less opening stock	(4,200)	(5,614)	(6,127)	(5,774)
Add closing stock				
16,040 x 7/20	5,614			
17,507 x 7/20		6,127		
16,498 x 7/20			5,774	
16,200 x 7/20				5,670
Purchases	15,530	16,553	17,154	16,394

Labour budget – hours

	Hours	Hours	Hours	Hours
Standard hours				
Production x 2	6,352	7,218	7,878	7,424
Idle time (hours x 20/80)	1,588	1,805	1,970	1,856
Total hours	7,940	9,023	9,848	9,280

Labour budget – £

	£	£	£	£
7,940 x £8	63,520			
8,000 x £8		64,000	64,000	64,000
1,023 x £12		12,276		
1,848 x £12			22,176	
1,280 x £12				15,360
	63,520	76,276	86,176	79,360

12 a) i) Production days = 12 x 5 = 60 days

    ii) Closing stock of finished goods:

        Aye = 1,500 x 5/60 = 125 units
        Bee = 2,400 x 5/60 = 200 units

    iii) Labour hours available before overtime

        = 12 weeks x 35 hours x 70 employees
        = 29,400 hours

preparing budgets: answers

b) i) Production budget

	Aye Units	Bee Units
Sales	1,500	2,400
Less opening stock	(160)	(300)
Add closing stock	125	200
	1,465	2,300
Faulty production		
1,465 x 2/98	30	
2,300 x 2.5/97.5		59
	1,495	2,359

ii) Materials purchases

	Kg
1,495 x 4kg	5,980
2,359 x 7kg	16,513
	22,493
Less opening stock	(2,800)
Add closing stock (22,493 x 6/60)	2,250
	21,943

Materials budget – value £219,430

iii) Labour budget – hours

	Hours
Standard hours	
Aye 1,495 x 10 hours	14,950
Bee 2,359 x 7 hours	16,513
	31,463

Labour budget – value

	£
29,400 hours x £8	235,200
2,063 hours x £12	24,756
	259,956

c) Cost savings

	Opening stock	Closing stock	Reduction	Saving £
Aye	160	125	35 x £6 =	210
Bee	300	200	100 x £7 =	700
Raw materials	2,800	2,250	550 x £2 =	1,100
				2,010

preparing budgets: answers

13 a) i) 1) Number of production days in quarter 1 = 12 weeks × 5 days = 60 days

2) Quarter 1 closing finished goods stock:
Exe = 8 days × (930 ÷ 60 per day) = 124 units
Wye = 9 days × (1,320 ÷ 60 per day) = 198 units

3) Quarter 1 labour hours available before overtime

= 12 weeks × 35 hours × 46 employees = 19,320 hours

ii) 1) Production budget for quarter 1, twelve weeks ending 24 March 2006

		Exe Units		Wye Units
Budgeted sales		930		1,320
Required closing stock (from (a))		124		198
Opening stock		172		257
Decrease in stock		(48)		(59)
Good production required		882		1,261
Failed product allowance (W)	(× 2/98)	18	(× 3/97)	39
Total production required		900		1,300

Working

Good production represents (100 − 2)% of total Exe production.
882 units = 98% of total production
Total production = 882/98 × 100%
Alternatively, allowance = 2/98 of 882 = 2/98 × 882

2) Material purchases budget for quarter 1, twelve weeks ending 24 March 2006

			Litres
Material required for production:	Exe (900 units × 6 litres)		5,400
	Wye (1,300 units × 9 litres)		11,700
			17,100
Required closing stock	(5 days × (17,100/60) litres per day)	1,425	
Opening stock		(1,878)	
Decrease in stock			(453)
Material purchases required			16,647
Value of material purchases required (× £15)			£249,70

301

preparing budgets: answers

3) **Production labour budget for quarter 1, twelve weeks ending 24 March 2006**

		Hours
Labour hours required for production:	Exe (900 units × 12 hours)	10,800
	Wye (1,300 units × 7 hours)	9,100
Total hours required		19,900
Labour hours available before overtime (from a)i)3))		19,320
Overtime hours required		580

Cost of budgeted labour hours

	£
Basic pay (19,900 hours × £6)	119,400
Overtime premium (580 hours × £1.80)	1,044
Total budgeted labour cost	120,444

iii)

	Opening stock	Closing stock	Stock reduction	Storage cost per quarter £ per unit	Saving £
Product Exe	172 units	124 units	48 units	4	192
Product Wye	257 units	198 units	59 units	5	295
Raw material	1,878 litres	1,425 litres	453 litres	1	453
Savings arising from changes in required stock levels					940

b) i)

	Q 1 Units	Q 2 Units	Q 3 Units	Q 4 Units
Quarterly sales before seasonal variations (20,000 ÷ 4)	5,000	5,000	5,000	5,000
Seasonal variations	(+20%) 1,000	(+30%) 1,500	(−10%) (500)	(−40%) (2,000)
Budgeted sales volume of Zed	6,000	6,500	4,500	3,000

ii)

	A	B	C	D	E	F
1		Unit selling price	£90			
2		Annual volume	20,000			
3		Seasonal variations	20%	30%	−10%	−40%
4			Quarter 1	Quarter 2	Quarter 3	Quarter 4
5		Seasonal variations (units)	= (C2/4) * C3	= (C2/4) * D3	= (C2/4) * E3	=(C2/4) * F3
6		Quarterly volume	= (C2/4)+C5	= (C2/4)+D5	= (C2/4)+E5	= (C2/4)+F5
7		Quarterly turnover	= C6 * C1	= D6 * C1	= E6 * C1	= F6 * C1

c) **Step 1. Confirm that material is a limiting factor**

	Litres
Material requirements	
Exe (1,120 × 6)	6,720
Wye (1,480 × 9)	13,320
	20,040
Available supplies	18,870
Shortfall	1,170

Step 2. Identify the contribution earned per unit of limiting factor.

The limiting factor is material and so we need to calculate, for each of the products, the contribution earned per unit for each litre of material used in the product.

	Exe	Wye
	£	£
Selling price	360	420
Variable cost	240	258
Unit contribution	120	162
Litres required per unit	6	9
Contribution per litre of material	£20	£18
Priority for production	1	2

Although Wyes have a higher unit contribution than Exes, Wyes require 50% more material that Exes. Because material is in short supply, it is more profitable to make Exes than Wyes.

Step 3. Work out the profit-maximising sales and production mix

Sufficient Exes will be made to meet the full sales demand, and the remaining litres available will then be used to make Wyes.

preparing budgets: answers

Product	Demand Units	Litres required	Litres available	Units produced
Exe	1,120	6,720 (W1)	6,720	1,120
Wye	1,480	13,320 (W2)	12,150 (W3)	1,350 (W4)
		20,040	18,870	

Workings

1. Demand x 6
2. Demand x 9
3. 18,870 – 6,720
4. 12,150 litres/ 9 litres per unit

Given the limited availability of material, production in quarter 4 should be 1,120 units of Exe and 1,350 units of Wye.

14 a) i) Gross production budget

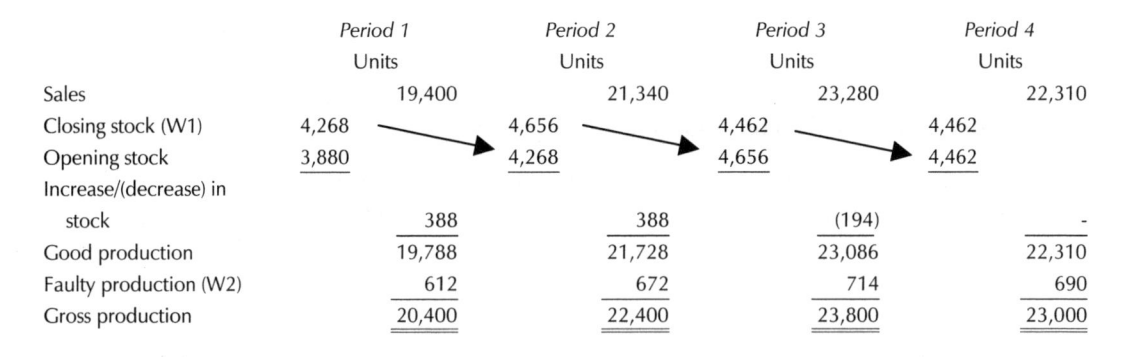

	Period 1 Units	Period 2 Units	Period 3 Units	Period 4 Units
Sales	19,400	21,340	23,280	22,310
Closing stock (W1)	4,268	4,656	4,462	4,462
Opening stock	3,880	4,268	4,656	4,462
Increase/(decrease) in stock	388	388	(194)	-
Good production	19,788	21,728	23,086	22,310
Faulty production (W2)	612	672	714	690
Gross production	20,400	22,400	23,800	23,000

Workings

1. There are 4 x 5 days in each period.

   Closing stock = 4 days' sales in the next period = 4/20 of next period's sales
   Closing stock in period 1 = 4/20 x 21,340 = 4,268
   Closing stock in period 2 = 4/20 x 23,280 = 4,656
   Closing stock in period 3 = 4/20 x 22,310 = 4,462
   Closing stock in period 4 = 4/20 x 22,310 = 4,462

2. 3% of gross production is scrapped. Good production therefore represents 97% (or 97/100) of gross production. Faulty production is 3% (or 3/100) of gross production and hence 3/97 of good production.

   Faulty production is 3/97 x good production.

ii) Material purchases budget

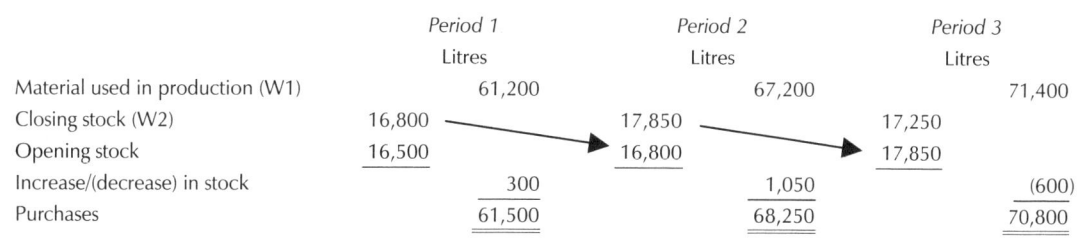

	Period 1 Litres	Period 2 Litres	Period 3 Litres
Material used in production (W1)	61,200	67,200	71,400
Closing stock (W2)	16,800	17,850	17,250
Opening stock	16,500	16,800	17,850
Increase/(decrease) in stock	300	1,050	(600)
Purchases	61,500	68,250	70,800

Workings

1. Each Gamma requires three litres of material.

   Material used in production = 3 × gross production (from a)i))
   Material used in production, period 1 = 3 × 20,400 = 61,200
   Material used in production, period 2 = 3 × 22,400 = 67,200
   Material used in production, period 3 = 3 × 23,800 = 71,400

2. - As we have already worked out, there are 20 days in each period.
   - Closing stock must equal five days' gross production in the next period.
   - Each Gamma requires three litres of material.
   - Closing stock in period 1 = 5/20 × 22,400 (from a)i)) × 3 = 16,800
     Closing stock in period 2 = 5/20 × 23,800 × 3 = 17,850
     Closing stock in period 3 = 5/20 × 23,000 × 3 = 17,250

iii) Cost of material purchases

	Period 1	Period 2	Period 3
Material to be purchased (from a)ii))	61,500 litres	68,250 litres	70,800 litres
Cost per litre	× £8	× £8	× £8
Cost of material purchases	£492,000	£546,000	£566,400

iv) Labour budget

	Period 1	Period 2	Period 3
Gross production (units) (from a)i))	20,400	22,400	23,800
Labour hrs required per unit	× 0.5	× 0.5	× 0.5
Labour hrs required	10,200	11,200	11,900
Basic labour hrs available *	11,200	11,200	11,200
Surplus hrs/(overtime hrs)	1,000	–	(700)

* 70 workers × 40 hrs per wk × 4 wks = 11,200

preparing budgets: answers

v) **Cost of labour budget**

	Period 1 £	Period 2 £	Period 3 £
Labour cost per period (guaranteed) *	67,200	67,200	67,200
Cost of overtime (700 × £9)	–	–	6,300
Cost of labour	67,200	67,200	73,500

* 70 workers x £240 x 4 wks

b) **Memo**

To: Production director
From: Management accountant
Date: xx.xx.xx
Subject: **Budget 2006 – overtime and faulty production**

I have investigated the points you raised about the budget for 2006 and have set out my findings below.

i) **The value of possible overtime savings**

In period 3, 700 hours of overtime are needed to produce the required number of units. There are 1,000 surplus labour hours available in period 1, however. If an extra 1,400 units (700 hrs ÷ 0.5 hrs) were produced in period 1, using 700 of the surplus hours available, the need for overtime in period 3 would be removed and £6,300 (£9 overtime rate x 700 hrs) saved.

ii) **Extra costs to achieve overtime savings**

The extra 1,400 units produced in period 1 are not needed until period 3 and so would need to be stored until then. This would incur additional storage costs.

The cost of the raw materials for the extra units produced in period 1 will not be covered by the sales revenue from the units until period 3 at the earliest. Additional financing may therefore be required to purchase this raw material, with the result that the company incurs financing costs.

iii) **Advantages of using sampling to determine reasons for faulty production**

Instead of checking every Gamma produced to see whether or not it is faulty, a sample of Gammas can be inspected. This has a number of advantages.

1) It is likely to be cheaper to inspect a sample of Gammas rather than all those produced.

2) Inspection of all production would be extremely time-consuming and would slow down the time between the start of production and the transfer to finished goods.

3) Inspection may sometimes require destruction of the item in question. For example, testing fireworks involves setting them off.

iv) **Differences between various methods of sampling**

1) **Random sampling** involves selecting a sample (of Gammas in this instance) in such a way that every item in the population (ie all Gammas produced) has an equal chance of being included. Random samples are drawn up by listing all items in the population (sampling frame), numbering them and then selecting items using random number tables or random numbers generated by computer.

2) **Systematic sampling** can provide a good approximation to random sampling. It works by selecting every nth item after a random start. For example, if it was decided to select a sample of 20 from a population of 800, then every 40th (800 ÷ 20) item after a random start in the first 40 should be selected. If (say) 23 was chosen, the sample would include the 23rd, 63rd, 103rd, 143rd, …, 783rd items.

3) **Stratified sampling** can often be the best method of choosing a sample (although it must be possible to divide the population into strata or categories for stratified sampling to be applied).

Suppose we wanted to know whether the area of a particular country in which students live has any bearing on their success in the AAT exams. If we took a random sample of all AAT students in the country, it is conceivable that the entire sample might consist of AAT students living in one particular region. Stratified sampling removes this possibility.

If the country's population of AAT students is divided into categories depending on where they live, random samples of students can be taken from each area of the country, the number in each sample being proportional to the total number of students in each category. So if there are 50,000 AAT students in the country in total, and 5,000 live in the north-west area, 10% of the sample should be chosen (randomly) from those living in the north-west.

v) **The form of sampling appropriate for our company**

Given that the faulty Gammas are thought to be caused by poor work practices of some of the production workers, those production workers need to be identified. It is therefore important to sample the work of every employee. By dividing the population of Gammas into categories based on the production worker who manufactured them, and applying **stratified sampling**, work of every employee would be inspected.

preparing budgets: answers

15 a) i) Production = sales + closing stock − opening stock.

Production budget for Antelopes for the four weeks ending 26 July 2006

		Units
Sales		141,120
Closing stock (W1)	42,336	
Opening stock	(30,576)	
Increase in stock		11,760
Good production required		152,880
Faulty production (W2)		3,120
Gross production		156,000

Workings

1   Demand in period 9 = 141,120 × 150% = 211,680
    Number of days in period 9   = 4 × 5 = 20
    Closing stock in period 8   = 4 days' sales in period 9
                                 = 4/20 × 211,680 = 42,336

2   Faulty production = 2% (or 2/100) of gross production
    100/2 × faulty production = gross production   (1)

    98% of gross production is good
    good production = 98% (or 98/100) of gross production
    100/98 × good production = gross production   (2)

    Equating (1) and (2):

    100/2 × faulty production   = 100/98 × good production
    Faulty production   = 2/98 × good production
                                = 2/98 × 152,880 = 3,120

Production budget for Bears for the four weeks ending 26 July 2006

		Units
Sales		95,000
Closing stock (W1)	30,875	
Opening stock	(25,175)	
Increase in stock		5,700
Good production required		100,700
Faulty production (W2)		5,300
Gross production		106,000

Workings

1   Demand in period 9 = 95,000 × 130% = 123,500
    Closing stock in period 8   = 5 days' sales in period 9
                                = 5/20 × 123,500 = 30,875

preparing budgets: answers

  2 Faulty production = 5/95 × good production
            = 5/95 × 100,700 = 5,300

ii) Material purchases = materials used in production + closing stock – opening stock

Material purchases budget for the four weeks ending 26 July 2006

		Kgs
Materials used in production		
Antelopes: 156,000 (from a)i)) × 0.75 kgs		117,000
Bears: 106,000 (from a)i)) × 0.50 kgs		53,000
		170,000
Closing stock	40,000	
Opening stock	30,000	
Increase in stock		10,000
Material purchases		180,000

iii) **Cost of material purchases budget for the four weeks ending 26 July 2006**

    = 180,000 kgs × £8
    = £1,440,000

iv) **Labour budget in hours for the four weeks ending 26 July 2006**

	Hrs
Hours for Antelope production: 156,000 × 0.1 hrs	15,600
Hours for Bear production: 106,000 × 0.05 hrs	5,300
	20,900

v) **Cost of labour budget for the four weeks ending 26 July 2006**

  = 140 employees × 4 weeks × guaranteed weekly wage of £228 = £127,680

b) i) **Labour**

  Number of available labour hours in period 8 = 140 employees × 4 weeks × 38 hours
  = 21,280

  Budgeted labour hours required in period 8 (from task a)iv)) = 20,900

  Spare labour hours in period 8 = 21,280 – 20,900 = 380

  In 380 hours, an extra 380/0.1 = 3,800 Antelopes could be produced.

  Powdered rock

  3,000 extra kgs of powdered rock could be purchased in period 8.

  3,000/0.75 = 4,000 Antelopes could be made from this extra material.

  Limiting factor

  Extra production is therefore limited by the availability of labour to 3,800 Antelopes.

preparing budgets: answers

2% of production is faulty, however.

3,800 × 98% = 3,724 fault-free Antelopes could be produced.

ii) **Revised material purchases budget for the four weeks ending 26 July 2006**

	Kgs
Original budgeted material purchases (from task a)iii))	180,000
Additional material purchases required for 3,800 Antelopes	
(3,800 × 0.75 kgs)	2,850
	182,850

16 a) i) Production budget

	Quarter 1 Tins	Quarter 2 Tins	Quarter 3 Tins	Quarter 4 Tins
Sales volume	2,910	3,395	3,880	4,365
Closing stocks (W1)	679	776	873	873
Opening stocks (W2)	(582)	(679)	(776)	(873)
Increase in stock	97	97	97	-
Good production	3,007	3,492	3,977	4,365
Faulty production (W3)	93	108	123	135
Gross production	3,100	3,600	4,100	4,500

Workings

1. Closing stocks in each quarter must equal 12 days' sales volume of the next quarter. There are 5 x 12 = 60 working days in each quarter. So closing stocks = 12/60 × next quarter's sales volume. With sales volume being the same as quarter 4 in quarter 5, closing stocks in quarter 4 will be the same as closing stocks in quarter 3.

   Sample working: closing stocks in quarter 1 = 12/60 x 3,395 = 679

2. Opening stocks of one quarter are the same as closing stocks of the previous quarter.

3. 3% of finished production is faulty. Good production therefore represents 97% (or 97/100) of gross production. Faulty production is 3% (or 3/100) of gross production and hence 3/97 of good production.

   Therefore faulty production is 3/97 x good production.

   Sample working: faulty production in quarter 1 = 3/97 x 3,007 = 93

ii) Material purchases budget

	Quarter 1	Quarter 2	Quarter 3	Quarter 4
Gross production	3,100 tins	3,600 tins	4,100 tins	4,500 tins
	kg	kg	Kg	Kg
Material used in production (W1)	21,700	25,200	28,700	31,500
Closing stock (W2)	2,520	2,870	3,150	3,150
Opening stocks (W3)	(2,170)	(2,520)	(2,870)	(3,150)
Increase in stocks	350	350	280	0
Purchases (kilograms)	22,050	25,550	28,980	31,500

Workings

1. Each tin requires 7 kgs of material and so material used in production = 7 × gross production (from (i))

2. Closing stocks in each quarter must equal six days' gross production and we already know there are 60 working days in each quarter. Therefore closing stocks = 6/60 × next quarter's material requirements.

    Sample calculation: closing stocks in period 1 = 6/60 × material requirements in period 2 = 6/60 × 25,200 = 2,520

3. Opening stocks of one quarter are the same as closing stocks of the previous quarter.

iii) Cost of material purchases budget

	Quarter 1	Quarter 2	Quarter 3	Quarter 4
Material to be purchased (from ii))	22,050 kgs	25,550 kgs	28,980 kgs	31,500 kgs
Cost per kg	× £12	× £12	× £12	× £12
Cost of material purchases	£264,600	£306,600	£347,760	£378,000

iv) Labour budget

	Quarter 1	Quarter 2	Quarter 3	Quarter 4
Gross production units (from i))	3,100	3,600	4,100	4,500
Labour hours required per unit	× 3	× 3	× 3	× 3
Labour hours required	9,300	10,800	12,300	13,500
Guaranteed hours (W)	12,180	12,180	12,180	12,180
Surplus hours/ (overtime hours)	2,880	1,380	(120)	(1,320)

Working

Guaranteed hours = 35 hours × 12 weeks × 29 workers

preparing budgets: answers

v) **Cost of labour budget**

	Quarter 1 £	Quarter 2 £	Quarter 3 £	Quarter 4 £
Guaranteed wages per period (W1)	97,440	97,440	97,440	97,440
Overtime (W2)			1,320	14,520
	97,440	97,440	98,760	111,960

Workings

1. Guaranteed wages = £280 x 12 weeks x 29 workers = £97,440
2. Overtime = overtime hours x £11.00 per overtime hour.

b) **Memo**

To: Jemma Hughes
From: Accounting technician
Date: xx.xx.xx
Subject: **Cost savings and forecasting**

Following our discussions, I have looked into the points you raised and set out my findings below.

i) **Revised budget of labour hours to reduce overtime**

By rescheduling overtime as shown in the budget below, the total overtime hours can be reduced, with production being carried out within guaranteed hours in quarters 1 and 2, when there are surplus hours.

	Quarter 1	Quarter 2	Quarter 3	Quarter 4
Surplus hours/ (overtime hours)	2,880	1,380	(120)	(1,320)
Original hours worked (from a) iv))	9,300	10,800	12,300	13,500
Reschedule quarter 3's overtime		120	(120)	
Reschedule quarter 4's overtime	60	1,260		(1,320)
Revised labour hours	9,360	12,180	12,180	12,180

ii) **Revised production budget**

A revised production budget which takes account of the rescheduling in (a) is shown below.

	Quarter 1	Quarter 2	Quarter 3	Quarter 4
Revised labour hours (from i))	9,360	12,180	12,180	12,180
Revised production budget (tins) (W)	3,120	4,060	4,060	4,060

Working

Each tin requires three labour hours and so the revised production budget = revised labour hours ÷ three labour hours per tin.

iii) **Forecast trend**

Using the regression line y = 1,000 + 100x established by the sales director, the trend for quarters 1 to 4 can be established (with x in quarter 1 = 25).

Quarter 1:   1,000 + (100 × 25) = 3,500 tins
Quarter 2:   1,000 + (100 × 26) = 3,600 tins
Quarter 3:   1,000 + (100 × 27) = 3,700 tins
Quarter 4:   1,000 + (100 × 28) = 3,800 tins

iv) **Forecast sales volume**

The forecast sales volume is established by adjusting the trend values set out in (iii) above by the seasonal variations calculated by the sales director.

Quarter 1:   3,500 − 500 = 3,000 tins
Quarter 2:   3,600 − 300 = 3,300 tins
Quarter 3:   3,700 + 300 = 4,000 tins
Quarter 4:   3,800 + 500 = 4,300 tins

v) **Reasons why linear regression might give inaccurate estimates of demand**

There are several reasons why linear regression might give inaccurate estimates of the demand for tins of A120. (You were required to provide only three reasons.)

- The level of demand for A120 may not be dependent on time but instead might be influenced by one or more other factors (such as economic factors and changes in taste and fashion).

- The relationship between sales of A120 and time might not be linear but instead might follow a curvilinear pattern

- There is no guarantee that what has happened in the past will provide a reliable guide to the future. For example, a new competitor entering the market could have a significant impact on levels of demand for Dobra's products.

- The amount of data used to determine the regression equation (24 observations) may be too small to provide accurate enough estimates.

answers to chapter 12: RECONCILING BUDGETS AND ACTUAL FIGURES

1   A fixed budget is a budget that is set in advance of a period and its purpose is to provide a single achievable target for the entire organisation to work to. This target level of activity means that all areas of the business will be coordinated towards achieving this goal. The purpose of the fixed budget is to aid in the planning processes of the business. The budget will set out the resources that are required in order to achieve that target.

   A flexed budget is a budget that is prepared once the actual results are known. The flexed budget is prepared at the actual activity level that was achieved in the period in order to show what the standard costs should have been at that activity level. When these costs are then compared to the actual costs meaningful variances can be calculated. The comparison of the flexed budget to the actual figures is therefore part of the control process.

2   £15,000 is the cost of 3 supervisors therefore each one costs £5,000 per period.

   At a production level of 330,000 units 4 production supervisors will be required costing £20,000 for the period.

3

	112,000 units £
Materials (112,000 x £2.40) (W)	268,800
Labour (112,000 x £1 + 24,000) (W)	136,000
Production overhead (fixed)	38,000

Working

Materials	100,000 units	£2.40 per unit
	120,000 units	£2.40 per unit

Therefore a variable cost – £2.40 per unit

Labour	100,000 units	£1.24 per unit
	120,000 units	£1.20 per unit

Therefore a semi-variable cost

Variable element = £20,000/20,000 units
 = £1 per unit

315

reconciling budgets and actual figures: answers

		£
At 100,000 units:		
Variable cost		100,000
Fixed cost (bal fig)		24,000
Total cost		124,000

4   Production overhead (72,000 x £7 + £104,000) (W) = £608,000

Working

Variable element of cost = $\dfrac{£664,000 - 524,000}{20,000 \text{ units}}$

= £7 per unit

	£
At 60,000 units:	
Variable element 60,000 x £7	420,000
Fixed element (bal fig)	104,000
Total cost	524,000

5

	Quarter 4 budget
	£
Sales 15,000 units	97,500
Material	(41,250)
Labour (8 x £3,500)	(28,000)
Production overhead	(18,000)
Gross profit	10,250
General expenses (6,400 + 15,000 x £0.28)	10,600
Operating loss	(350)

6   i)

	Budget	Actual	Variances
	28,000 units	31,500 units	
	£	£	£
Sales	406,000	441,000	35,000 Fav
Materials	165,200	180,400	15,200 Adv
Labour	100,800	115,600	14,800 Adv
Production overhead	37,500	39,000	1,500 Adv
Gross profit	102,500	106,000	3,500 Fav
General expenses	55,600	68,900	13,300 Adv
Operating profit	46,900	37,100	9,800 Adv

reconciling budgets and actual figures: answers

ii)

	Flexed Budget 31,500 units £	Actual 31,500 units £	Variances £
Sales	456,750	441,000	15,750 Adv
Materials	185,850	180,400	5,450 Fav
Labour	113,400	115,600	2,200 Adv
Production overhead	37,500	39,000	1,500 Adv
Gross profit	120,000	106,000	14,000 Adv
General expenses (W)	60,850	68,900	8,050 Adv
Operating profit	59,150	37,100	22,050 Adv

Working

General expenses:

At 28,000 units – Variable element = £55,600 – 13,600/28,000
 = £1.50 per unit

At 31,500 units: £
Variable element 31,500 x £1.50   47,250
Fixed element   13,600
Total cost   60,850

iii) The variances calculated when using the original fixed budget show favourable sales and gross profit variances and fairly large adverse cost variances culminating in an adverse net profit variance.

When the actual results are compared to the flexed budget the variances are different.

There is an adverse sales variance and an adverse gross profit variance. The materials now show a favourable variance and the other variances are not so large. The final net profit variance however is much larger than the variance when compared to the fixed budget.

7

	Flexed budget 230,000 units £ £	Actual 230,000 units £ £	Variances £
Sales	1,564,000	1,532,000	32,000 Adv
Materials	793,500	783,200	10,300 Fav
Labour	433,500	428,600	4,900 Fav
Production expenses	180,000	173,500	6,500 Fav
Production cost	1,407,000	1,385,300	
Gross profit	157,000	146,700	10,300 Adv
General expenses	72,000	74,700	2,700 Adv
Operating profit	85,000	72,000	13,000 Adv

reconciling budgets and actual figures: answers

Working

Labour – semi-variable cost

$$\text{Variable element} = \frac{£449,000 - 387,000}{40,000}$$

$$= £1.55$$

Fixed element = £387,000 − (200,000 × 1.55)

= £77,000

At 230,000 = £77,000 + (230,000 × 1.55)

= £433,500

Production expenses – semi-variable cost

$$\text{Variable element} = \frac{£186,000 - 162,000}{40,000}$$

= £0.60 per unit

Fixed element = £162,000 − (200,000 × 0.60)

= £42,000

At 230,000 = £42,000 + (230,000 × 0.60)

= £180,000

8 i) **Quarter 2 budget**

	£	£
Sales 50,000 units		400,000
Materials	165,400	
Labour	69,800	
Cost of production		
56,000 units	235,200	
Less: closing stock	25,200	
Cost of sales		210,000
Gross profit		190,000
Production overhead		56,000
General expenses		52,000
Operating profit		82,000

reconciling budgets and actual figures: answers

ii)
	£
Profit per absorption costing budget	88,000
Less: production overhead included in closing stock (6,000 x £1)	(6,000)
Profit per marginal costing budget	82,000

9 Budgeted level of activity = $\dfrac{£3,034,000}{£16.40}$

= 185,000 units

10 Budgeted level of activity = $\dfrac{£331,200}{£1.20}$

= 276,000 units

11 Overhead absorption rate = $\dfrac{£84,000}{24,000 \text{ units}}$

= £3.50 per unit

Overhead absorbed = £93,600 – £3,650

= £89,950

Actual activity level = $\dfrac{£89,950}{£3.50}$

= 25,700 units

12 Overhead absorption rate = $\dfrac{£483,000}{70,000 \text{ units}}$

= £6.90 per unit

Overhead absorbed = £490,000 + £15,080

= £505,080

Actual activity level = $\dfrac{£505,080}{£6.90}$

= 73,200 units

13 i) A responsibility centre is an area of a business for which costs or revenues are gathered and compared to budgets for control purposes. Responsibility centres are known as such due to the fact that each of these areas of the business has a manager that is responsible for the activities of that area.

ii) Responsibility accounting is a method of budgeting and comparing actual costs to budgets for each of the responsibility centres with the manager of that responsibility centre being answerable for variances that are under his control.

iii) An expense centre is an area of the business for which costs can be ascertained. This may be the entire factory or a smaller area such as a single machine.

iv) A profit centre is an area of the business for which both revenues and costs can be ascertained and therefore a profit or loss for a period can be determined. Often profit centres are larger areas of the business such as an entire division or geographical sales area.

14 The importance of identifying controllable variances is in the area of motivation or de-motivation of management. If variances are reported as part of the responsibility of a manager over which he has no control then this will have a de-motivational effect. If a manager is constantly held responsible for an adverse variance in a cost, the level of which he cannot influence, then this will not have a positive effect on the performance of this manager.

Investigating the causes of variances and determining any interdependence between the variances is an important aspect of management control as in a system of responsibility accounting the managers responsible for various elements of the business will be held accountable for the relevant variances. However they should only be held accountable for variances that are within their control.

There may be variances caused by factors which are beyond the manager's control such as an increase in rent or business rates. There may also be variances in a manager's responsibility centre which have not been caused by his actions but by those of another responsibility centre manager.

An example is a favourable material price variance caused by purchasing a lower grade of material which leads directly to an adverse materials usage variance as the lower grade of material means that there is greater wastage. The initial reaction might be to give credit to the purchasing manager for the favourable variance and to lay blame for the adverse usage variance on the production manager. However the true picture is that, in the absence of any further reasons for the variance then the responsibility for both variances lies with the purchasing manager.

15 The process of continual comparison of actual results to budgeted results is known as feedback.

The budget period is normally for the forthcoming year; however, the feedback process should take place on a much more frequent basis .The calculation and reporting of variances should take place on a regular basis and will be daily, weekly or monthly depending upon the organisation. Any resulting action that must be taken in order to eliminate variances or improve efficiency should then be taken as soon as possible.

The information that is being received about the current performance of the business in terms of the current actual results can then also be used to influence the budget for future periods. This system of using information about the current performance for budgeting for the future is known as feedforward.

reconciling budgets and actual figures: answers

16 a) i) Budgeted unit selling price $= \dfrac{£660,000}{30,000}$

$= £22$ per unit

ii) Budgeted unit material cost $= \dfrac{£252,000}{30,000}$

$= £8.40$ per unit

iii) Marginal element of factory power $= £83,600 - £20,600$

$= £63,000$

Budgeted marginal cost per unit $= \dfrac{£63,000}{30,000}$

$= £2.10$ per unit

iv) Actual marginal cost $= £88,600 - £20,600$

$= £68,000$

Actual marginal cost per unit $= \dfrac{£68,000}{34,000}$

$= £2.00$ per unit

b)

Units	Flexed budget 34,000		Actual 34,000		Variance
	£	£	£	£	£
Sales (34,000 x £22)		748,000		697,000	51,000 A
Direct costs					
Materials (34,000 x £8.40)	285,600		299,200		13,600 A
Factory power					
(34,000 x £2.10)	71,400		68,000		3,400 F
		357,000		367,200	
Contribution		391,000		329,800	
Labour	180,000		192,600		12,600 A
Factory power	20,600		20,600		–
Fixed overheads	75,000		79,000		4,000 A
Fixed costs		275,600		292,200	
Operating profit		115,400		37,600	77,800 A

c) The original budget was a fixed budget based upon the budgeted sales and production of 30,000 units. The flexed budget is based upon sales of 34,000 units therefore the anticipated increases in sales revenue and variable costs is built into this budget.

The original fixed budget and actual results were based on absorption costing whereas the flexed budget is based upon marginal costing. Under absorption costing the fixed production overheads are included in the closing stock valuation and therefore carried forward to be charged in the next accounting period. Under marginal costing all of the fixed overheads are charged in the current period. As the stock levels are rising, under absorption costing more costs are being carried forward to the next period resulting in a higher budgeted profit figure than under marginal costing.

d) One reason for the flexed budget being a better measure of management performance is that when comparing the budget to the actual results it is comparing like with like. As the activity level has increased above the original budgeted level the flexed budget reflects the related expected increases in variable costs and revenues.

Furthermore, the flexed budget has been produced under marginal costing principles whereas the original budget was prepared under absorption costing principles; under the latter profits can be boosted by increasing stock levels, as we have here, as more costs can be deducted from this period's figures to be charged in the next period's figures.

17 a) i) **Calculation of fixed costs and variable unit costs**

	Original budget	Revised budget	Difference		Variable cost per unit
Production and sales units	24,000	20,000	4,000		
	£	£	£		£
Variable costs					
Material	216,000	180,000	36,000	(÷ 4,000)	9
Labour	288,000	240,000	8,000	(÷ 4,000)	12
Semi-variable costs					
Heat, light and power	31,000	27,000	4,000	(÷ 4,000)	1

The fixed element of heat, light and power costs can now be determined using figures from the original budget.

	£
Total costs	31,000
Variable cost (24,000 units × £1)	24,000
∴ Fixed costs of heat, light and power	7,000

reconciling budgets and actual figures: answers

ii) **Flexible budget comparison for the year ended 31 May 2006**

		Flexible budget		Actual results	Variance
Fasta production and sales units		22,000		22,000	
		£		£	£
Variable costs					
Material	22,000 × £9	198,000	(£206,800 + £7,520)	214,320	16,320 (A)
Labour	22,000 × £12	264,000		255,200	8,800 (F)
Semi-variable costs					
Heat, light and power:					
variable 22,000 × £1		22,000			
fixed		7,000			
		29,000	(£33,400 − £7,520)	25,880	3,120 (F)
Fixed costs					
Rents, rates and depreciation		40,000		38,000	2,000 (F)
		531,000		533,400	2,400 (A)

Note. (A) denotes an adverse variance. (F) denotes a favourable variance.

b) **Memorandum**

To: Steven Jones, managing director
From: Management accountant
Date: xx.xx.xx
Subject: **Flexible budget statement for the year ended 31 May 2006**

This memorandum deals with your queries regarding the latest flexible budget statement.

i) **Why the flexible budgeting variances differ from those in the original statement**

The variances in the original statement were derived from a comparison of the budgeted costs for 20,000 units with the actual costs for 22,000 units. Since variable costs increase when output increases, the actual costs are almost certain to be higher than the budget costs, with consequent adverse variances.

The flexible budget statement compares like with like, by determining the budgeted costs for the actual volume of 22,000 units and comparing these with the actual results.

The resulting mixture of adverse and favourable variances is much more realistic. Your assertion that the large reduction in adverse variances is due to the introduction of participative budgeting is not necessarily true.

ii) **Two reasons why a favourable cost variance may have arisen**

1) **Managers may have included unrealistically high costs in the original budget.** This is a problem which can arise with participative budgeting; managers include extra cost allowances to ensure that they achieve their budgets. The submitted budgets therefore need careful checking, although this may be difficult because the managers themselves are the ones with the technical expertise.

323

reconciling budgets and actual figures: answers

      2) **Costs may have been lower than the level expected when the original budget was determined.** For example, an expected rise in rent or rates costs may not have occurred. Such savings are not necessarily the result of management control action.

  iii) **Two reasons why higher sales volume may not be the result of improved motivation**

      1) The **market** for Fastas may have **expanded** and Rivermede could have reaped the benefit of a general increase in the demand for this product. This general market increase is not necessarily the result of improved motivation of sales staff.

      2) The sales staff may have **submitted an unrealistically low sales target** for the budget, to ensure that they achieve the target. Thus the fact that the sales volume is higher than budget may be a result of participative budgeting, but it may be due to manipulation of the system rather than improved motivation.

18 a) i) 1) Budgeted selling price = £960,000 turnover ÷ 20,000 units = £48 per unit

      2) Budgeted material cost = £240,000 material cost ÷ 20,000 units
                               = £12 per unit

      3) Total budgeted marginal cost of light, heat and power

                  = £68,000 − fixed cost £20,000 = £48,000

         Budgeted marginal cost of light, heat and power per unit

                  = £48,000 ÷ 20,000 = £2.40 per unit

      4) Actual marginal cost of light, heat and power

                  = £74,500 production cost − fixed costs £12,000
                  = £62,500

         Actual marginal cost of light, heat and power per unit

                  = £62,500 ÷ 25,000 units produced = £2.50 per unit

ii) **HFD Processes Ltd**
Flexible budget statement for year ended 30 November 2006

	Flexible budget 22,000 units		Actual results 22,000 units		Variance
Sales units					
	£	£	£	£	£
Turnover					
(22,000 × £48 (from a)i)1))		1,056,000		1,012,000	44,000 (A)
Variable costs					
Material (22,000 × £12)	264,000		261,800		2,200 (F)
Light, heat and power					
(22,000 × £2.40)	52,800		55,000*		2,200 (A)
		316,800		316,800	
Contribution		739,200		695,200	
Fixed costs					
Production labour	260,000		273,000		13,000 (A)
Light, heat and power	20,000		12,000		8,000 (F)
Fixed overheads	400,000		430,000		30,000 (A)
		680,000		715,000	
Operating profit/(loss)		59,200		(19,800)	79,000 (A)

Note. (A) denotes an adverse variance; (F) denotes a favourable variance.

*Variable cost of light, heat and power = £2.50 (from (a)) ÷ 22,000 = £55,000

b) **Memorandum**

To: Chief executive of HFD plc
From: Management accountant
Date: xx.xx.xx
Subject: **Flexible budget statement for year ended 30 November 2006**

This memorandum addresses your concerns regarding the results shown in the flexible budget statement.

i) **Why the flexible budget operating statement shows different results from the original operating results**

1) The flexible budget is prepared on a marginal cost basis whereas the original budget and actual results were prepared on an absorption cost basis. Since production was higher than sales, some fixed overhead was carried forward in stock with absorption costing. With marginal costing, however, all of the fixed overheads are charged as period costs against the sales for the period, resulting in a lower reported profit figure.

2) The flexible budget is a realistic target for costs and revenues for the actual activity level of 22,000 units sold. The 2,000 units sold in excess of the original budgeted amount would be expected to increase both revenue and variable costs. The flexible budget makes allowances for these increases caused by the change in volume.

reconciling budgets and actual figures: answers

ii) **Why the flexible budget operating statement might be a better measure of management performance**

The flexible budget statement compares like with like. When the activity level changes, the expected revenue and variable costs also change. It is therefore logical to alter the budget to allow for these changes. The resulting variances will provide a better measure for management performance.

Furthermore the profit shown in the original statement, which was prepared on an absorption costing basis, can be distorted by increases or decreases in stock, as fixed overheads are carried forward in, or 'released from', stock. The use of marginal costing, however, avoids such profit distortions.

19 a) i) 1) Budgeted selling price per Omega

Turnover ÷ sales volume = selling price
£1,440,000 ÷ 36,000 = selling price
£40 = selling price

2) **Budgeted material cost per Omega**

Material is a variable cost and so total material cost ÷ sales volume * = material cost per unit

£432,000 ÷ 36,000 = material cost per unit
£12 = material cost per unit

* Production equals sales and so material cost of production is the same as material cost of sales.

3) **Budgeted labour cost per Omega**

Labour is a variable cost and so total material cost ÷ sales volume = labour cost per unit

£216,000 ÷ 36,000 = labour cost per unit
£6 = labour cost per unit

4) **Budgeted variable cost of light, heat and power per Omega**

	£
Total budgeted cost	92,000
Fixed element	20,000
Variable element	72,000

Variable cost per unit = £72,000/36,000 = £2

5) **% of cost of production carried forward in closing stock**

Cost of production = £1,318,000

Closing stock = £164,750

Closing stock as a % of the cost of production = (164,750/1,318,000) x 100% = 12.5%

6) Material cost of sales = 87.5% x £500,000 = 87.5/100 x £500,000 = £437,500

   Labour cost of sales = 87.5% x £232,000 = 87.5/100 x £232,000 = £203,000

   Variable production cost of light, heat and power = £(96,000 – 12,000) = £84,000

   Variable cost of sales of light, heat and power = 87.5% x £84,000 = 87.5/100 x £84,000 = £73,500

   Actual variable cost of sales

	£'000
Material	437.5
Labour	203.0
Light, heat and power	73.5
	714.0

7) **Total actual fixed costs**

	£'000
Light, heat and power	12.0
Deprecation	70.0
Other fixed overheads	420.0
	502.0

327

reconciling budgets and actual figures: answers

ii) **Hall Ltd – Flexible budget statement for year ended 30 November 2006**

	Original budget	Flexed budget		Actual results		Variances	
Sales volume (units)	36,000	35,000		35,000		–	
	£	£		£		£	
Turnover	1,440,000	1,400,000	(W1)	1,365,000		35,000	(A)
Variable costs							
Material	432,000	420,000	(W2)	437,500	(from vi))	17,500	(A)
Labour	216,000	210,000	(W3)	203,000	(from vi))	7,000	(F)
Light, heat, power	72,000	70,000	(W4)	73,500	(from vi))	3,500	(A)
	720,000	700,000		714,000		14,000	(A)
Contribution	720,000	700,000		651,000		49,000	(A)
Fixed costs							
Light, heat, power	20,000	20,000		12,000		8,000	(F)
Depreciation	100,000	100,000		70,000		30,000	(F)
Other fixed o'ds	400,000	400,000		420,000		20,000	(A)
	520,000	520,000		502,000		18,000	(F)
Profit	200,000	180,000		149,000		31,000	(A)

Workings

1. 35,000 × £40 = £1,400,000
2. 35,000 × £12 = £420,000
3. 35,000 × £6 = £210,000
4. 35,000 × £2 = £70,000

b) **Memo**

To: Harry Easton, Chief executive
From: Assistant management accountant
Date: xx.xx.xx
Subject: **Hall Ltd – Flexible budget statement for year ended 30 November 2006**

This memorandum addresses your concerns regarding the results shown in the flexible budget.

i) 1) **Why there is a difference between the original budget and the flexible budget**

The original budget was for planning purposes and was based on sales and production volumes of 36,000 units. It provided a target at which management should have aimed. The flexible budget is based on sales and production volumes of 35,000 units. It is for control purposes and shows what costs and revenues should have been given actual sales and production volumes. The revenue and variable costs in the flexible budget will therefore be less than those in the original budget given the different volumes, although the fixed costs are the same.

reconciling budgets and actual figures: answers

2) **Why there is a difference between the original actual operating profit and the flexible budget actual operating profit**

The original actual results were prepared using absorption costing, which involves matching all costs (including fixed costs) against revenue. Units in closing stock are therefore valued at full cost so that all costs including fixed costs can be matched against the revenue from the units when they are eventually sold in a later period. So not all fixed costs are charged in the period. Marginal costing, on the other hand, which was used to prepare the flexible budget, requires that all fixed costs are written off in the period in which they are incurred.

ii) **Why the actual operating profit was greater than the budgeted operating profit, despite a lower sales volume**

1) Because the actual level of production was greater than the actual level of sales, the use of absorption costing means that some of the fixed overhead is carried forward in the closing stock valuation to be charged against next year's profit.

2) The actual contribution per unit was higher than the budgeted contribution per unit, and actual fixed costs were lower than budgeted fixed costs.

---

20 a) i) **Budgeted selling price per CD player** = turnover/sales volume
(£3,200,000/80,000 or £4,000,000/100,000) £40.00

ii) **Budgeted bought-in material cost per CD player** = bought-in materials/ production volume (£1,600,000/80,000 or £2,000,000/100,000) £20.00

iii) **Labour unit variable cost**

Using the incremental approach:

	Volume		Cost
	100,000		£760,000
	80,000		£640,000
Incremental volume of	20,000	has an incremental cost of	£120,000

Therefore variable cost per unit = £120,000/20,000 = £6 per unit

iv) **Budgeted total labour fixed cost**

	£
Total cost	760,000
Total variable cost (£6 × 100,000)	600,000
Fixed cost	160,000

An identical answer is possible by using the total cost for 80,000 CD players and deducting the total variable cost based on 80,000 CD players.

329

reconciling budgets and actual figures: answers

v) **Budgeted variable cost of light, heat and power**

Using the incremental approach:

	Volume		Cost
	100,000		£450,000
	80,000		£370,000
Incremental volume of	20,000	has an incremental cost of	£80,000

Therefore variable cost per unit = £80,000/20,000 = £4 per unit

vi) **Budgeted total light, heat and power fixed cost**

Total cost	450,000
Total variable cost (£4 × 100,000)	400,000
Fixed cost	50,000

An identical answer is possible by using the total cost for 80,000 CD players and deducting the total variable cost based on 80,000 CD players.

b) **Flexible budget statement for the year ended 31 May 2006**

	Flexible budget	Actual results	Variances
Production and sales volume (CD players)	140,000	140,000	
	£'000	£'000	£'000
Conversion costs			
Labour (W1)	1,000	972	28 (F)
Light, heat and power (W2)	610	586	24 (F)
Rent, rates and insurance (W3)	200	200	–
Deprecation (W4)	150	132	18 (F)
Total conversion costs	1,960	1,890	70 (F)
Bought-in materials (W5)	2,800	3,220	420 (A)
Total expenses	4,760	5,110	350 (A)
Turnover (W6)	5,600	6,440	840 (F)
Operating profit	840	1,330	490 (F)

Workings

1. Variable cost of 140,000 CD players + labour fixed cost = (£6 × 140,000) + £160,000 = £1,000,000

2. Variable cost of 140,000 CD players + light, heat and power fixed cost = (£4 × 140,000) + £50,000 = £610,00

3. Fixed cost so the same at all levels of production

4. Fixed cost so the same at all levels of production

5. Cost of 140,000 CD players = £20 × 140,000 = £2,800,000

6. Turnover from 140,000 CD players = £40 × 140,000 = £5,600,000

c) **Memo**

To: Mike Jones
From: Assistant management accountant
Date: xx.xx.xx
Subject: **Performance related pay**

i) **Possible reasons for improved profit**

The improved profitability may have occurred even without the introduction of performance related pay.

1) KBV Sound cannot control the volume of sales as the only customer is the parent company. It therefore depends entirely on the level of demand from KBV Motors. This year KBV Motors required 40,000 more CD players than budgeted and so, even without performance related pay, the sales volume target would have been exceeded. All other things being equal (ie no increase in fixed costs and variable costs per unit), this increase in demand would have increased profit.

2) Part of the improved profit arose from a change in accounting policy on depreciation. There were no fixed asset purchases or sales and hence the actual annual depreciation figure would have been known and should have been the same as the budgeted figure. The actual figure was less than the budgeted figure and so actual profit was greater than budgeted.

3) The selling price per CD player is set at twice the cost of the bought-in materials. This means the more managers pay for the bought-in materials, the higher the price they can charge KBV Motors and so the higher the profit KBV Sound can report. (Such a policy leads to inefficiencies, however, as managers are motivated to pay as much as possible for bought-in materials.)

4) Fixed costs are the same irrespective of the level of production and sales. Hence the contribution will increase, all other things being equal, if actual volumes are greater than budgeted volumes and, with fixed costs remaining constant, so will profitability.

Note. You were required to provide only three reasons.

ii) **General conditions for improved performance**

There are several conditions necessary if performance related pay is to lead to improved performance.

1) Managers need to know the objectives of the organisation.
2) Budgets must tie in with those objectives.
3) Managers must feel that the objectives are achievable (although they should provide a challenge).
4) Managers must want to achieve those objectives.
5) Managers must be able to influence the achievement of the objectives.

reconciling budgets and actual figures: answers

6) The level of rewards – both financial and non-financial – should motivate managers.

7) Managers must have the skills necessary to achieve the targets.

8) There should be a short period of time between effort and reward.

9) The actual results should not be capable of being manipulated.

Note. You were required to provide only three reasons.

UNIT 8

PRACTICE EXAM 1

LNG LTD

ANSWERS

unit 8 – practice exam 1: answers

SECTION 1

Task 1.1

a) i) Actual price of ink per litre: Actual cost(£)/Actual purchases (l)

$$\frac{£95,120}{23,200 \text{ litres}} = £4.10$$

ii) Standard usage of ink for actual production: Actual production (units) × standard usage (l)

$$\frac{600,000 \text{ newspapers}}{1,000 \text{ newspapers}} \times 40 \text{ litres} = 24,000 \text{ litres}$$

iii) Actual labour rate per hour: Actual cost (£)/Actual hours worked

$$\frac{£38,440}{6,200 \text{ hours}} = £6.20$$

iv) Standard labour hours for actual production = Actual production (units) × standard hours

$$\frac{600,000 \text{ newspapers}}{1,000 \text{ newspapers}} \times 10 \text{ hrs} = 6,000 \text{ hours}$$

v) Budgeted production overheads: Budgeted production (units) × standard fixed production overheads (£)

$$\frac{560,000}{1,000} \times £120 = £67,200$$

b) i) Price variance for ink: (Actual price per litre (a) i) above) – standard price per litre) × actual purchases

£(4.10 – £4.00) × 23,200 litres = £2,320 (A)

ii) Usage variance for ink: (Actual usage (l) - standard usage for actual production (a) ii) above)) × standard price per litre

(23,200 litres – 24,000 litres) × £4 = £3,200 (F)

iii) Labour rate variance: (Actual labour rate/hr (a) iii) above) – standard labour rate) × actual hours worked

(£6.20 – £6.00) × 6,200 hours = £1,240 (A)

iv) Labour efficiency variance: (Actual hours worked – standard hours for actual production (a) iv) above) × standard rate (£)

(6,200 hours – 6,000 hours) × £6 = £1,200 (A)

v) Fixed overhead expenditure variance: Actual fixed overhead - budgeted fixed overhead (a) v) above)

£70,000 − £67,200 = £2,800 (A)

vi) Fixed overhead volume variance: (Actual production − budgeted production) at absorption rate

$$\frac{(600,000 \text{ units} - 560,000 \text{ units})}{1,000} \times £120 = £4,800 \text{ (F)}$$

vii) Fixed overhead capacity variance: (Actual hours − budgeted hours) at standard rate

(6,200 hours − (560,000/1,000) × 10 hours) × £12 = £7,200 (F)

viii) Fixed overhead efficiency variance: Actual hours for actual production − budgeted hours for actual production at standard rate

(6,200 hours − 6,000 hours) × £12 = £2,400 (A)

c) **Reconciliation statement for November**

	£	£	£
Fixed overheads incurred			70,000
	Favourable	*Adverse*	
Fixed overhead expenditure variance		2,800	
Fixed overhead capacity variance	7,200		
Fixed overhead efficiency variance		2,400	
	7,200	5,200	
			2,000
Fixed overheads absorbed (600,000/1,000 × £120)			72,000

Task 1.2

a) i) Actual exchange rate when paper was purchased

$$\frac{\$110,565}{£58,500} = \$1.89:£$$

Decrease in value of dollar $\frac{(\$1.89 - \$1.80)}{\$1.80} \times 100 = 5\%$

ii) Actual price = £58,500/130,000 kg = £0.45

Price variance = (£0.45 − £0.50) × 130,000 = £6,500 (F)

iii) US$ standard cost of paper at $1.80 = £0.50 × $1.80 = $0.90

£ standard cost at new exchange rate = $0.90/$1.89 = £0.47619

		£
Price variance caused by dollar devaluation = (£0.50 − £0.47619) × 130,000 kgs		3,095 (F)
Price variance caused by other factors = (0.45 − 0.47619) × 130,000 kgs		3,405 (F)
		6,500 (F)

b) **To:** Finance Director
From: Accounting Technician
Date: xx.xx.xx
Subject: Materials price variances and exchange rates

In November there was a favourable materials price variance of £6,500 on purchases of 130,000 kgs of materials. Further analysis of the data shows that the standard cost was based on a £:$ exchange rate of $1.80:£, whereas during November the actual exchange rate was $1.89:£, that is the dollar devalued. In total, £3,095 of the favourable variance was caused by this devaluation. This should be excluded from the purchasing manager's performance report, as it is a fluctuation over which he had no control.

Task 1.3

a) **Increase in ink cost July - November**

$$\frac{£4.10 - £4.00}{£4.00} \times 100\% = 2.5\% \text{ increase}$$

b) **Increase in Ink Producers' Price Index July - November**

$$\frac{116.2 - 107.6}{107.6} \times 100\% = 7.99\% \text{ increase}$$

c) While the managing director is justified in being concerned at a 2.5% increase in the price of a material over only 5 months, in fact the increase suffered by LNG Ltd is far less than that experienced in the industry as a whole, as indicated by the producers' index. An industry increase of nearly 8% compared with an individual firm's increase of only 2.5% suggests that the purchasing manager at LNG Ltd is doing very well to avoid the increase in costs suffered by competitors.

SECTION 2

Task 2.1

a) Benchmarking is a technique used by individual firms to improve their operational effectiveness. With competitor benchmarking, the performance of a directly comparable competitor such as Ads Ltd is analysed into a set of performance indicators, which are then compared with a similar set for LNG Ltd calculated on the same basis. Where this highlights poorer performance on the part of LNG Ltd, further analysis of operations and performance can be carried out, in order to identify any areas in which performance may be improved.

b) i) **Gross profit margin: gross profit (£)/advertising sales (£) × 100%**

   = 990/4,200 × 100%
   = 23.6%

   ii) **Operating profit margin: operating profit (£)/advertising sales (£) × 100%**

   = 210/4,200 × 100%
   = 5%

   iii) **Return on capital employed (ROCE): Operating profit (£)/net assets (£) × 100%**

   = 210/3,800
   = 5.5%

   iv) **Average age of debtors in months: Year-end debtors (£)/Annual advertising sales (£) × 12 months**

   = 1,050/4,200 × 12 months
   = 3 months

   v) **Average advertising revenue per newspaper produced: Annual advertising sales (£)/number of newspapers produced**

   = £4,200,000/7,500,000
   = £0.56

   vi) **Advertising revenue per employee: Annual advertising sales (£)/Number of employees**

   = £4,200,000/70
   = £60,000

   vii) **Average advertising revenue per advertising transaction: Annual advertising sales (£)/number of advertising transactions**

   = £4,200,000/40,000
   = £105

Task 2.2

a) **LNG Ltd Profit and loss accounts for the year ended 30 November 2005**

	Original £'000		Restated £'000
Advertising sales	4,200	× 1.05	4,410
Less cost of sales			
Materials	(1,900)	× 0.97	(1,843)
Direct labour	(430)		(430)
Fixed production overheads	(880)		(880)
Gross profit	990		1,257
Sales and distribution costs	(540)		(540)
Administration costs	(240)	+ (25)	(265)
Operating profit	210		452

b) **Memo**

To:	Board of Directors
From:	Accounting technician
Date:	xx.xx.xx
Subject:	**Performance indicators**

The improvements in operations identified at the management meeting will affect our performance indicators as follows.

Performance indicators	**Effect of improvement**
i) **Gross profit margin** 23.6% to 28.5%	This will rise to $\frac{£1,257}{£4,410} \times 100\% = 28.5\%$ due to: a) rise in advertising revenues b) fall in materials cost
ii) **Operating profit margin** 5% to 10.2%	This will rise to £452/4,410 × 100% = 10.2%, for the same reasons as listed above. The rise would have been higher but for the £25,000 rise in administration costs caused by taking on a credit controller.
iii) **ROCE** 5.5% to 12.8%	The return earned rises from £210,000 to £452,000. Capital employed is affected by this change in operating profits, and also by the sale of land, but not by the reduction in debtors which is a change in working capital rather than fixed capital. Thus ROCE will rise to: £452/(3,800 − 210 + 452 − 500) = 12.8%.

iv) **Average age of debtors in months:**

3 months to 2.3 months

The level of debtors will fall due to better collection, though the rise in sales will create a rise in debtors. The average age of debtors will fall to £850/£4,410 x 12 months = 2.3 months.

v) **Average advertising revenue per newspaper produced**
56p to 58.8p

This will rise, due to the increase in advertising prices, to: £4,410,000/7,500,000 = £0.588

vi) **Average revenue per employee**

£60,000 to £63,000 (or £62,113)

This will rise, following the rise in advertising prices, to: £4,410,000/70 = £63,000 (or to £4,410,000/71 = £62,113 if we assume the credit controller raises the average employee level to 71 people).

vii) **Average advertising revenue per advertising transaction**
£105 to £110.25

This will increase to £(4,410,000/40,000) = £110.25.

UNIT 8

PRACTICE EXAM 2

BELL PLC

ANSWERS

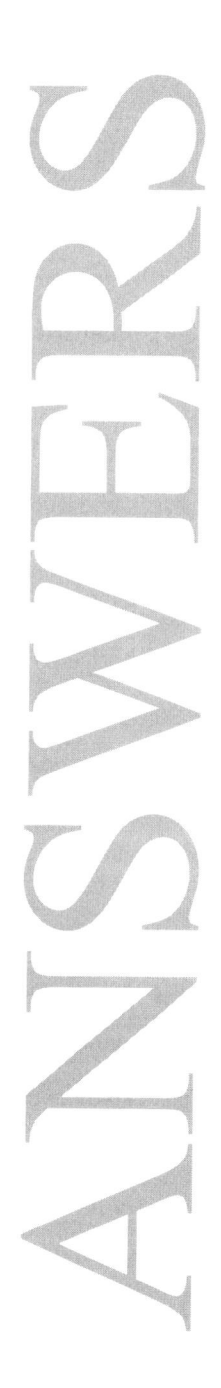

unit 8 – practice exam 2: answers

SECTION 1

Task 1.1

a) i) **Actual price of materials per kg**

$$\frac{\text{Actual cost (£)}}{\text{Actual purchases (kg)}} = \frac{£675,500}{350,00 \text{ kgs}} = £1.93$$

ii) **Standard usage of materials for Model F**

Actual production (units) × Standard usage in kgs = 9,800 units × 20 kgs = 196,000 kgs

iii) **Standard hours for the production of Model F**

Actual production (units) × standard hours per unit = 9,800 units × 5 hours = 49,000 hours

iv) **Actual direct labour hour rate for producing Model F**

$$\frac{\text{Actual cost (£)}}{\text{Actual hours}} = \frac{£254,800}{52,000 \text{ hours}} = £4.90 \text{ per hour}$$

v) **Budgeted fixed production overheads**

Budgeted output (units) × standard fixed overheads per unit

= (10,000 units × £30) + (1,000 units × £48) = £348,000

b) i) **Materials price variance**

(Standard price per kg – actual price per kg ((a) i) above)) × Actual purchases (kg)

= (£2.00 - £1.93) × 350,000 kg = £24,500 (F)

ii) **Fixed overhead expenditure variance**

Actual fixed overhead - budgeted fixed overhead ((a) v) above)

= £360,000 – £348,000 = £12,000 (A)

iii) **Fixed overhead volume variance**

(Actual production at absorportion rate – budgeted production at absorption rate)

= [(9,800 units × £30) + (1,000 units × £48)] – [(10,000 units × £30) + (1,000 units × £48)]

= £6,000 (A)

iv) **Fixed overhead capacity variance**

(Budgeted hours – actual hours worked) × absorption rate

= [(10,000 units × 5 hrs) + (1,000 units × 8 hrs)] – 58,600 hrs) × £6 = £3,600 (F)

342

v) **Fixed overhead efficiency variance**

(Standard hours for actual production − actual hours for actual production) at absorption rate

= [[(9,800 units × 5 hrs) + (1,000 units × 8 hrs) - 58,600 hrs] × £6 = £9,600 (A)

c) i) **Materials usage variance for Model F**

(Actual quantity − standard quantity of materials for actual production) at standard price

= (210,000 kgs − 196,000 kgs) × £2 = £28,000 (A)

ii) **Labour rate variance for Model F**

Actual hours at (standard rate − actual rate for labour)

= (£5.00 − £4.90 (a) iv) above) × 52,000 hrs = £5,200 (F)

iii) **Labour efficiency variance for Model F**

(Actual hours − standard hours) at standard rate

= (52,000 hrs − 49,000 hours) × £5 = £15,000 (A)

Task 1.2

a)

	Purchased kg A	Std price £ B	Std cost £ C (A × B)	Variance £ D	Actual Cost £ E (C − D)	Cost/kg £ (E/A)
January	200,000	2	400,000	(4,000)	396,000	1.98
February	250,000	2	500,000	(10,000)	490,000	1.96
March	280,000	2	560,000	(11,200)	548,800	1.96
April	300,000	2	600,000	(18,000)	582,000	1.94

b) **Memo**

To: Finance Director
From: Accounting technician
Date: xx.xx.xx
Subject: **Materials prices January - April**

i) Over the four month period from January to April, prices for materials have fallen from £1.98 per kg to £1.94 per kg, a fall of 2%. In May, the unit price is budgeted to fall further, to £1.93 per kg.

ii) The change in unit prices may be due to market forces, whereby prices are forced down due to many suppliers competing for our custom. It is also probable that the purchasing department has been able to secure bulk discounts. Our level of purchases has risen from

unit 8 – practice exam 2: answers

200,000 kgs at £1.98/kg to 300,000 kgs at £1.94/kg; a rise of 50% in volume, and a fall of
$$\frac{£(1.98-1.94)}{£1.98} = 2\% \text{ in unit price.}$$

iii) The movement in materials prices may encourage the purchasing department to continue to place large orders with the supplier(s) offering the bulk discounts. In the short term this will improve Bell plc's profitability, and if further discounts are available for even larger orders this improvement should continue in the medium term. It is very important, however, to identify how far materials are being purchased for production and how far for stock. Any increase in stock levels of materials means that stockholding costs (warehousing, insurance etc) and stock financing costs (interest on cash tied up in stock) will increase. Cash flow may become a problem for the company. Furthermore, there is a danger that holding high levels of materials stocks over time will increase the risk of damage to stock, its obsolescence, and its pilferage.

Task 1.3

a)

	£	£
Material handling	80,000	20,000
Production set-up	65,000	20,000
Quality inspection	85,000	40,000
Production supervision	20,000	18,000
	250,000	98,000
Budgeted output (units)	10,000	1,000
Standard overhead cost per unit	£25.00	£98.00

b) i) *Workings*

	£	£
Standard cost using labour hours:		
Materials	40.00	80.00
Labour	25.00	40.00
	65.00	120.00
Fixed overheads using labour hours	30.00	48.00
Per task data	95.00	168.00

344

		£	£
ABC cost:			
Materials and labour (as above)		65.00	120.00
Fixed overheads using ABC (from a))		25.00	98.00
		90.00	218.00

	Model F	Model H	
Finished goods stock @ 31 May (units)	1,000	500	Total
	£	£	£
Valued at standard cost	95,000	84,000	179,000
Valued at ABC cost	90,000	109,000	199,000
Change	(5,000)	25,000	20,000

MEMO

To: Finance Director
From: Accounting Technician
Date: xx.xx.xx
Subject: **Stock valuation using activity based costing (ABC)**

Valuing the closing stocks of stoves at standard cost, as currently calculated, with fixed overheads absorbed on the basis of labour hours, will lead to a total stock valuation at 31 May of £179,000 (see working). Valuing them using ABC will see the valuation of Model F stoves fall from £95,000 to £90,000, as each of the 1,000 units will absorb £5 less fixed overhead (£30 - £25), while the valuation of Model H stoves will rise from £84,000 to £109,000, as each of the 500 units will absorb £50 more fixed overhead (£98 - £48). Total stock valuation would therefore rise £20,000 from £179,000 to £199,000. Assuming the valuation of opening stock (which comprises the same units as closing stock) remains at standard cost, the effect of the increase in valuation will be to carry forward £20,000 more fixed overheads to a further period - and so reported profit for May will rise by £20,000.

Introducing an ABC system involves identifying which activities give rise to costs, collecting together those costs, identifying which activities are used by each product, and then attributing the costs to the products. This is more detailed information than a traditional standard cost system uses, but the accounting analysis, collection and processing of information is greatly facilitated by computer software.

The benefit of information must outweigh the time and other costs involved in obtaining it, and without software ABC systems would probably not be worthwhile. ABC packages however facilitate the initial analysis of what drives costs, and which products use which activities and cost drivers. Packages also mean that data on the cost drivers can be collected easily (often directly from the machines on the factory floor) and processed directly into the costing system. Processing time is minimised by using powerful software on appropriate hardware, and very little user intervention is needed (once the system is set up). This means that appropriate software enables detailed, accurate and relevant information to be collected quickly and at low transaction cost.

SECTION 2

Task 2.1

a) i)   **Budgeted contribution margin:** budgeted contribution/budgeted turnover × 100%

   Model F: £(343,000/980,000) × 100% = 35.0%

   Model H: £(90,000/198,000) × 100% = 45.5%

   ii) **Actual contribution margin:** actual contribution/actual turnover × 100%

   Model F: (£334,000/1,010,000) × 100% = 33.1%

   Model H: £(104,000/187,000) × 100% = 55.6%

   iii) **Budgeted gross profit margin:** budgeted gross profit/budgeted turnover × 100%

   Model F: £(49,000/980,000) × 100% = 5.0%

   Model H: £(46,800/198,000) × 100% = 23.6%

   iv) **Actual gross profit margin:** actual gross profit/actual turnover × 100%

   Model F: £(40,000/1,010,000) × 100% = 4.0%

   Model H: £(60,800/187,000) × 100% = 32.5%

   v)   **Actual capacity ratio:** actual labour hours/budgeted direct labour hours × 100%

   Model F: 50,200/50,000 × 100% = 100.4%

   Model H: 7,800/8,000 × 100% = 97.5%

   vi) **Actual efficiency ratio:** budgeted hours for actual production/actual hours worked × 100%

   Model F: 50,000/50,200 × 100% = 99.6%

   Model H: 8,000/7,800 × 100% = 102.6%

b) **MEMO**

   To: Finance Director
   From: Accounting Technician
   Date: xx.xx.xx
   Subject: **Gross profit margin (Model F)**

The actual gross profit margin for Model F in April was 4%, compared with 32.5% for Model H, and a budgeted gross profit margin for Model F of 5%.

Gross profit is measured as actual turnover less actual variable costs less fixed production overheads, so to improve gross profit we should look at each of these elements in turn.

Increase turnover

Bell plc could aim to increase its sales volume (so fixed production overheads are spread over a greater number of units sold) or to increase its unit sales prices. Already we have seen volumes exceed budget, so it may be possible to sell more. Whether it will be possible to maintain or increase volume at a higher unit price requires consideration of how much customers want the product - will they be prepared to pay a higher price? As volumes have risen recently, it is possible that a price rise is indeed feasible.

Reduce variable costs

There are significant adverse variable cost variances for Model F, and the causes of these need to be examined. Materials and labour costs need to be analysed carefully. The actual efficiency ratio for Model F is less than 100% so it should be feasible to increase efficiency and so obtain lower variable costs per unit.

Reduce fixed overhead costs per unit

We know that the current standard fixed production overheads for Model F are inaccurate, and result in too much fixed overhead per unit being attributed to Model F. Changing the standard cost for this will increase Model F's gross margin.

Using gross profit margin for decision-making

On gross profit margin alone, it appears that Model H is a more profitable product, and it may be tempting to switch production resources to Model H for that reason. However, gross profit margin has a number of significant limitations as a basis for making decisions.

1) The basis for absorption of fixed production overheads can often distort the real profitability of a product. We know that on an activity basis Model H should be attributed with more fixed production overheads. Currently it appears to be more profitable than it actually is. In addition, fixed production overheads remain fixed in the short term and so decisions made for the short term should ignore them, focusing instead on the variable elements of a product's profitability - its sales price and volume, and its variable costs.

2) Gross profit margin is calculated as a percentage which necessarily ignores the absolute amounts involved. Although Model H has a much higher margin, it is a much lower volume product. It may be that the market for Model H cannot increase in volume, and therefore any attempt to switch production to Model H will be doomed to failure. As things currently stand, Model F produces greater gross profit than Model H, albeit at a lower gross margin, and this is something Bell plc should not ignore.

Task 2.2

BOARD REPORT

To: Board of Directors, Bell plc
From: Accounting Technician, Bell plc
Date: xx.xx.xx
Subject: **Sub-contracting production of Model H**

In order to evaluate whether Model H production should be sub-contracted, we need first to compare its current contribution to fixed costs (based on April data) with the effect of the proposal that Chime Ltd should make the product.

	Current contribution per unit £	Sub-contracting £
Revenue		
(£187,000/850)	220.00	220.00
Variable costs		
(£(102,000 – 19,000)/850	(97.65)	
Per question		(180.00)
Contribution/unit	122.35	40.00

On this analysis alone, we would reject the proposal since contribution per unit declines by £82.35, or about £82,350 per month (assuming 1,000 units are sold).

However, as the Managing Director has pointed out, some substantial savings will be made in relation to the activities that comprise fixed production overheads, in the amount of £78,000 per month. The Finance Director has also stated that £12,000/12 = £1,000 per month will be saved in relation to stockholding costs of Model H finished goods. In total therefore it appears that there will be a decrease of £(78,000 + 1,000 - 82,350) = £3,350 in gross profit.

If we assume that each month we make and sell 1,000 units of Model H, and that variable costs per unit are monitored, the effect of sub-contracting is as follows on unit cost.

	£
Contribution per unit lost	(82.35)
Production overheads saved (£78,000/1,000)	78.00
Stockholding costs saved (£12,000/12/1,000)	1.00
Net contribution per unit lost	(3.35)

Of course, we may not sell 1,000 units per month; in April we only sold 850. If we can produce Model H stoves at £97.65 per unit, and we can buy them for £180 per unit, we can afford to spend up to (£180 - 97.65) = £82.35 per unit on fixed production costs. Monthly savings are £79,000, so if we produced and sold £79,000/£82.35 = 960 units we would be indifferent as to whether to make or buy. At a higher level we would be better off producing in-house; any lower than 960 units would be better produced by Chime Ltd.

The Board must therefore attempt to reach a conclusion on the sub-contracting proposal based on its expectation for further sales of Model H.

UNIT 8

PRACTICE EXAM 3

BLOSSOM LTD

ANSWERS

unit 8 – practice exam 3: answers

SECTION 1

Task 1.1

a) i)   Standard price of materials per kg

$$\frac{£90,000}{22,500 \text{ kg}} = £4 \text{ per kg}$$

   ii) Actual price of materials per kg

$$\frac{£91,000}{20,800 \text{ kg}} = £4.40 \text{ per kg}$$

   iii) Standard usage of materials for actual production

$$\frac{22,500 \text{ kg}}{7,500 \text{ units}} \times 6,500 \text{ units} = 19,500 \text{ kg}$$

   iv) Standard labour rate per hour

$$\frac{£45,000}{7,500 \text{ hours}} = £6 \text{ per hour}$$

   v)   Actual labour rate per hour

$$\frac{£44,330}{7,150 \text{ hours}} = £6.20 \text{ per hour}$$

   vi) Standard labour hours for actual production

$$\frac{7,500 \text{ hours}}{7,500 \text{ units}} \times 6,500 \text{ units} = 6,500 \text{ hours}$$

   vii) Budgeted overhead absorption rate

$$\frac{£15,000}{7,500 \text{ hours}} = £2 \text{ per hour}$$

b) i)   Material price variance

   (20,800 kg × £4) – £91,520 = £8,320 adverse

   ii) Material usage variance

   (19,500 kg – 20,800 kg) × £4 = £5,200 adverse

   iii) Labour rate variance

   (7,150 hours × £6) – £44,330 = £1,430 adverse

iv) Labour efficiency variance

(7,150 − 6,500 hours) × £6 = £3,900 adverse

v) Fixed overhead expenditure variance

£15,850 − £15,000 = £850 adverse

vi) Fixed overhead volume variance

(7,500 − 6,500 hours) × £2 = £2,000 adverse

vii) Fixed overhead capacity variance

(7,500 − 7,150 hours) × £2 = £700 adverse

viii) Fixed overhead efficiency variance

(7,150 − 6,500 hours) × £2 = £1,300 adverse

c) **Operating statement for November**

	Variances Adverse £	Variances Favourable £	£
Standard cost of actual production			
$\dfrac{£150,000}{7,500} \times 6,500$			130,000
Variances			
Material price	8,320		
Material usage	5,200		
Labour rate	1,430		
Labour efficiency	3,900		
Fixed overhead expenditure	850		
Fixed overhead capacity	700		
Fixed overhead efficiency	1,300		
			21,700
Actual cost of actual production			151,700

Task 1.2

REPORT

To: Managing Director
From: Accounting Technician
Date: xx.xx.xx
Subject: November variance report

At the recent meeting of senior management to discuss the November variance data a number of points were raised concerning those cost variances.

Purchasing manager

The purchasing manager was concerned about the material price variance as the standard price is clearly an out of date standard. If the standard price for materials was revised to reflect the current price index then this would be £4.48 (£4 x 123.2/110). Using this revised standard price the material price variance would become a favourable variance of £1,664 ((20,800kg x £4.48) – £91,520) rather than the original adverse variance of £8,320. Therefore the purchasing manager may well have benefited the company by superior buying when prices are increasing.

Production manager

The purchasing manager was concerned about one batch of 500kg of material of inferior quality which had to be scrapped and caused 150 hours of idle time.

One effect of this is that the materials usage variance would have been affected by this. Therefore of the total materials usage variance of £5,200 then £2,000 (500kg x £4) was caused by this batch of materials. However this still leaves the problem of the cause of the remaining material usage variance.

A further effect of the inferior quality material is the impact on labour efficiency. This batch of materials caused idle time of 150 hours which would have contributed £900 (150 hours x £6) of the total labour efficiency adverse variance of £3,900. The remaining £3,000 of adverse variance must have been caused by other factors.

Personnel manager

According to the personnel manager there have been problems with recruitment recently leading to overtime being worked. This may have been the cause of the £1,430 adverse labour rate variance.

Measurement of performance

In general there were some concerns expressed about the use of financial variances to assess performance. It is certainly the case that out of date standard costs, such as the materials cost, and other unforeseen factors can lead to questions being asked about the validity of the financial variances. Also fixed overhead variances often have little relevance to the operational managers as to them the fixed overheads are non-controllable costs.

Therefore it might be more useful for operational managers and certainly for operational personnel to express performance by way of measures of physical output. Such measures might include:

- Total daily production
- Production of units per employee
- Production of units per hour
- Scrapped units as a percentage of materials input
- Scrapped units as a percentage of good output

(Note that only three suggested measures were required by the task).

SECTION 2

Task 2.1

		Factory A	Factory B
a)	**Gross profit margin**		

$$\frac{880}{2,200} \times 100 \qquad 40.0\%$$

$$\frac{1,198}{2,850} \times 100 \qquad\qquad\qquad 42.0\%$$

b) **Operating profit margin**

$$\frac{150}{2,200} \times 100 \qquad 6.8\%$$

$$\frac{308}{2,850} \times 100 \qquad\qquad\qquad 10.8\%$$

c) **Return on capital employed**

$$\frac{150}{1,500} \times 100 \qquad 10.0\%$$

$$\frac{308}{7,700} \times 100 \qquad\qquad\qquad 4.0\%$$

d) **Stock turnover**

$$\frac{120}{660} \times 12 \qquad 2.2 \text{ months}$$

$$\frac{142}{784} \times 12 \qquad\qquad\qquad 2.2 \text{ months}$$

e) **Age of creditors**

$$\frac{60}{660} \times 12 \qquad 1.1 \text{ months}$$

$$\frac{100}{784} \times 12 \qquad\qquad\qquad 1.5 \text{ months}$$

		Factory A	Factory B

f) **Age of debtors**

$\dfrac{183}{2,200} \times 12$ 1.0 months

$\dfrac{238}{2,850} \times 12$ 1.0 months

g) **Labour capacity ratio**

$\dfrac{75,000}{70,000} \times 100$ 107.1%

$\dfrac{85,000}{140,000} \times 100$ 60.7%

Task 2.2

Revised profit and loss account for Factory B

	£'000
Turnover ((2,200 x 40%) + 2,850)	3,730.0
Materials ((660 x 40%) + 784) x 95%	995.6
Direct labour ((440 x 40%) + 448)	624.0
Fixed production overheads (420 + 100)	520.0
Cost of sales	2,139.6
Gross profit	1,590.4
Sales and distribution expenses (640/2,850 x 3,730)	(837.6)
Administration costs (250 + 60)	(310.0)
Operating profit	442.8

Task 2.3

MEMO

To: Board of Directors
From: Accounting Technician
Date: xx.xx.xx
Subject: Proposed closure of factory A

It has been proposed that factory A should be closed and that factory B should take over factory A's non-local customers, being 40% of factory A's current turnover. Allied to this closure there would be an increase in fixed costs for factory B of £160,000 and closure costs of £250,000, but a 5% reduction in materials costs as a just-in-time system would be introduced.

As far as the performance of factory B is concerned if the closure were to go ahead then the profit of factory B would increase to £442,800 which would mean an increase in operating profit margin from 10.8% to 11.9%. Perhaps more significantly the labour capacity ratio of factory B would improve from the current figure of 60.7% to 82.1%.

However the improvement of the factory B performance at the expense of factory A is not all that should be considered. By closing factory A costs of £250,000 would be incurred leaving a net operating profit for the company of just £192,800 (£442,800 – £250,000). This compares with the joint profit of the two factories if factory A were not closed of £458,000 (£308,000 + 150,000).

It can be assumed that the 5% savings on materials costs can be introduced for both factory A and factory B giving a total company saving of £72,200 (£660,000 + £784,000 x 5%). When this is added to the currently anticipated profits of the two factories then the company profit would be £530,200 (£458,000 + £72,200). This clearly exceeds the profit from just operating factory B after closure of factory A significantly.

Therefore it has to be concluded that for the company as a whole continued operation of both factories and introduction of the just-in-time system is the best option.

UNIT 8

PRACTICE EXAM 4

BROWN LTD

ANSWERS

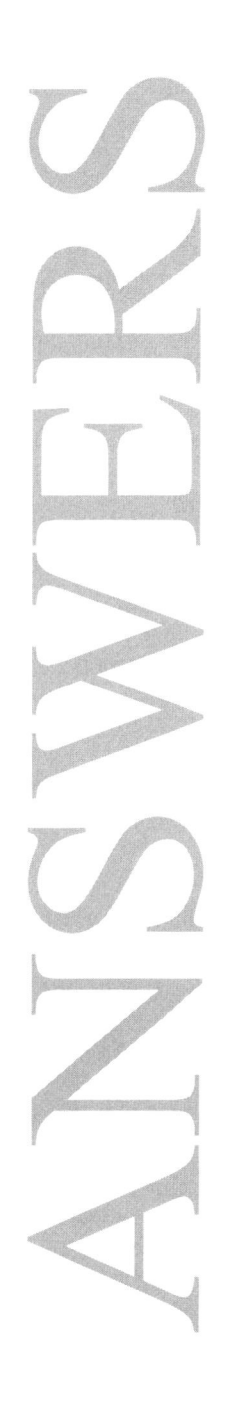

unit 8 – practice exam 4: answers

SECTION 1

Task 1.1

a) i) Actual price of materials per kg

$$\frac{£143,000}{27,500 \text{ kgs}} = £5.20 \text{ per kg}$$

ii) Standard usage of materials for actual production

900 x 30 kgs = 27,000 kgs

iii) Actual direct labour rate per hour

$$\frac{£26,040}{4,200 \text{ hours}} = £6.20 \text{ per hour}$$

iv) Standard labour hours for actual production

900 x 5 hours = 4,500 hours

v) Budgeted production overheads

1,000 x £20 = £20,000

b) i) **Material price variance**

	£
Standard cost of actual materials (27,500 x £5)	137,500
Actual cost of actual materials	143,000
Variance	5,500 (A)

ii) **Material usage variance**

	£
Standard usage at standard cost (27,000 (part a) x £5)	135,000
Actual usage at standard cost (27,500 x £5)	137,500
Variance	2,500 (A)

iii) **Labour rate variance**

	£
Standard cost of actual hours (4,200 x £6)	25,200
Actual cost of actual hours	26,040
Variance	840 (A)

iv) **Labour efficiency variance**

	£
Standard hours at standard cost (4,500 (part a) x £6)	27,000
Actual hours at standard cost (4,200 x £6)	25,200
Variance	1,800 (F)

358

v) Fixed overhead expenditure variance

	£
Budgeted fixed overhead (part a)	20,000
Actual fixed overhead	23,000
Variance	3,000 (A)

vi) Fixed overhead volume variance

	£
Actual production at standard rate (900 x £20)	18,000
Budgeted production at standard rate (1,000 x £20)	20,000
Variance	2,000 (A)

vii) Fixed overhead capacity variance

	£
Actual hours at standard rate (4,200 x £4)	16,800
Budgeted hours at standard rate ((1,000 x 5 hours) x £4)	20,000
Variance	3,200 (A)

viii) Fixed overhead efficiency variance

	£
Standard hours at standard rate (4,500 (part a) x £4)	18,000
Actual hours at standard rate (4,200 x £4)	16,800
Variance	1,200 (F)

c) Operating statement – May 2006

	Variances Adverse £	Favourable £	£
Standard cost of actual production (900 x £200)			180,000
Variances			
Material price	5,500		
Material usage	2,500		
Labour rate	840		
Labour efficiency		1,800	
Fixed overhead expenditure	3,000		
Fixed overhead capacity	3,200		
Fixed overhead efficiency		1,200	
	15,040	3,000	
			12,040
Actual cost of actual production (143,000 + 26,040 + 23,000)			192,040

unit 8 – practice exam 4: answers

d)

MEMO

To: Sam Thomas, Finance Director
From: Accounting Technician
Date: xx.xx.xx
Subject: Operating statement – May 2006

The production of executive desks in May 2006 was 900 compared to the budgeted figure of 1,000. The budgeted cost of these 900 desks was £180,000 but the actual cost incurred was £12,040 higher than this figure at £192,040.

The operating statement gives indications as to why this higher cost figure was incurred. The operating statement indicates the following areas:

- The unit price of materials was higher than budgeted.
- The amount of materials used in production was higher than budgeted.
- The labour rate actually paid was higher than budgeted.
- The number of hours worked was lower than budgeted.
- The fixed overheads incurred were higher than budgeted.
- The hours worked in total were less than those budgeted but the hours worked were done more efficiently than budgeted.

The operating statement is a useful indication of factors that led to the higher than budgeted cost for the production for the month but the statement does not indicate the reasons for the adverse and favourable variances. The operating statement could be more useful if reasons for the variances were included. The operating statement also does not distinguish between variances that are controllable by management and those which are non-controllable.

Task 1.2

a)

	Monthly price £	Three month moving average £
January	5.05	
February	5.02	5.05
March	5.08	5.07
April	5.11	5.13
May	5.20	

Working

February three month moving average = $\dfrac{5.05+5.02+5.08}{3}$ = 5.05

March three month moving average = $\dfrac{5.05+5.08+5.11}{3}$ = 5.07

April three month moving average = $\dfrac{5.08+5.11+5.20}{3}$ = 5.13

b)   **MEMO**

To: Sam Thomas, Finance Director
From: Accounting Technician
Date: xx.xx.xx
Subject: Direct materials price

i) The three month moving average for the direct materials price indicates that the price is increasing over time with a higher rate of increase in the most recent months. The three month moving average shows the trend in prices more clearly than the individual monthly prices.

ii) The standard unit cost of direct materials currently being used is £5 per unit which is clearly out of date. The trend in the increase in the direct materials price could be used as a basis for setting a higher standard direct materials cost for each remaining month of 2006. This could be done by using the three month moving average by extrapolation.

iii) In order to set the standard cost for direct materials for 2006 the following additional information would also be required:

- Any known supplier price changes.
- Whether the trend in price increases is likely to continue.
- Any seasonal variations in price of the direct materials.
- Any changes of supplier anticipated which may lead to a different price charged.
- Increased demand for desks requiring more materials and possible bulk discounts.
- The estimated usage of the direct materials per desk.

(Note that only TWO more pieces of information were required for the task.)

unit 8 – practice exam 4: answers

SECTION 2

Task 2.1

			Actual	Budgeted
a)	i)	**Gross profit margin**		
		$\dfrac{460,400}{2,750,000} \times 100$	16.7%	
		$\dfrac{600,000}{3,000,000} \times 100$		20.0%
	ii)	**Operating profit margin**		
		$\dfrac{115,400}{2,750,000} \times 100$	4.2%	
		$\dfrac{240,000}{3,000,000} \times 100$		8.0%
	iii)	**Return on capital employed**		
		$\dfrac{115,400}{1,075,400} \times 100$	10.7%	
		$\dfrac{240,000}{1,200,000} \times 100$		20.0%
	iv)	**Stock turnover (average stock)**		
		$\dfrac{220,000}{2,289,600} \times 12$	1.15 months	
		$\dfrac{200,000}{2,400,000} \times 12$		1.0 months
	v)	**Labour capacity ratio** Actual hours/budgeted hours × 100		
		$\dfrac{58,200}{60,000} \times 100$	97%	
		$\dfrac{60,000}{60,000} \times 100$		100%
	vi)	**Labour efficiency ratio** Standard hours for actual production/ actual hours worked × 100		
		$\dfrac{(11,200 \times 5)}{58,200} \times 100$	96.2%	
		$\dfrac{(12,000 \times 5)}{60,000} \times 100$		100%

unit 8 – practice exam 4: answers

b)   MEMO

To: Sam Thomas, Finance Director
From: Accounting Technician
Date: xx.xx.xx
Subject: Performance indicators

I have calculated a variety of performance indicators for the production and sales of executive desks for the year to May 2006 and compared these to the budgeted performance indicators. There are a number of ways in which these actual performance indicators could be improved.

Gross profit margin

Gross profit margin could be improved by any of the following actions:

- Increase in sales price
- Negotiation of trade discounts with suppliers
- Improve labour efficiency thereby reducing labour element of production cost

Operating profit margin

If the gross profit margin improves this will have an effect on the operating profit margin but other courses of action could also improve the operating profit margin:

- Reduce distribution and administration costs as a percentage of sales value (they are currently 12.5% of sales value compared to 12% budgeted). Although these costs have reduced in absolute terms they are still higher than budget in terms of the sales value.

- Increase volume of sales as many distribution and administration costs will be fixed rather than variable costs.

Return on capital employed

The return on capital employed is a factor of both the operating profit margin and asset turnover. Return on capital employed could be improved by:

- increases in gross profit margin and operating profit margin (see above)
- more efficient use of assets thereby increasing asset turnover (however this is actually currently higher, at 2.56 times, than the budgeted figure of 2.5 times)
- reduction in assets employed in the business for example sale of unused fixed assets

Stock turnover

Stocks of desks have increased by 200 as there were 200 fewer desks sold than were produced in the year. This has increased the stock turnover period to 1.15 months from 1.0 month. The stock turnover period could be improved by:

- increasing the number of desks sold to match the amount of desks to the production amount
- decreasing production amounts to match sales quantities more exactly, particularly as there appear to be 1,000 desks in stock at the start of the period (each valued at £200) and 1,200 desks at the end of the year. With this level of stock there is unlikely to be a stock-out and stock levels could therefore be reduced.

Labour capacity

The amount of hours worked were only 97% of the hours that were budgeted to be worked. However only 93% (11,200/12,000) of the desks budgeted to be produced were actually produced. Labour capacity can only be improved by production of more desks with increased labour efficiency. However without additional demand for desks it would be unwise to increase production levels as this will simply increase the levels of stock of desks.

Labour efficiency

Each desk is taking longer to produce than was budgeted for. Methods of improving labour efficiency include:

- increased training and supervision for production workers
- use of better direct materials requiring less production work
- elimination of idle time hours
- introduction of a bonus scheme to encourage more efficient work practices

(Note that in the task only ONE course of action was required for each performance indicator. More have been given here for a fuller answer.)

Task 2.2

MEMO

To: Sam Thomas, Finance Director
From: Accounting Technician
Date: xx.xx.xx
Subject: Value engineering or value analysis

The purpose behind value engineering and value analysis is to reduce the cost of a product or service without any reduction in the value to the customer. Value analysis is where every aspect of a product or service is analysed to determine whether it does provide value to the customer and whether its function can be achieved in any other way at a lower cost.

The aims of value engineering and value analysis are to produce a product with the required degree of quality whilst keeping costs as low as possible. Value engineering takes place at the design stage of the product, ensuring that a new product is designed for quality but at low cost by analysing how every part of the design enhances value. Value analysis is used to analyse the value of existing products by questioning whether their function can be achieved some other way at a lower cost.

As the executive desk is currently in production then it is value analysis which is most relevant here to a potential reduction of costs. Each aspect of the design and production of the desk should be examined to determine what is the value provided to the customer of each aspect and whether this level of quality can be kept or improved whilst costs are reduced.

With regard to the production cost of the executive desk the types of questions that might be asked include the following:

- What is the customer looking for in an executive desk and is this provided?
- Are all the functions of the desk essential to the customer?

- Are all features of the executive desk necessary for customer satisfaction eg could it be made of just one wood type rather than a choice of woods and still satisfy the customer?

- Can the desk be made smaller, or of lesser quality of material, in order to reduce costs but still retaining the value aspects required by the customer?

- Can components of the executive desk be standardised with other office furniture produced in order to reduce costs?

- Is there a more efficient way of producing the desk on the factory floor regarding machinery layout, working practices and schedules etc?

When all of these aspects have been considered it may be possible to modify the production of the executive desk in order to produce a product with the required elements of value to the customer but at a lower cost to the company.

UNIT 8

PRACTICE EXAM 5

ECONAIR LTD

ANSWERS

unit 8 – practice exam 5: answers

SECTION 1

Task 1.1

a) i) Standard price of fuel per gallon = $\frac{£50,400}{33,600 \text{ gallons}}$ = £1.50 per gallon

ii) Standard fuel usage for 160 flights = $33,600 \times \frac{160}{168}$ = 32,000 gallons

iii) Standard hourly rate for pilots = $\frac{£67,200}{1,344 \text{ hours}}$ = £50 per hour

iv) Standard pilot hours per flight = $\frac{1,344 \text{ pilot hours}}{168 \text{ flights}}$ = 8 pilot hours per flight

v) Standard pilot hours for 160 flights = 160 x 8 = 1,280 standard pilot hours

vi) Standard fixed overhead cost per budgeted flying hour = $\frac{£75,600}{672 \text{ hours}}$ = £112.50

vii) Standard flying hours per flight = $\frac{672 \text{ hours}}{168}$ = 4 hours

viii) Standard flying hours for 160 flights = 160 x 4 = 640 hours

ix) Standard fixed O/H absorbed by the 160 flights = £112.50 x 640 = £72,000

x) **Standard cost of actual operations**

		£
Fuel	32,000 gallons @ £1.50 per gallon	48,000
Pilots' remuneration	1,280 pilot hours @ £50 per hour	64,000
Aircraft fixed overheads		72,000
		184,000

b) i) **Fuel price variance**

	£
Actual cost of actual fuel used	61,440
Standard cost of actual fuel used (38,400 x £1.50)	57,600
	3,840 (A)

ii) **Fuel usage variance**

	£
Standard cost of actual fuel used	57,600
Standard cost of standard fuel usage for actual number of flights (32,000 x £1.50)	48,000
	9,600 (A)

iii) Pilots' labour rate variance

	£
Actual pilot hours at actual rate	79,872
Actual pilot hours at standard rate (1,536 x £50)	76,800
	3,072 (A)

iv) Pilots' labour efficiency variance

	£
Actual pilot hours at standard rate	76,800
Standard pilot hours for actual number of flights at standard rate (1,280 x £50)	64,000
	12,800 (A)

v) Fixed overhead expenditure variance

	£
Actual fixed overhead	76,200
Budgeted fixed overhead	75,600
	600 (A)

vi) Fixed overhead volume variance

	£
Standard flying hours for actual number of flights x standard fixed overhead absorption rate	72,000
Budgeted fixed overheads	75,600
	3,600 (A)

vii) Fixed overhead capacity variance

	£
Actual flying hours x standard absorption rate (768 hours x £112.50)	86,400
Budgeted fixed overheads	75,600
	10,800 (F)

viii) Fixed overhead efficiency variance

	£
Actual flying hours x standard absorption rate	86,140
Standard flying hours for actual number of flights x standard absorption rate: 4 hours x 160 flights x £112.50	72,000
	14,400 (A)

c) **Standard costing reconciliation statement for the 28 days ended 30 November**

	F £	A £	£
Standard absorption cost of actual operations			184,000
Variances			
Fuel price		3,840	
Fuel usage		9,600	
Pilots' labour rate		3,072	
Pilots' labour efficiency		12,800	
Fixed overhead expenditure		600	
Fixed overhead capacity	10,800		
Fixed overhead efficiency		14,400	
	10,800	44,312	33,512
Actual absorption cost of actual operations			217,512

Task 1.2

MEMO

To: Lisa Margoli **From:** Accounting Technician

Date: xx.xx.xx **Subject:** Absorption of fixed overheads

a) **An alternative method of charging standard fixed overheads**

A rate per flight basis is a more appropriate method of charging standard fixed overheads than the current flying hours basis, since the nature of the overheads (maintenance, insurance, luggage handling etc.) suggests that the overheads arise due to flights being operated rather than as the number of flying hours increases.

b) **Effect on fixed overhead capacity and efficiency variances**

The capacity and efficiency variances would be different from those calculated using the flying hours method as the entire volume variance of £3,600 (A) would be due to capacity, with no efficiency variance. This is because the new basis is similar to a per unit basis; efficiency variances only arise when the basis used is labour hours, machine hours or, as in the original method, flying hours.

c) **Reallocation of budgeted fixed overheads to the Alpha City route.**

	£
Aircraft maintenance £116,480 × $\frac{672}{2,912}$ based on flying hours *	26,880
Insurance £98,020 × $\frac{20}{100}$ based on aircraft insurance value	19,604
Luggage handling and in-flight facilities	–
Budgeted fixed overheads apportioned	46,484

* Aircraft maintenance may be needed after intervals of so many flying hours. Alternatively, maintenance may be carried out at regular intervals on each aircraft, in which case the apportionment should be based on number of aircraft, and the Alpha city route would receive (£116,480 x $^2/_6$ = £38,827).

unit 8 – practice exam 5: answers

SECTION 2

Task 2.1

a) Selling price per Zeta $\dfrac{£14.4m}{360,000} = £40$

b) Material cost per Zeta $\dfrac{£5.76m}{360,000} = £16$

c) Labour cost per Zeta $\dfrac{£3.6m}{360,000} = £10$

d) Contribution per Zeta (£40 – £16 – £10) = £14

e) Contribution percentage $\dfrac{14}{40} \times 100 = 35\%$

f) Net profit (or sales) margin $\dfrac{576}{14,400} \times 100 = 4\%$

g) Return on capital employed $\dfrac{576}{9,600} \times 100 = 6\%$

h) Asset turnover $\dfrac{14,400}{9,600} = 1.5$ times

i) Average age of debtors in months = $\dfrac{2,400}{14,400} \times 12 = 2$ months

j) Average age of stock in months = $\dfrac{1,440}{5,760} \times 12 = 3$ months

k) Average age of creditors in months = $\dfrac{1,200}{5,760} \times 12 = 2.5$ months ✓

l) Added value per employee = £44,000 $\dfrac{(£14.4m - £5.76m - £0.72m)}{180}$

m) Average delay in completing an order in months $\dfrac{390,000 - 360,000}{360,000} \times 12 = 1$ month

n) Cost of quality = (£80,000 + £40,000 + £200,000)
   = £320,000

372

Task 2.2

a) **Sales volume**

		Units
Indexing the 2006 sales volume	360,000 × $\frac{84}{70}$	432,000
Completing unsatisfied 2006 orders	390,000 – 360,000	30,000
Total forecast sales volume		462,000

b) **Purchases**

	£
Sales volume	432,000
Less: opening stock	(90,000)
Purchases	342,000

Note. There are no forecast closing stocks.

c) Cost of purchases (unit cost of material will be the same as in the year to 30 November 2005).

372,000 × £16 = £5,952,000

d) Selling price per Zeta   £40 × $\frac{171}{180}$ = £38

e) Turnover (38 × 462,000) = £17,556,000

f) Total contribution = £5,444,000 as calculated below

	£'000	£'000
Turnover		17,556
Purchases	5,952	
Add: opening stock	1,440	
	7,392	
Production labour 3,600 × $\frac{462}{360}$	4,620	
Variable costs		12,012
Contribution		5,544

g) **Fixed costs**

	£'000
Heat, light and power	720
Depreciation	1,000
Production overhead	2,000
Marketing and administrative expenses	424
	4,144

h) Operating profit (£5,544 – £4,144) = £1.4m

unit 8 – practice exam 5: answers

i) **Net assets at 30 November 2007**

		£'000	£'000
Fixed assets:	cost	8,000	
	cumulative depreciation	3,000	
Net book value			5,000
Debtors (17,556,000 x 2/12)			2,926
Creditors (5,952,000 x 1/12)			(496)
Cash			960
			8,390

j) Net profit (or sales) margin $\dfrac{1.4m}{17.556m} \times 100 = 8.0\%$

k) Return on capital employed $\dfrac{1.4m}{8.39m} \times 100 = 16.7\%$

UNIT 9

PRACTICE EXAM 6

MERANO LTD

ANSWERS

unit 9 – practice exam 6: answers

SECTION 1

Task 1.1

Production budget for period 1 (units)

	Exe (units)	Wye (units)
Opening stock	(140)	(184)
Budgeted sales Period 1	3,200	2,344
Closing stock: 3,000 × 2/20	300	
2,500 × 4/20		500
Production required	3,360	2,660
Faulty production: 4/96 × 3,360	140	
5/95 × 2,660		140
Actual production	3,500	2,800

Task 1.2

a) **Material purchases budget (kgs) for Period 1**

	Exe	Wye
Production	3,500 units	2,800 units

Materials required for production:	kgs
Exe: 3,500 × 6 kg	21,000
Wye: 2,800 × 8 kg	22,400
	43,400
Less: opening stock	(2,000)
Add: closing stock	2,400
Purchases in Period 1	43,800 kg

b) **Cost of materials budget (£) for Period 1:** 43,800 × £20 = £876,000

Task 1.3

a) **Labour hours budget (kgs) for Period 1**

Labour hours required for production:	Hrs
Exe: 3,500 × 8 hours	28,000
Wye: 2,800 × 5 hours	14,000
Total hours required	42,000
Normal hours available	(40,000)
Overtime hours required	2,000

376

b) Cost of labour budget for Period 1 (£)

	£
Normal hours (40,000 × £6)	240,000
Overtime hours (2,000 × £9)	18,000
	258,000

Task 1.4

a) Budgeted marginal cost of production for Period 1 (£)

		Exe £	Wye £
Material:	21,000 kgs × £20	420,000	
	22,400 kgs × £20		448,000
Labour:	28,000 hours × £6	168,000	
	14,000 hours × £6		84,000
		588,000	532,000

b) Unit cost of fault-free production for Period 1 (£)

	Exe	Wye
Good production (units)	3,360	2,660
Total cost	£588,000	£532,000
Unit cost of good production	£175	£200

c) Budgeted operating statement for Period 1 (£)

	Exe £	Wye £
Turnover: 3,200 × £200	640,000	
2,344 × £250		586,000
Expenses/cost of sales:		
Opening stock	140	184
Good production sold	3,060	2,160
	3,200 @ £175	2,344 @ £200
	(560,000)	(468,800)

Task 1.5

a) Extra good production of Exe given labour hours constraint

Total hours planned	42,000
Extra overtime hours available (4,000 − 2,000)	2,000
Total hours available	44,000

In 2,000 hours, Golden can produce (2,000 hours/8 hours) = 250 units of production. Of these, 96% (250 × 96%) = 240 units will be fault-free (good) units.

unit 9 – practice exam 6: answers

b) **Extra good production of Exe given materials constraint**

Extra material now available   1,200 kgs

With 1,200 kgs of material, Golden can produce (1,200 kg/6 kg) = 200 units. Of these, 96% (200 × 96%) = 192 units will be fault-free (good) units.

c) **Revised fault-free production of Exes**

	Exe Units
Original planned production	3,360
Add: extra prodution possible (materials are the limiting factor)	192
Revised fault-free producftion	3,552

SECTION 2

Task 2.1

a) i) **Budgeted selling price per Kat (£)**

Budgeted turnover (£)/budgeted sales volume (units): $\dfrac{£990,000}{1,100} = £900$

ii) **Budgeted material cost per Kat (£)**

Budgeted materials cost (£)/budgeted production volume (units): $\dfrac{£264,000}{1,100} = £240$

iii) **Budgeted labour cost per Kat (£)**

Budgeted labour cost (£)/budgeted production volume (units): $\dfrac{£132,000}{1,100} = £120$

iv) **Budgeted variable cost of electricity per Kat (£)**

	£
Budgeted total cost	260,000
Budgeted fixed cost	(40,000)
Budgeted variable cost	220,000

Budgeted variable cost per Kat: $\dfrac{£220,000}{1,100} = £200$

b) i) **Actual selling price per Kat (£)**

Actual turnover (£)/Actual sales volume (units): $\dfrac{£897,000}{1,000} = £897$

ii) **Actual material cost per Kat (£)**

Actual materials cost (£)/Actual production volume (units): $\dfrac{£291,600}{1,200} = £243$

iii) **Actual labour cost per Kat (£)**

Actual labour cost (£)/Actual production volume (units): $\dfrac{£147,600}{1,200} = £123$

c) **Fixed cost of electricity per Kat (£)**

Actual marginal cost: Actual production (units) x Actual marginal cost of electricty

= 1,200 × £198
= £237,600

unit 9 – practice exam 6: answers

		£
Actual fixed cost		
Total actual electricity cost		279,600
Less: marginal cost		(237,600)
		42,000

d) **Otzal Ltd: Revised operating statement 12 months ended 30 November**

	Flexed budget £	Actual £	Variance £
Turnover: 1,000 × £900	900,000		
1,000 × £897		897,000	(3,000) (A)
Cost of sales			
Variable costs			
Material: 1,000 × £240	240,000		
1,000 × £243		243,000	(3,000) (A)
Labour: 1,000 × £120	120,000		
1,000 × £123		123,000	(3,000) (A)
Electricity: 1,000 × £200	200,000		
1,000 × £198		198,000	2,000 (F)
	560,000	564,000	
Contribution	340,000	333,000	
Fixed costs			
Electricity	40,000	42,000	(2,000) (A)
Depreciation	40,000	36,000	4,000 (F)
Rates	70,000	69,000	1,000 (F)
Property expenses	80,000	78,000	2,000 (F)
Operating profit	110,000	108,000	2,000 (A)

Task 2.2

EMAIL

From   Managementaccountant@merano.co.uk
To   Winston Smith, winston.smith@merano.co.uk
Date   xx.xx.xx
Subject **Operating statements**

a) i) The original budget in the original operating statement was drawn up in advance of the 12 months to which it related, that is, it was a planning budget. The flexed budget in the revised operating statement was drawn up on the basis of the actual sales volume experienced (1,000 units). So the figures have been 'flexed' to reflect how the original budget would have looked had actual volumes been known at the time it was prepared.

ii) The operating profit of £145,500 in the original operating statement was based on a system of full or absorption costing. This means that the figures for materials, labour and electricity in the statement cover all 1,200 items produced, even though only 1,000 of them were sold. Total fixed costs are then deducted, to arrive at a 'cost of production' of £901,800. The 200 items left in stock at 30 November are then valued on a full cost basis as follows:

£901,800/1,200 × 200 = £150,300.

The effect of this is that 200/1,200 of the fixed costs incurred in the period are carried forward in closing stock, as well as the variable costs (materials, labour and electricity) of producing those units.

The revised operating statement relates only to the variable costs of those 1,000 items both produced and sold in the period - that is, it is prepared on a marginal cost basis. Once variable costs are deducted from turnover we have a figure for the 'contribution' that operations have made to the fixed costs incurred in the period. We then deduct all these fixed costs from contribution to arrive at operating profit for the period. This means that there are no fixed costs carried forward in stock; the 200 units remaining at 30 November will be valued at marginal/variable cost only.

The difference between the two profits is therefore made up of the level of fixed costs carried forward in stock, and can be reconciled as follows:

	£
Actual profit as originally reported	145,500
Less: fixed costs carried forward in stock	
(42,000 + 36,000 + 69,000 + 78,000 × 200/1,200)	(37,500)
Revised actual profit	108,000

b) In controlling costs, the revised operating statement is more helpful.

c) The revised operating statement is more helpful since it concentrates on costs which can be changed in the short term (fixed costs are, by definition, fixed in the short term, and therefore should be ignored for decision-making purposes).

In addition, as the revised operating statement has both budget and actual figures geared to the same quantities, the variances calculated are more meaningful. For instance, we know that the turnover variance is caused not by sales volume (since both are based on 1,000 units) but rather by a fall in sales price. SImilarly, we can see how much 1,000 items should have cost us clearly mapped against what they did cost us.

Excluding fixed costs from closing stock allows us, in the revised statement, to see clearly the fixed cost variances. Writing off all fixed costs in the period in which they were incurred, as we have done in the revised statement, also prevents manipulation of profit figures in the short term by building up stocks.

UNIT 9

PRACTICE EXAM 7

ARUSHA LTD

ANSWERS

unit 9 – practice exam 7: answers

SECTION 1

Task 1.1

a) **Production budget for Period 7 (4 weeks from 1 July) (units)**

	Aston units	Brum units
Sales	1,840	2,625
Add: closing stocks: 4 × $\frac{2,520}{28}$	360	
7 × $\frac{3,000}{28}$		750
Less: opening stock	(200)	(875)
Budgeted production	2,000	2,500

b) **Materials purchases budget for Period 7**

	A1 litres	B2 litres
Production: 2,000 × 6 litres	12,000	
2,500 × 12 litres		30,000
Evaporation before issued to production: 12,000 = 96% of issues needed, so evaporation is 4%/96% × 12,000	500	–
Total needed is 100%/96% × 12,000	12,500	30,000

c) **Cost of materials purchase budget for Period 7**

	A1 £	B2 £
Cost: 12,500 litres × £8	100,000	
30,000 litres × £7		210,000

d) **Labour hours budget for Period 7**

	Hours
Production hours: Aston (2,000 × 2)	4,000
Brum (2,500 × 3)	7,500
	11,500
Labour hours available (75 × 35 × 4)	10,500
Overtime hours required	1,000

384

e) **Cost of labour budget for Period 7**

Total hours (11,500 × £8)	92,000
Overtime premium ((11,500 − 10,500) × £(12 − 8))	4,000
	96,000

	£
OR	
Normal hours (10,500 × £8)	84,000
Overtime hours (1,000 × £12)	12,000
	96,000

f) **Cost of overheads budget for Period 7**

	Aston £	Brum £
Cost of overheads: 4,000 × £4	16,000	
7,500 × £4		30,000

g) **Absorption cost of production budget for Period 7**

	Aston £	Brum £
Materials (c) above)	100,000	210,000
Labour: 4,000 × £8	32,000	
7,500 × £8		60,000
Overheads (f) above)	16,000	30,000
	148,000	300,000

h) **Unit absorption cost of production for Period 7**

	Aston	Brum
Absorption cost of all production	£148,000	£300,000
Units produced	2,000	2,500
Unit absorption cost: $\dfrac{£148,000}{2,000}$	£74	
$\dfrac{£300,000}{2,500}$		£120

unit 9 – practice exam 7: answers

i) **Budgeted operating statement for Period 7**

		Aston £	Brum £
Budgeted turnover:	1,840 × £100	184,000	
	2,625 × £140		367,500
Budgeted expenses:			
Opening stock (given)		16,000	96,250
Production cost ((g) above)		148,000	300,000
Less: closing stocks:	360 × £74 ((h) above)	(26,640)	
	750 × £120 ((h) above)		(90,000)
Budgeted expenses		137,360	306,250
Budgeted operating profit		46,640	61,250

Task 1.2

a) As a way of identifying which employees are responsible for poor production, testing only a sample (less than 100% of the Guards) as opposed to testing all of them will be less expensive and time-consuming. Sampling is actually the only feasible method in the case of Guards, as the testing process destroys the Guards; a 100% test of all production therefore would mean that no Guards could be sold at all.

b) Simple random sampling involves taking items for testing from the whole population of Guards, such that each and every Guard has an equal chance of being selected.

Systematic sampling means that the first item to be tested is selected on a random basis (ie each Guard has an equal chance of selection), but then the rest of the sample is selected on a systematic basis, such a 'every 40th item'. For instance, if there were 20,000 Guards produced in a month, a sample of 750 items was required, and the fist item randomly selected was Guard number 35, the remaining 749 items would then be selected at intervals of $\left(\frac{20,000-35}{749}\right)$ = 26 items approximately.

With both random and systematic sampling, a group of items may be missed out, such as all the production of 'Employee 20'. Where a population can be identified into groups (for instance, the production of each of the 200 workers), we may want to make sure that some at least of each group is included in the sample. This is achieved by stratified sampling, where items are selected from every group within the population, so that the number of items from each group is in proportion to the relative size of the group to the population as a whole. Thus if each of the 200 workers produces 100 items each (20,000 produced in all), and a sample of 750 items is required (1/200 x 750) = 3.75 items on average should be selected from each worker's production.

c) As each worker is solely responsible for the Guards they produce, each worker's output should be included in the sample, so a form of stratified sampling should be performed by Arusha.

SECTION 2

Task 2.1

a) **Budgeted selling price per M9** (same for Plan A and Plan B)

Planned turnover (£)/planned volume (units) = $\dfrac{690{,}000}{300{,}000}$

= £23 per M9

(Check: Plan B $\dfrac{9{,}200{,}000}{400{,}000}$ = £23)

b) **Budgeted variable cost per M9** (same for Plan A and Plan B)

i) **Materials:** Planned expenditure (£)/planned volume

$= \dfrac{£2{,}400{,}000}{300{,}000}$

= £8 per M9

(Check: Plan B $\dfrac{£3{,}200{,}000}{400{,}000}$ = £8)

ii) **Labour:** Planned expenditure (£)/planned volume

$= \dfrac{£1{,}500{,}000}{300{,}000}$

= £5 per M9

(Check: Plan B $\dfrac{£2{,}000{,}000}{400{,}000}$ = £5)

iii) **Electricity** (variable element): Change in planned expenditure (£)/Change in planned volume

$= \dfrac{£1{,}800{,}000 - £1{,}400{,}000}{400{,}000 - 300{,}000}$

= £4.00 per M9

unit 9 – practice exam 7: answers

c) Budgeted fixed cost of electricity

	£
Total electricity cost (Plan A)	1,400,000
Less: variable cost (300,000 × £4)	(1,200,000)
Fixed cost	200,000

		£
(Check: Plan B	Total cost	1,800,000
	Less variable cost (400,000 × £4)	(1,600,000)
	Fixed cost	200,000

d) Operating statement for year ended 31 May

	Flexed budget £'000	Actual £'000	Variance £'000
Turnover (380,000 × £23)	8,740	8,626	(114) (A)
Materials (380,000 × £8)	3,040	3,116	(76) (A)
Labour (380,000 × £5)	1,900	1,938	(38) (A)
Electricity ((380,000 × £4) + £200,000)	1,720	1,624	96 (F)
Quality control	480	358	122 (F)
Rent and rates	200	200	0
Depreciation	400	100	300 (F)
Operating profi	1,000	1,290	290 (F)

Task 2.2

MEMO

To: Tara Williams
From: Management Accountant
Date: xx.xx.xx
Subject: **Performance-related pay**

a) During the year to 31 May, CityEng's profit was £290,000 more than the budget for volume of 380,000 units, and was also greater than either Plan A or Plan B (volume of 300,000 and 400,000 M9s) that were suggested. The profit improvement arises despite the fact that there was a shortfall of 40,000 M9s between what Car Makers plc wanted (420,000 M9s) and what CityEng Ltd was able to supply (380,000 M9s).

The operating statement shows a number of variances between actual and flexed budget performance. The adverse variance on turnover is caused by a lower selling price than planned (£8,626,000/380,000 = £22.70 per M9). Similarly, materials were purchased at a higher price than planned (£3,116,000/380,000 = £8.20 per M9), and more was paid for labour than planned (£1,938,000/380,000 = £5.10 per M9). Performance in these key areas therefore - management of sales price, materials price and labour - appears to have been relatively poor.

These decreases in profitability are more than offset, however, by positive variances on electricity, quality control and depreciation:

i) the decreases in both fixed and variable charges for electricity were due to independent action by the supplier;

ii) reducing quality control costs by 25% from budget (122/480) has created a high positive variance, but this may be a tactic that will rebound on CityEng Ltd, since Car Makers plc have very strict quality requirements;

iii) the £300,000 positive variance on depreciation is unlikely to relate to performance, but rather to a change in accounting policy.

Thus there are few if any grounds to suggest that performance-related pay for managers has increased short-term profitability. In relation to cutting quality control costs, it may actually damage long-term profitability.

b) Performance-related pay is a method of remunerating managers in such a way that their total remuneration increases if they meet organisational goals and targets. It may take the form of bonuses, share options or other incentives.

Performance-related pay will only be successful in motivating managers to improve performance if the following conditions are met.

i) The organisation has specific objectives and goals of which managers are aware.

ii) Targets are set for managers which relate specifically to achieving the organisation's objectives and goals.

iii) The relationship between objectives and targets is clear to managers.

iv) The overall objectives are ones which managers want to help to achieve.

v) The targets set for managers must be challenging but achievable.

vi) Managers must be in full control of the factors which impact on achieving their targets, and must have appropriate skills.

vii) Achieving an individual manager's targets must not be contingent on another manager achieving their target, although there may be an element of team bonuses so co-operation and support are encouraged.

viii) The rewards being offered must be sufficient to motivate managers to meet their challenging targets.

ix) The timescale between achieving targets and receiving rewards should be as short as possible.

x) The achievement of long-term targets must not be sacrificed by managers concentrating on achieving short-term targets.

xi) Care must be taken that actual results are not manipulated, and that good results are down to good management, not just good luck.

(Note that any four conditions were required).

UNIT 9

PRACTICE EXAM 8

JORVIK LTD

ANSWERS

SECTION 1

Task 1.1

a) **Production budget (units)**

	1	2	Period 3	4	5
Sales	19,200	23,040	28,800	34,560	30,720
Add: closing stock (8/20 × next period sales)	9,216	11,520	13,824	12,288	
Less: opening stock	(7,680)	(9,216)	(11,520)	(13,824)	
Good production required	20,736	25,344	31,104	33,024	
Faulty production 4/96 × good production	864	1,056	1,296	1,376	
Total production	21,600	26,400	32,400	34,400	

b) **Material purchases budget (litres)**

	1	Period 2	3	4
Production in units	21,600	26,400	32,400	34,400
Material required in litres (production × 2 litres)	43,200	52,800	64,800	68,800

Task 1.2

a) **Materials shortages/surpluses (litres)**

	1	Period 2	3	4
Material required	43,200	52,800	64,800	68,800
Material available	60,000	60,000	60,000	60,000
(Shortage)/surplus	16,800	7,200	(4,800)	(8,800)

b) **Rescheduling of purchases (litres)**

	1	Period 2	3	4
Original purchases	43,200	52,800	64,800	68,800
Reschedule period 3 shortfall		4,800	(4,800)	
Reschedule period 4 shortfall	6,400	2,400		(8,800)
Revised purchases	49,600	60,000	60,000	60,000

unit 9 – practice exam 8: answers

c) **Revised materials purchases budget (litres)**

	Period 1	Period 2	Period 3	Period 4
Revised purchases	49,600	60,000	60,000	60,000

d) **Revised production budget**

	Period 1	Period 2	Period 3	Period 4
Production capacity (materials/2)	24,800	30,000	30,000	30,000
Less: faulty production (4%)	992	1,200	1,200	1,200
Good production	23,808	28,800	28,800	28,800

Task 1.3

a) **Revised material purchases budget**

	Period 1	Period 2	Period 3	Period 4
Revised purchases (litres)	49,600	60,000	60,000	60,000
Revised purchases (× £2.10)	104,160	126,000	126,000	126,000

b) **Labour budget (hours)**

	Period 1	Period 2	Period 3	Period 4
Production (units)	24,800	30,000	30,000	30,000
Labour hours required (production/5)	4,960	6,000	6,000	6,000
Basic hours available (40 × 35 hours × 4 weeks)	(5,600)	(5,600)	(5,600)	(5,600)
(Idle time)/Overtime	(640)	400	400	400

c) **Labour cost budget**

	Period 1 £	Period 2 £	Period 3 £	Period 4 £
Productive hours at basic rate				
4,960 × £6	29,760			
6,000 × £6		36,000	36,000	36,000
Factory overheads				
Idle time 640 × £6	3,840			
Overtime premium 400 × £3		1,200	1,200	1,200
Total labour cost	33,600	37,200	37,200	37,200

d) Cost of production budget

	Period 1 £	Period 2 £	Period 3 £	Period 4 £
Materials (Task 1.3 a)	104,160	126,000	126,000	126,000
Labour (Task 1.3c)	29,760	36,000	36,000	36,000
Factory overheads (150% x labour + idle time + overtime) (Task 1.3c) (see note below)	48,480	55,200	55,200	55,200
Total cost of production	182,400	217,200	217,200	217,200

Note. We have calculated factory overheads as 150% of the labour cost of production and then added idle time and the overtime premium, as these are charged to factory overheads according to the question.

Task 1.4

Cell	Formula
B7	=B1+(B2*(B3+B5))
C7	=B1+(B2*(B3+C5))
B8	=SUM(B6:B7)
C8	=SUM(C6:C7)

SECTION 2

Task 2.1

a) **Budgeted selling price**

$$\frac{£1,680,000}{70,000} = £24 \text{ per Yorker}$$

b) i) **Budgeted material cost**

$$\frac{£350,000}{70,000} = £5 \text{ per Yorker}$$

ii) **Budgeted labour cost**

$$\frac{£420,000}{70,000} = £6 \text{ per Yorker}$$

iii) **Budgeted variable electricity cost**

$$\frac{(£230,000 - 20,000)}{70,000} = £3 \text{ per Yorker}$$

c) **Budgeted maintenance cost per 10,000 Yorkers**

$$\frac{£140,000}{70,000 \times 10,000} = £20,000 \text{ per 10,000 Yorkers}$$

d) **Operating statement for year ended 30 November 2006**

	Flexed budget		Actual		Variance
Volume	85,000		85,000		
	£'000	£'000	£'000	£'000	£'000
Turnover 85,000 × £24		2,040		1,955	85 (A)
Material 85,000 × £5	425		442		17 (A)
Labour 85,000 × £6	510		493		17 (F)
Electricity					
20,000 + (85,000 × £3)	275		230		45 (F)
Maintenance (£20,000 × 9)	180		160		20 (F)
Rent and rates	400		420		20 (A)
Administration	100		95		5 (F)
Total expenses		(1,890)		(1,840)	
Operating profit		150		115	35 (A)

Task 2.2

E-MAIL

To: Carol Brown
From: Accountant
Date: xx.xx.xx
Subject: Budgets and variances

Thank you for your e-mail. Here are my thoughts on the points that you raised.

a) I agree that having two budgets might appear confusing. However the two budgets have different purposes.

   The original budget from the software package was prepared prior to the start of the budget year and its purpose was to aid in planning the operations of the business for the forthcoming year. The budget set out the aims of the company over the year ie to produce and sell 70,000 Yorkers and the costs associated with that aim.

   The budget that I have prepared however is part of the control process. I have revised the original budget to reflect the fact that the actual sales and production were in fact 85,000 Yorkers during the year. This revised budget shows the revenue and costs that would have been expected at this activity level. This can then be compared to the actual revenue and costs and meaningful variances calculated. By comparing the actual figures to this revised, flexed budget we are comparing like with like.

b) When deciding whether or not to investigate individual variances a number of factors should be taken into account.

   In general terms the cost of investigating the variance should be less than the likely benefit from the investigation. Therefore most variances will only be investigated if they are either above an absolute amount such as £5,000 or a percentage amount of the budget such as 10%.

   Variances that are smaller than the limits set by the organisation may however on occasion be investigated if there is a trend in the variance. If it is a small amount but has been appearing as a variance period after period, the cause would be likely to be investigated.

   Variances will only be investigated if their causes are controllable. If the variance is not controllable then there is little point in knowing more about it.

c) As part of the control process variances are calculated. A variance is the difference between what the actual production should have cost and what it actually cost. Therefore the appropriate budget to use for this purpose is the flexed budget as this has been calculated to show how much it should have cost to produce 85,000 units. That can then be compared to how much it actually cost to produce those units.

I hope that this has been helpful.

UNIT 9

PRACTICE EXAM 9

NEWMARKET LTD

ANSWERS

SECTION 1

Task 1.1

a) **Production budget (units)**

		Alpha Units	Beta Units
Sales in period		8,460	9,025
Add: closing stock	(10,575 × 5/25)	2,115	
	(12,635 × 10/25)		5,054
Less: opening stock		(1,692)	(3,610)
Required finished units		8,883	10,469
Wastage	(8,883 × 10/90)	987	
	(10,469 × 5/95)		551
Production quantity		9,870	11,020

b) **Materials purchases budget (kgs)**

	Kgs
Required for production	
Alpha 9,870 × 20kgs	197,400
Beta 11,020 × 40kgs	440,800
Add: closing stock	52,600
Less: opening stock	(64,800)
Materials purchases	626,000

c) **Cost of materials budget**

	£
Purchases 626,000kgs × £0.50	313,000

d) **Budgeted labour hours**

	Hours
Required for production	
Alpha 9,870 × 2 hours	19,740
Beta 11,020 × 3 hours	33,060
	52,800
Basic hours available (300 × 35 hours × 5 weeks)	(52,500)
Overtime hours required	300

e) **Cost of labour budget**

	£
Basic pay (52,800 hours × £7)	369,600
Overtime premium (300 hours × £3)	900
Total labour cost	370,500

f) **Total absorption cost of production budget**

	Alpha £	Beta £
Materials cost		
Alpha (9,870 × 20kgs × £0.50)	98,700	
Beta (11,020 × 40kgs × £0.50)		220,400
Labour cost		
Alpha (9,870 × 2 hours × £7)	138,180	
Beta (11,020 × 3 hours × £7)		231,420
Factory overheads		
Alpha (9,870 × 2 hours × £62)	1,223,880	
Beta (11,020 × 3 hours × £58)		1,917,480
Total absorption cost	1,460,760	2,369,300

g) **Absorption cost per unit of good production**

	Alpha £	Beta £
Alpha (1,460,760/8,883)	164.44	
Beta (2,369,300/10,469)		226.32

h) **Value of closing stock**

	Alpha £	Beta £
Alpha (2,115 (part a) × £164.44)	347,790.60	
Beta (5,054 (part a) × £226.32)		1,143,821.28

Task 1.2

MEMO

To: Bob Scott, Chief Executive
From: Management accountant
Date: xx.xx.xx
Subject: Production of Alphas – period 8

a) It has been brought to our attention that sales of Alpha in period 8 will be 10,460 units rather than the originally budgeted figure of 8,460 units. This additional production will therefore require additional materials and additional labour hours.

   i) **Materials required**

   If sales of Alphas are to increase by 2,000 units then 2,223 (2,000 × 100/90) additional units will need to be produced due to faulty production. This will require an additional 44,460 kgs (2,223 × 20kgs) of materials. However the supplier of this material can only produce an additional 34,000 kgs during period 8 therefore this shortage will limit the production of Alphas.

Labour hours required

If an additional 2,223 units of Alpha are to be made this will require 4,446 hours (2,223 × 2 hours) of overtime. Under the current production plan only 300 hours of overtime were required giving a total of 4,746 hours of overtime which can be worked. Therefore the additional labour hours required will not limit the production of Alphas.

ii) **Revised production budget for Alphas for period 8**

	Units
Original production of Alphas	9,870
Additional units produced $\left(\dfrac{34,000 \text{ kgs}}{20 \text{ kgs per unit}}\right)$	1,700
Revised production in units	11,570

iii)

	Units
Additional Alpha units produced	1,700
Additional good Alpha units produced (1,700 × 90/100)	1,530
Additional sales required	2,000
Shortfall in sales	470

iv) The shortfall in the planned sales of Alphas for period 8 could potentially be overcome in a number of ways. However we are told that closing stock (inventory) of finished goods is to remain the same and also that there is only this particular supply of raw materials then subcontracting is not an option. Therefore the only remaining method of overcoming the problem is to reduce the closing stock (inventory) levels of the raw material from the 52,600 kgs budgeted and use these in period 8 to make the additional units of Alphas and replenish these stocks (inventories) in period 9 when purchase of the materials is not a limiting factor.

b) A budget might be imposed on staff without consultation for the following reasons:

i) if the management of the organisation is highly centralised with little autonomy or independence within areas of the business

ii) only the senior management in the business have enough knowledge and overview of the business to be able to set a fully integrated budget for all aspects of the business

iii) managers and employees, other than senior management, do not possess the skills required or desire to set their own budgets

iv) an imposed budget can generally be prepared more quickly than a participative budget

v) imposed budgets may be set when circumstances change and these changes need to be reflected at short notice in operations and budgets.

(Note that only TWO reasons were required for this task.)

SECTION 2

Task 2.1

a) i) **Budgeted selling price** = $\dfrac{£630,000}{9,000}$ = £70 per Zylo

ii) **Budgeted material cost** = $\dfrac{£45,000}{9,000}$ = £5 per Zylo

iii) **Budgeted labour cost** = $\dfrac{£55,800}{9,000}$ = £6.20 per Zylo

iv) **Budgeted variable cost of electricity** = $\dfrac{(£38,000 - 20,000)}{9,000}$ = £2 per Zylo

v) **Actual selling price** = $\dfrac{£616,000}{8,800}$ = £70 per Zylo

vi) **Actual material cost** = $\dfrac{£52,000}{10,000}$ = £5.20 per Zylo

vii) **Actual labour cost** = $\dfrac{£65,000}{10,000}$ = £6.50 per Zylo

viii) **Actual variable cost of electricity** = $\dfrac{(£42,000 - 21,000)}{10,000}$ = £2.10 per Zylo

unit 9 – practice exam 9: answers

b) **Marginal costing operating statement**

	Flexible budget 10,000 units £	Actual £	Variance £
Turnover (8,800 units)	616,000	616,000	–
Variable costs			
Materials (10,000 × £5)	50,000	52,000	2,000 (A)
Labour (10,000 × £6.20)	62,000	65,000	3,000 (A)
Electricity – variable (10,000 × £2))	20,000	21,000	1,000 (A)
Variable cost of production	132,000	138,000	
Less: closing stock			
(1,200 × £13.2)	(15,840)		
(1,200 × £13.8)		(16,560)	720 (F)
Variable cost of sales	116,160	121,440	
Fixed costs			
Electricity – fixed	20,000	21,000	1,000 (A)
Depreciation	70,000	65,000	5,000 (F)
Rent and rates	24,000	25,000	1,000 (A)
Other fixed overheads	40,000	42,000	2,000 (A)
Total production cost	270,160	274,440	4,280 (A)
Operating profit	345,200	341,560	

c) **Note to operating statement**

The actual profit calculated by the manager is £359,920 whereas the actual profit shown in this operating statement is £341,560. The reason for this difference is that the original profit was calculated under absorption costing whereas this profit statement has been calculated using variable costing. The difference in the two profit figures is due to the fixed overheads included in the valuation of closing stock in the original profit statement.

	£
Original profit	359,920
Fixed overheads included in closing stock	
$\frac{(21,000+65,000+25,000+42,000)}{10,000} \times 1,200$ units	(18,360)
Revised marginal costing profit	341,560

Task 2.2

Notes for Mike Town – Weaknesses of current report

- The report concentrates upon the budget to date and the cash expenditure to date, however there is no information about the current month expenditure and current month budget. Therefore to isolate any variances in the current month the General Manager would have to compare the figures to the previous similar report. Individual columns showing current month figures would be more useful.

- Although the costs are split according to their type, they are not analysed according to the relevant areas of the business. If the report is being sent to individual managers in the business then it might be more useful if the costs were classified as to the swimming pool, gymnasium, sauna and sports hall. Particularly if individual managers are responsible for each of these areas then they will be interested in the costs that relate to their responsibility centre rather than the costs overall.

- Only costs are included in the statement with no mention of revenues. It is likely that each separate area of the business will be a revenue centre and therefore revenue information will be useful to management as well.

- The report includes figures for 'central services recharge'. This is presumably not a cost that either the General Manager or individual managers can control and therefore is not useful information for them.

- The actual expenditure to date is reported as 'cash expenditure' rather than the amount of expenditure that has actually been incurred to date which may be misleading.

- There is no distinction in the report between fixed costs and variable costs. Fixed costs will often not be controllable by individual managers whereas variable costs may well be.

- The report deals with both revenue and capital expenditure. Although individual managers may have control over revenue expenditure it is normally only higher levels of management who control capital expenditure.

- Although the 'under/over spend' to date is reported it is done so in terms of 'Dr' and 'Cr' which may not be understandable to a non-financial manager.

- There is no information about activity levels which may affect the variable expenses. A flexed budget could be produced based upon visitor numbers to the leisure centre which may provide more useful information.

- The 'budget to date' is clearly not just 3 months of the total budget and therefore it would appear that seasonal factors have been built into the budget. However this is not particularly clear from the budget itself. For example why is there only £2,000 of the annual repairs and maintenance budget relating to the first three months of the year out of a total budget of £44,000? Similarly the lighting and heating budget for the first three months is only one twelfth of the total budget for the year.

- The budget remaining column could also be misleading. This actually means the amount of budget not yet allocated to the period to date rather than the amount remaining to be spent. For example the fixed asset budget is £240,000 and although £60,000 of that has already been spent the budget remaining figure appears as £240,000.

(Note that only SIX weaknesses were required for the task).

UNIT 9

PRACTICE EXAM 10

TIPTON LTD

ANSWERS

unit 9 – practice exam 10: answers

SECTION 1

Task 1.1

a) **Production budgets**

		Exe Units		Wye Units
Sales		8,820		5,800
Less: opening stock		(4,410)		(2,320)
Add: closing stock	(10/20 × 8,820 × 1.2)	5,292	(8/20 × 5,800 × 1.3)	3,016
Production		9,702		6,496

b) **Material purchases budget**

	Square metres
Production of Exes (5 × 9,702)	48,510
Wyes (7 × 6,496)	45,472
	93,982
Lost through wastage (²/₉₈ × 93,982)	1,918
Gross issues to production	95,900
Less: opening stock	(16,950)
Add: closing stock	18,000
Purchases	96,950

c) **Cost of materials purchases budget**

96,950 × £2 = £193,900

d) **Budgeted labour hours**

		Hours
Exes:	$\dfrac{9,702}{6}$	1,617
Wyes:	$\dfrac{6,496}{4}$	1,624
		3,241

e) **Cost of labour budget**

		£
Normal pay rate (3,241 hours × £8)		25,928
Overtime premium:		
Total hours	3,241	
Normal hours = (22 × 35 × 4)	3,080	
Therefore overtime hours	161	
x overtime premium	x £4	
		644
		26,572

f) Cost of production budgets

		Exe £	Wye £
Materials	(48,510 × £2)	97,020	
	(45,472 × £2)		90,944
Labour	(1,617 × £8)	12,936	
	(1,624 × £8)		12,992
Production overheads	(1,617 × £12)	19,404	
	(1,624 × £12)		19,488
		129,360	123,424

Task 1.2

MEMO

To: Susan Fellows
From: Management Accountant
Date: xx.xx.xx
Subject: Production capacity constraints in periods 1 and 2

a) Constraints on extra Exe production

Surplus capacity in period 1 is sufficient to produce (88 hours × 6 units per hour) 528 Exes in terms of labour hours available, and (2,000 square metres/5 square metres per unit) 400 Exes in terms of materials available. Therefore availability of materials in period 1 is the constraint that limits extra Exe production.

b) Revised production budget for period 1

	Exe Units	Wye Units
Original budget	9,702	6,496
Additional production to meet demand in period 2	400	
Revised budget	10,102	6,496

c) Other short-term ways of overcoming the capacity constraint in period 2

1. Obtain additional resources. Hire-in temporary labour and source materials from alternative suppliers, as long as any additional cost still enables a contribution to be made on the products. An extra shift may be needed in the factory.

2. Buy-in containers to satisfy the shortfall.

SECTION 2

Task 2.1

a) Budgeted selling price per Omega $\dfrac{£4,800,000}{120,000} = £40$

b) Budgeted variable cost per Omega of:

  i) Material A $\dfrac{£480,000}{120,000} = £4$

  ii) Material B $\dfrac{£840,000}{120,000} = £7$

  iii) Material C $\dfrac{£360,000}{120,000} = £3$

c) i) Budgeted fixed cost of light, heat and power = £50,000

	£
Total cost budgeted	290,000
Less: variable cost (120,000 × £2)	240,000
Fixed cost	50,000

  ii) Budgeted variable cost of water per Omega = £1.60

	£
Total cost budgeted	212,000
Less: fixed cost	(20,000)
Total variable cost	192,000

Variable cost per Omega = $\dfrac{£192,000}{120,000} = £1.60$

d) **Shifnal Ltd – flexed budget statement for the 12 months ended 30 November 2006**

	Budget	Actual	Variance
Production and sales volume of Omegas	95,000	95,000	
	£'000	£'000	£'000
Sales (95,000 × £40)	3,800	3,990	190 (F)
Variable expenses			
Material A (95,000 × £4)	380	456	76 (A)
Material B (95,000 × £7)	665	665	–
Material C (95,000 × £3)	285	266	19 (F)
Semi-variable expenses			
Light, heat and power (£50,000 + 95,000 × £2)	240	249	9 (A)
Water (£20,000 + 95,000 × £1.60)	172	182	10 (A)
Stepped expenses			
[1]Labour (96,000 ÷ 3,000 × £5,000)	160	168	8 (A)
Maintenance (100,000 ÷ 20,000 × £10,000)	50	54	4 (A)
Fixed expenses			
Rent and rates	360	355	5 (F)
Distribution expenses	600	620	20 (A)
Administrative expenses	300	280	20 (F)
Operating profit	588	695	107 (F)

[1]Although only 95,000 Omegas were made, the stepped nature of the cost means that sufficient labour cost to produce 96,000 Omegas had to be incurred. Similarly, with maintenance, sufficient had to be spent to make 100,000 Omegas.

Task 2.2

a) Forecast turnover using Model A, y = £200,000 + £58,000x

	Quarter 17 £	Quarter 18 £	Quarter 19 £
(£200,000 + £58,000 × 17)	1,186,000		
(£200,000 + £58,000 × 18)		1,244,000	
(£200,000 + £58,000 × 19)			1,302,000

Forecast turnover using Model B, y = £1,000,000 + £60,000(1.1)^x

	Quarter 17 £	Quarter 18 £	Quarter 19 £
(£1,000,000 + £60,000(1.1)^{17})	1,303,268		
(£1,000,000 + £60,000(1.1)^{18})		1,333,595	
(£1,000,000 + £60,000(1.1)^{19})			1,366,955

unit 9 – practice exam 10: answers

b) Model B gives the better estimate of the seasonally adjusted actual data for the three quarters in question, as the differences between the actual and forecast figures are smaller for Model B than Model A.

	Quarter 17 £'000	Quarter 18 £'000	Quarter 19 £'000
Seasonally adjusted actual data (SAAD)	1,300	1,350	1,390
(SAAD – Model A)	+114	+106	+88
(SAAD – Model B)	–3	+16	+23

c)

MEMO

To: Barry Jones
From: Accounting technician
Date: xx.xx.xx
Subject: Quarter 20 sales forecast

As requested, I have used a mathematical model to forecast the seasonally adjusted turnover of Ironbridge Ltd for the three months ending 31 December 2005 (quarter 20).

i) Seasonally adjusted turnover for quarter 20

Using model B, forecast sales are $(£1,000,000 + £60,000(1.1)^{20}) = £1,403,650$

ii) Limitations of the model as a forecasting technique

This model has been formulated based on a substantial volume of historical data. However, the further into the future it is used to forecast, the less likely it is that the conditions prevailing during the observed data will continue to apply; there are often random elements which cause a trend to change. Furthermore, it ignores any changes in the political, economic or technological environment in which the business operates, even if such changes are expected.